PRAISE
FREAKONOMICS

A *New York Times Book Review* Notable Book

Named a Best Book of the Year by *The Economist, New York* Magazine, Amazon.com, and Barnesandnoble.com

Winner—Book Sense Nonfiction Book of the Year

Winner—Quill Award for Business Book of the Year

Finalist—*Financial Times*/Goldman Sachs Business Book of the Year

"Levitt and Dubner's clever juxtapositions, the way they consistently mine illuminating truths by contrasting seemingly unrelated topics, is what makes *Freakonomics* a romp of a read. . . . *Freakonomics* is a splendid book, full of unlikely but arresting historical details that distinguish the authors from the run of pop social scientists."

—*The New York Times*

"If Indiana Jones were an economist, he'd be Steven Levitt. . . . A maverick treasure hunter who relies for success on his wit, pluck and disregard for conventional wisdom. . . . *Freakonomics* reads like a detective novel. . . . Economists, ever wary of devaluing their currency, tend to be stinting in their praise. I therefore tried hard to find something in this book that I could complain about. But I give up. Criticizing *Freakonomics* would be like criticizing a hot fudge sundae. . . . The cherry on top of the sundae is Mr. Levitt's co-author, Stephen Dubner, a journalist who clearly understands what he is writing about and explains it in prose that has you chuckling one minute and gasping in amazement the next. Mr. Dubner is a treasure of the rarest sort; we are fortunate that Mr. Levitt managed to find him."

—*The Wall Street Journal*

"A delight. . . . It shows, in fact, what plain old-fashioned economics can do in the hands of a boundlessly curious and superbly skilled practitioner. . . . The material is quite fascinating. . . . Always it finds questions that are mischievously intriguing in themselves but that also shed light on broader matters as well—and then it finds ingenious ways of answering them."

—*The Economist*

"An engaging and always interesting work, rich in insights, full of surprises. . . . *Freakonomics* is packed with fascinating ideas."

—*Washington Post Book World*

"We think we know how the world operates, but we really don't. . . . *Freakonomics* uses the science of economics and concrete data to challenge our assumptions about everything. . . . You'll walk away with not only a few good party tidbits, but also a more critical eye to many things presented as fact."

—*Harvard Business Review*

"Instructive and entertaining . . . the trivia alone is worth the cover price. . . . It might appear presumptuous of Steven Levitt to see himself as an all-purpose intellectual detective, fit to take on whatever puzzle of human behavior grabs his fancy. But on the evidence of *Freakonomics,* the presumption is earned."

—*The New York Times Book Review*

"Imagine a whip-smart economist with a sprawling imagination. Now imagine he's 9 years old and wants to know everything. That is the basic profile of Steven Levitt. . . . Each chapter is an enlightening field trip, like the investigations into human nature in Malcolm Gladwell's books, *The Tipping Point* and *Blink*."

—*Time*

"Steven Levitt has the most interesting mind in America, and reading *Freakonomics* is like going for a leisurely walk with him on a sunny summer day, as he waves his fingers in the air and turns everything you once thought to be true inside out. Prepare to be dazzled."

—Malcolm Gladwell

"Levitt employs statistical tools that are simple yet elegant. He cuts to the heart of a question and picks topics that are fascinating. All social scientists should ask themselves if the problems they are working on are as interesting or important as those in this superb work."

—*Los Angeles Times Book Review*

"The funkiest study of statistical mechanics ever by a world-renowned economist . . . Levitt (along with coauthor Dubner) searches for logic in the messy mathematics of human behavior. His conclusions are often eye-opening and sometimes eye-popping (his theory that high abortion rates help reduce crime probably won't get him invited to the White House anytime soon). . . . fun to read."

—*Entertainment Weekly*

"While legions of his fellow economists toil to decipher the intricacies of, say, monetary policy, Steven D. Levitt has become something of a sensation by using its models to tease out the answers to livelier questions."

—*San Francisco Chronicle*

"Maverick economist Steven Levitt explains why a lot of the things you thought you knew about money are wrong. . . . A fresh look at everyday topics through an economic lens."

—*Money*

"Principles of economics are used to examine daily life in this fun read."

—*People* (Great Reads)

"*Freakonomics* unfolds much less like a typical arcane economic treatise and more like the type of detective story that has you reading late into the night. . . . compelL[ing]."

—*Chicago Tribune*

"*Freakonomics* presents Levitt's findings in accessible, nonacademic terms. It is an engaging and always interesting work, rich in insights, full of surprises. . . . *Freakonomics* is packed with fascinating ideas."

—*Houston Chronicle*

"Imagine the best of Levitt put into readable form by an excellent journalist. When it comes to the popular exposition of contemporary economic research, this book is a milestone."

—Tyler Cowen, MarginalRevolution.com

"It's not often an economist writes a book that people untutored in the complicated science might actually want to read. But University of Chicago economist Steven Levitt seems to have pulled it off."

—*Chicago Sun-Times*

"An econ tome for both freaks and geeks. . . . Armed with the attitude of a puzzle solver and the tools of statistical economics, Levitt finds different ways to get answers. . . . In his hands, economics, far from being a dismal science, is a tool for the curious."

—*Fortune*

"Fun yet substantial . . . a mind-bending variety of questions in fascinating ways."

—*Detroit Free Press*

"In recent memory, there has not been an economics text that has gripped the popular consciousness like this intriguing and strikingly original collaborative offering. . . . One of the singular accomplishments of this book is its ability to bring together analyses of seemingly unrelated situations, and explain all of them through imparting a simple truth; namely, that people respond, more or less rationally, to economic incentives."

—*Washington Times*

"There's plenty in these pages to warrant a long-form treatment of Levitt's peculiar points of view. . . . Levitt never fails to emerge left-of-center from a mountain of data, with ideas that make us do a double take on wisdom we've long taken for granted. . . . Levitt extrapolates his material with an apparent lack of agenda.

Neither politically correct nor pushing a political viewpoint, he displays rare common sense-and uncommon sense as well."

—*Time Out New York*

"*Freakonomics,* shows Levitt at his best, asking questions that nobody else thought of and sometimes finding answers that nobody else imagined."

—*Atlanta Journal-Constitution*

"Forget your image of an economist as a crusty professor worried about fluctuating interest rates: Levitt focuses his attention on more intimate real-world issues. . . . Underlying all [Levitt's] research subjects is a belief that complex phenomena can be understood if we find the right perspective. Levitt has a knack for making that principle relevant to our daily lives, which could make this book a hit."

—*Publishers Weekly* (starred review)

"In an age of too much wishful, faith-based conventional wisdom on the right and left, and too much intellectual endeavor squeezed into pre-fab ideological containers, *Freakonomics* is politically incorrect in the best, most essential way. Levitt and Dubner suss out all kinds of surprising truths—sometimes important ones, sometimes merely fascinating ones—by means of a smart, deep, rigorous, open-minded consideration of facts, with a fearless disregard for whom they might be upsetting. This is bracing fun of the highest order."

—Kurt Andersen

"A showcase for Levitt's intriguing explorations into a number of disparate topics. . . . Plenty of fun."

—Salon.com

"*Freakonomics* [is] an addictive, irresistible crash course in the populist application of economics. . . . Levitt has a remarkable gift for gazing into a dry pile of statistics and coming away with a novel, exciting theory about how the world works, and in *Freakonomics,* it's well matched by Dubner's gift for conveying Levitt's ideas and theories in vivid, fun, conversational language."

—*The Onion*

"Riveting, funny, and surprising. I can't think of a single adult I know who wouldn't enjoy reading it."

—*San Francisco Weekly*

"[An] innovative and brilliant way of looking at the world. . . . In spite of the controversy that *Freakonomics* is almost certain to cause, Levitt has produced a work full of stunning insights that can rightfully be called genius. . . . In spite of the dense and complex nature of its many arguments, it is from start to finish a good read. . . . Levitt has described aspects of that 'actual world' with stunning originality and breathtaking audacity. How our society responds to these realities is of course an open question, but Levitt and Dubner have done their job. They have written one of the decade's most intelligent and provocative books."

—*The Daily Standard* (UK)

"*Freakonomics* is full of stunning data analysis, the kind that shatters conventional wisdom and leads you to yell across the room to your spouse, 'Hey, listen to this . . . '"

—*Toronto Star*

"*Freakonomics* just might be the first data-analysis book that also qualifies as a beach read. . . . [It] is a series of provocative but persuasive, clearly articulated conclusions about hot-button social issues—crime, abortion, cheating on tests, class consciousness, parenting—leavened by anecdotes and dryly humorous asides."

—*Minneapolis Star Tribune*

"In non-stick prose *Freakonomics* explains how the world really works, popularizing a science or scientific insight while forever hitting the reader on the head with how damnably clever the author is. . . . Entertaining."

—*New York Observer*

"The lasting reason Levitt and Dubner's book will be remembered for decades to come is that it is a tour de force of analysis and logical rigor. *Freakonomics* can legitimately be called dazzling. . . . *Freakonomics'* intellectual fearlessness isn't just welcome. It's something to treasure.

—*Orange County Register*

"Levitt is a brilliant mind applying itself to the mysteries of everyday life, like an economic Sherlock Holmes . . . *Freakonomics* offers nonstop counterintuitive fun."

—*The Evening Standard* (UK)

"*Freakonomics* is about unconventional wisdom, using the raw data of economics in imaginative ways to ask clever and diverting questions . . . Levitt has a genius for wacky inquiry . . . Hallucinatory and mesmerizing . . . Brilliant."

—*The Observer* (UK)

"Vivid, readily understandable and consistently convincing. . . . Levitt tries to serve as a guide for us in opening up a different perspective on the world and its works. . . . He is a compellingly clever economist."

—*Canberra Times* (Australia)

"A thoughtful and provocative analysis."

—*Legal Times*

"Asking provocative and profound questions about human motivation and contemporary living, and reaching some astonishing conclusions, *Freakonomics* shows you a familiar world through a totally new lens. . . . Levitt puts forward a theory that keeps you wondering for a long time after finishing the last page."

—*Business Day* (South Africa)

"Anybody who is interested in the answers to [an] eclectic set of questions should read *Freakonomics,* one of the smartest, politically incorrect and definitely the most entertaining book you will ever read about economics. . . . So skillful is Dubner that even a two-page definition of regression analysis passes by not just painlessly, but pleasurably."

—*The Jakarta Post* (Indonesia)

"*Freakonomics* is Economics 101 meets Sherlock Holmes meets *Ripley's Believe It or Not.*"

—*Times Colonist* (Victoria, British Columbia)

"This book is a brilliant, provocative investigation into motives: what they are, how they can be changed, and how they affect what people do. It is also a deceptively easy read: its style is so light, its tone so sunny and humorous, that it is hard to realise the extent to which the arguments in *Freakonomics* attack some of our most basic assumptions about the way people, and society, work. . . . I can't recommend this book highly enough. Wherever you read it—on the beach, at home, on a train or in an office—you will be stimulated, provoked and entertained."

—*Sunday Telegraph* (UK)

"A thoughtful and provocative analysis"

—*The Legal Intelligencer*

"*Freakonomics* is filled with fascinating revelations.

—*Tulsa World*

"Levitt's curiosity is contagious. He has never lost that toddler's desire to know why, and with that he encourages us to keep questioning, to keep looking for answers and perhaps to look somewhere we hadn't thought of before. . . . An entertaining work highlighting economic theory. Something previously thought impossible."

—*Buffalo News*

"I can't imagine anyone reading this book and not stopping every once in a while and saying, 'Whoa, that goes against everything I've believed for a long time.' . . . Fascinating. I highly recommend it"

—*Green Bay Press Gazette*

"A fun and fascinating book that applies economics to interesting questions of our times . . . *Freakonomics* is a quick and enjoyable read that's thought-provoking at the same time. Levitt's use of statistical analysis to answer quirky questions may help corporate executives find new ways of looking at their problems."

—*Texas Lawyer*

"Levitt's interests are immediately attractive to non-specialists, and he and Dubner tackle them in a lively, conversational style. . . . For readers unfamiliar with the way economists think, *Freakonomics* is likely to be enlightening as well as entertaining."

—*New Statesman* (UK)

"*Freakonomics* is an incredibly stunning book, full of insights that will leave you gasping in amazement. . . . Stephen Levitt is one of the most original thinkers around."

—*Business World*

"An eye-opening, and most interesting, approach to the world."

—*Kirkus Reviews*

FREAKONOMICS

CONTENTS

Chapter 3

In which the conventional wisdom is often found to be a web of fabrication, self-interest, and convenience.

> *Why experts routinely make up statistics; the invention of chronic halitosis . . . How to ask a good question . . . Sudhir Venkatesh's long, strange trip into the crack den . . . Why prostitutes earn more than architects . . . What a drug dealer, a high-school quarterback, and an editorial assistant have in common . . . How the invention of crack cocaine mirrored the invention of nylon stocking . . . Was crack the worst thing to hit black Americans since Jim Crow?*

Chapter 4

In which the facts of crime are sorted out from the fictions.

> *What Nicolae Ceauşescu learned—the hard way—about abortion . . . Why the 1960s was a great time to be a criminal . . . Think the roaring 1990s economy put a crimp on crime? Think again . . . Why capital punishment doesn't deter criminals . . . Do police actually lower crime rates? . . . Prisons, prisons everywhere . . . Seeing through the New York City police "miracle" . . . What is a gun, really? . . . Why early crack dealers were like Microsoft millionaires and later crack dealers were like Pets.com . . . The superpredator versus the senior citizen . . . Jane Roe, crime stopper: how the legalization of abortion changed everything.*

Chapter 5

In which we ask, from a variety of angles, a pressing question: do parents really matter?

The conversion of parenting from an art to a science . . . Why parenting experts like to scare parents to death . . . Which is more dangerous: a gun or a swimming pool? . . . The economics of fear . . . Obsessive parents and the nature-nurture quagmire . . . Why a good school isn't as good as you might think . . . The black-white test gap and "acting white" . . . Eight things that make a child do better in school and eight that don't.

Chapter 6

In which we weigh the importance of a parent's first official act—naming the baby.

A boy named Winner and his brother, Loser . . . The blackest names and the whitest names . . . The segregation of culture: why Seinfeld *never made the top fifty among black viewers . . . If you have a really bad name, should you just change it? . . . High-end names and low-end names (and how one becomes the other) . . . Britney Spears: a symptom, not a cause . . . Is Aviva the next Madison? . . . What your parents were telling the world when they gave you your name.*

In which the dependability of data meets the randomness of life.

AN EXPLANATORY NOTE

In the summer of 2003, *The New York Times Magazine* sent Stephen J. Dubner, an author and journalist, to write a profile of Steven D. Levitt, a heralded young economist at the University of Chicago.

Dubner, who was researching a book about the psychology of money, had lately been interviewing many economists and found that they often spoke English as if it were a fourth or fifth language. Levitt, who had just won the John Bates Clark Medal (a sort of junior Nobel Prize for young economists), had lately been interviewed by many journalists and found that their thinking wasn't very . . . robust, as an economist might say.

But Levitt decided that Dubner wasn't a complete idiot. And Dubner found that Levitt wasn't a human slide rule. The writer was dazzled by the inventiveness of the economist's work and his knack for explaining it. Despite Levitt's elite credentials (Harvard undergrad, a PhD from MIT, a stack of awards), he approached economics in a notably unorthodox way. He seemed to look at the world not so much as an academic but as a very smart and curious explorer—a documentary filmmaker, perhaps, or a forensic investigator or a bookie whose markets ranged from sports to crime to pop culture. He professed little interest in the sort of monetary issues that come to mind when most people think about economics; he practically blustered with self-effacement. "I just don't know very much about the field of economics," he told Dubner at one point, swiping the hair from his eyes. "I'm not good at math, I don't know a lot of econometrics, and I also don't know how to do theory. If you ask me about whether the stock market's going to go up or down, if you ask me whether the economy's going to grow or shrink, if you ask me whether deflation's good or bad, if you ask me about taxes—I mean, it would be total fakery if I said I knew anything about any of those things."

What interested Levitt were the riddles of everyday life. His investigations were a feast for anyone wanting to know how the world really works. His singular attitude was evoked in Dubner's resulting article:

> As Levitt sees it, economics is a science with excellent tools for gaining answers but a serious shortage of interesting questions. His particular gift is the ability to ask such questions. For instance: If drug dealers make so much money, why do they still live with their mothers? Which is more dangerous, a gun or a swimming pool? What really caused crime rates to plunge during the past decade? Do real-estate agents have their clients' best interests at heart? Why do black parents give their children names that may hurt their career prospects?

Do schoolteachers cheat to meet high-stakes testing standards? Is sumo wrestling corrupt?

Many people—including a fair number of his peers—might not recognize Levitt's work as economics at all. But he has merely distilled the so-called dismal science to its most primal aim: explaining how people get what they want. Unlike most academics, he is unafraid of using personal observations and curiosities; he is also unafraid of anecdote and storytelling (although he is afraid of calculus). He is an intuitionist. He sifts through a pile of data to find a story that no one else has found. He figures a way to measure an effect that veteran economists had declared unmeasurable. His abiding interests— though he says he has never trafficked in them himself—are cheating, corruption, and crime.

Levitt's blazing curiosity also proved attractive to thousands of *New York Times* readers. He was beset by questions and queries, riddles and requests—from General Motors and the New York Yankees and U.S. senators but also from prisoners and parents and a man who for twenty years had kept precise data on his sales of bagels. A former Tour de France champion called Levitt to ask his help in proving that the current Tour is rife with doping; the Central Intelligence Agency wanted to know how Levitt might use data to catch money launderers and terrorists.

What they were all responding to was the force of Levitt's underlying belief: that the modern world, despite a surfeit of obfuscation, complication, and downright deceit, is *not* impenetrable, is *not* unknowable, and—if the right questions are asked—is even more intriguing than we think. All it takes is a new way of looking.

In New York City, the publishers were telling Levitt he should write a book.

"Write a book?" he said. "I don't want to write a book." He already had a million more riddles to solve than time to solve them. Nor did he think himself much of a writer. So he said that no, he wasn't interested—"unless," he proposed, "maybe Dubner and I could do it together."

Collaboration isn't for everyone. But the two of them— henceforth known as the two of *us*—decided to talk things over to see if such a book might work. We decided it could. We hope you agree.

FREAKONOMICS

INTRODUCTION:
THE HIDDEN SIDE OF EVERYTHING

Anyone living in the United States in the early 1990s and paying even a whisper of attention to the nightly news or a daily paper could be forgiven for having been scared out of his skin.

The culprit was crime. It had been rising relentlessly—a graph plotting the crime rate in any American city over recent decades looked like a ski slope in profile—and it seemed now to herald the end of the world as we knew it. Death by gunfire, intentional and otherwise, had become commonplace. So too had carjacking and crack dealing, robbery and rape. Violent crime was a gruesome, constant companion. And things were about to get even worse. Much worse. All the experts were saying so.

The cause was the so-called superpredator. For a time, he was everywhere. Glowering from the cover of newsweeklies. Swaggering his way through foot-thick government reports. He was a scrawny, big-city teenager with a cheap gun in his hand and nothing in his heart but ruthlessness. There were thousands out there just like him, we were told, a generation of killers about to hurl the country into deepest chaos.

In 1995 the criminologist James Alan Fox wrote a report for the U.S. attorney general that grimly detailed the coming spike in murders by teenagers. Fox proposed optimistic and pessimistic scenarios. In the optimistic scenario, he believed, the rate of teen homicides would rise another 15 percent over the next decade; in the pessimistic scenario, it would more than double. "The next crime wave will get so bad," he said, "that it will make 1995 look like the good old days."

Other criminologists, political scientists, and similarly learned forecasters laid out the same horrible future, as did President Clinton. "We know we've got about six years to turn this juvenile crime thing around," Clinton said, "or our country is going to be living with chaos. And my successors will not be giving speeches about the wonderful opportunities of the global economy; they'll be trying to keep body and soul together for people on the streets of these cities." The smart money was plainly on the criminals.

And then, instead of going up and up and up, crime began to fall. And fall and fall and fall some more. The crime drop was startling in several respects. It was ubiquitous, with every category of crime falling in every part of the country. It was persistent, with incremental decreases year after year. And it was entirely unanticipated—especially by the very experts who had been predicting the opposite.

The magnitude of the reversal was astounding. The teenage murder rate, instead of rising 100 percent or even 15 percent as James Alan Fox had warned, fell more than 50 percent within five years. By 2000 the overall murder rate in the United States had dropped to its lowest level in thirty-five years. So had the rate of just about every other sort of crime, from assault to car theft.

Even though the experts had failed to anticipate the crime drop—which was in fact well under way even as they made their horrifying predictions—they now hurried to explain it. Most of their theories sounded perfectly logical. It was the roaring 1990s economy, they said, that helped turn back crime. It was the pro-liferation of gun control laws, they said. It was the sort of innova-tive policing strategies put into place in New York City, where murders would fall from 2,262 in 1990 to 540 in 2005.

These theories were not only logical; they were also *encouraging*, for they attributed the crime drop to specific and recent human initiatives. If it was gun control and clever police strategies and better-paying jobs that quelled crime—well then, the power to stop criminals had been within our reach all along. As it would be the next time, God forbid, that crime got so bad.

These theories made their way, seemingly without friction, from the experts' mouths to journalists' ears to the public's mind. In short course, they became conventional wisdom.

There was only one problem: they weren't true.

There was another factor, meanwhile, that *had* greatly contrib-uted to the massive crime drop of the 1990s. It had taken shape more than twenty years earlier and concerned a young woman in Dallas named Norma McCorvey.

Like the proverbial butterfly that flaps its wings on one continent and eventually causes a hurricane on another, Norma McCorvey dramatically altered the course of events without intending to. All she had wanted was an abortion. She was a poor, uneducated, unskilled, alcoholic, drug-using twenty-one-year-old woman who had already given up two children for adoption and now, in 1970, found herself pregnant again. But in Texas, as in all but a few states at that time, abortion was illegal. McCorvey's cause came to be adopted by people far more powerful than she. They made her the lead plaintiff in a class-action lawsuit seeking to legalize abortion. The defendant was Henry Wade, the Dallas County district attorney. The case ultimately made it to the U.S. Supreme Court, by which time McCorvey's name had been disguised as Jane Roe. On January 22, 1973, the court ruled in favor of Ms. Roe, allowing legalized abortion throughout the United States. By this time, of course, it was far too late for Ms. McCorvey/Roe to have her abortion. She had given birth and put the child up for adoption. (Years later she would renounce her allegiance to legalized abortion and become a pro-life activist.)

So how did *Roe v. Wade* help trigger, a generation later, the greatest crime drop in recorded history?

As far as crime is concerned, it turns out that not all children are born equal. Not even close. Decades of studies have shown that a child born into an adverse family environment is far more likely than other children to become a criminal. And the millions of women most likely to have an abortion in the wake of *Roe v. Wade*—poor, unmarried, and teenage mothers for whom illegal abortions had been too expensive or too hard to get—were often models of adversity. They were the very women whose children, if born, would have been much more likely than average to become criminals. But because of *Roe v. Wade*, these children *weren't* being born. This powerful cause would have a drastic, distant effect: years later, just as these unborn children would have entered their criminal primes, the rate of crime began to plummet.

It wasn't gun control or a strong economy or new police strategies that finally blunted the American crime wave. It was, among other factors, the reality that the pool of potential criminals had dramatically shrunk.

Now, as the crime-drop experts (the former crime doomsayers) spun their theories to the media, how many times did they cite legalized abortion as a cause?

Zero.

It is the quintessential blend of commerce and camaraderie: you hire a real-estate agent to sell your home.

She sizes up its charms, snaps some pictures, sets the price, writes a seductive ad, shows the house aggressively, negotiates the offers, and sees the deal through to its end. Sure, it's a lot of work, but she's getting a nice cut. On the sale of a $300,000 house, a typical 6 percent agent fee yields $18,000. Eighteen thousand dollars, you say to yourself: that's a lot of money. But you also tell yourself that you never could have sold the house for $300,000 on your own. The agent knew how to—what's that phrase she used?—"maximize the house's value." She got you top dollar, right?

Right?

A real-estate agent is a different breed of expert than a criminologist, but she is every bit the expert. That is, she knows her field far better than the layman on whose behalf she is acting. She is better informed about the house's value, the state of the housing market, even the buyer's frame of mind. You depend on her for this information. That, in fact, is why you hired an expert.

As the world has grown more specialized, countless such experts have made themselves similarly indispensable. Doctors, lawyers, contractors, stockbrokers, auto mechanics, mortgage brokers, financial planners: they all enjoy a gigantic informational advantage. And they use that advantage to help you, the person who hired them, get exactly what you want for the best price.

Right?

It would be lovely to think so. But experts are human, and humans respond to incentives. How any given expert treats you, therefore, will depend on how that expert's incentives are set up. Sometimes his incentives may work in your favor. For instance: a study of California auto mechanics found they often passed up a small repair bill by letting failing cars pass emissions inspections—the reason being that lenient mechanics are rewarded with repeat business. But in a different case, an expert's incentives may work against you. In a medical study, it turned out that obstetricians in areas with declining birth rates are much more likely to perform cesarean-section deliveries than obstetricians in growing areas—suggesting that, when business is tough, doctors try to ring up more expensive procedures.

It is one thing to muse about experts' abusing their position and another to prove it. The best way to do so would be to measure how an expert treats you versus how he performs the same service for himself. Unfortunately a surgeon doesn't operate on himself. Nor is his medical file a matter of public record; neither is an auto mechanic's repair log for his own car.

Real-estate sales, however, *are* a matter of public record. And real-estate agents often do sell their own homes. A recent set of data covering the sale of nearly 100,000 houses in suburban Chicago shows that more than 3,000 of those houses were owned by the agents themselves.

Before plunging into the data, it helps to ask a question: what is the real-estate agent's incentive when she is selling her own home? Simple: to make the best deal possible. Presumably this is also your incentive when you are selling your home. And so your incentive and the real-estate agent's incentive would seem to be nicely aligned. Her commission, after all, is based on the sale price.

But as incentives go, commissions are tricky. First of all, a 6 percent real-estate commission is typically split between the seller's agent and the buyer's. Each agent then kicks back roughly half of her take to the agency. Which means that only 1.5 percent of the purchase price goes directly into your agent's pocket.

So on the sale of your $300,000 house, her personal take of the $18,000 commission is $4,500. Still not bad, you say. But what if the house was actually worth more than $300,000? What if, with a little more effort and patience and a few more newspaper ads, she could have sold it for $310,000? After the commission, that puts an additional $9,400 in your pocket. But the agent's additional share—her personal 1.5 percent of the extra $10,000—is a mere $150. If you earn $9,400 while she earns only $150, maybe your incentives aren't aligned after all. (Especially when she's the one paying for the ads and doing all the work.) Is the agent willing to put out all that extra time, money, and energy for just $150?

There's one way to find out: measure the difference between the sales data for houses that belong to real-estate agents themselves and the houses they sold on behalf of clients. Using the data from the sales of those 100,000 Chicago homes, and controlling for any number of variables—location, age and quality of the house, aesthetics, whether or not the property was an investment, and so on—it turns out that a real-estate agent keeps her own home on the market an average of ten days longer and sells it for an extra 3-plus percent, or $10,000 on a $300,000 house. When she sells her own house, an agent holds out for the best offer; when she sells yours, she encourages you to take the first decent offer that comes along. Like a stockbroker churning commissions, she wants to make deals and make them fast. Why not? Her share of a better offer—$150—is too puny an incentive to encourage her to do otherwise.

Of all the truisms about politics, one is held to be truer than the rest: money buys elections. Arnold Schwarzenegger, Michael Bloomberg, Jon Corzine—these are but a few recent, dramatic examples of the truism at work. (Disregard for a moment the contrary examples of Steve Forbes, Michael Huffington, and especially Thomas Golisano, who over the course of three gubernatorial elections in New York spent $93 million of his own money and won 4 percent, 8 percent, and 14 percent, respectively, of the vote.) Most people would agree that money has an undue influence on elections and that far too much money is spent on political campaigns.

Indeed, election data show it is true that the candidate who spends more money in a campaign usually wins. But is money the *cause* of the victory?

It might seem logical to think so, much as it might have seemed logical that a booming 1990s economy helped reduce crime. But just because two things are correlated does not mean that one causes the other. A correlation simply means that a relationship exists between two factors—let's call them X and Y—but it tells you nothing about the direction of that relationship. It's possible that X causes Y; it's also possible that Y causes X; and it may be that X and Y are both being caused by some other factor, Z.

Think about this correlation: cities with a lot of murders also tend to have a lot of police officers. Consider now the police/murder correlation in a pair of real cities. Denver and Washington, D.C., have about the same population—but Washington has nearly three times as many police as Denver, and it also has eight times the number of murders. Unless you have more information, however, it's hard to say what's causing what. Someone who didn't know better might contemplate these figures and conclude that it is all those extra police in Washington who are causing the extra murders. Such wayward thinking, which has a long history, generally provokes a wayward response. Consider the folktale of the czar who learned that the most disease-ridden province in his empire was also the province with the most doctors. His solution? He promptly ordered all the doctors shot dead.

Now, returning to the issue of campaign spending: in order to figure out the relationship between money and elections, it helps to consider the incentives at play in campaign finance. Let's say you are the kind of person who might contribute $1,000 to a candidate. Chances are you'll give the money in one of two situations: a close race, in which you think the money will influence the outcome; or a campaign in which one candidate is a sure winner and you would like to bask in reflected glory or receive some future in-kind consideration. The one candidate you *won't* contribute to is a sure loser. (Just ask any presidential hopeful who bombs in Iowa and New Hampshire.) So front-runners and incumbents raise a lot more money than long shots. And what about spending that money? Incumbents and front-runners obviously have more cash, but they only spend a lot of it when they stand a legitimate chance of losing; otherwise, why dip into a war chest that might be more useful later on, when a more formidable opponent appears?

Now picture two candidates, one intrinsically appealing and the other not so. The appealing candidate raises much more money and wins easily. But was it the money that won him the votes, or was it his appeal that won the votes *and* the money?

That's a crucial question but a very hard one to answer. Voter appeal, after all, isn't easy to quantify. How can it be measured?

It can't, really—except in one special case. The key is to measure a candidate against . . . himself. That is, Candidate A today is likely to be similar to Candidate A two or four years hence. The same could be said for Candidate B. If only Candidate A ran against Candidate B in two consecutive elections but in each case spent different amounts of money. Then, with the candidates' appeal more or less constant, we could measure the money's impact.

As it turns out, the same two candidates run against each other in consecutive elections all the time—indeed, in nearly a thousand U.S. congressional races since 1972. What do the numbers have to say about such cases?

Here's the surprise: the amount of money spent by the candidates *hardly matters at all.* A winning candidate can cut his spending in half and lose only 1 percent of the vote. Meanwhile, a losing candidate who doubles his spending can expect to shift the vote in his favor by only that same 1 percent. What really matters for a political candidate is *not* how much you spend; what matters is who you are. (The same could be said—and will be said, in chapter 5—about parents.) Some politicians are inherently attractive to voters and others simply aren't, and no amount of money can do much about it. (Messrs. Forbes, Huffington, and Golisano already know this, of course.)

And what about the other half of the election truism—that the amount of money spent on campaign finance is obscenely huge? In a typical election period that includes campaigns for the presidency, the Senate, and the House of Representatives, about $1 billion is spent per year—which sounds like a lot of money, unless you care to measure it against something seemingly less important than democratic elections.

It is the same amount, for instance, that Americans spend every year on chewing gum.

This isn't a book about the cost of chewing gum versus campaign spending per se, or about disingenuous real-estate agents, or the impact of legalized abortion on crime. It will certainly address these scenarios and dozens more, from the art of parenting to the mechanics of cheating, from the inner workings of a crack-selling gang to racial discrimination on *The Weakest Link*. What this book *is* about is stripping a layer or two from the surface of modern life and seeing what is happening underneath. We will ask a lot of questions, some frivolous and some about life-and-death issues. The answers may often seem odd but, after the fact, also rather obvious. We will seek out these answers in the data—whether those data come in the form of schoolchildren's test scores or New York City's crime statistics or a crack dealer's financial records. Often we will take advantage of patterns in the data that were incidentally left behind, like an airplane's sharp contrail in a high sky. It is well and good to opine or theorize about a subject, as humankind is wont to do, but when moral posturing is replaced by an honest assessment of the data, the result is often a new, surprising insight.

Morality, it could be argued, represents the way that people would like the world to work—whereas economics represents how it actually *does* work. Economics is above all a science of measurement. It comprises an extraordinarily powerful and flexible set of tools that can reliably assess a thicket of information to determine the effect of any one factor, or even the whole effect. That's what "the economy" is, after all: a thicket of information about jobs and real estate and banking and investment. But the tools of economics can be just as easily applied to subjects that are more—well, more *interesting*.

This book, then, has been written from a very specific worldview, based on a few fundamental ideas:

Incentives are the cornerstone of modern life. And understanding them—or, often, ferreting them out—is the key to solving just about any riddle, from violent crime to sports cheating to online dating.

The conventional wisdom is often wrong. Crime didn't keep soaring in the 1990s, money alone doesn't win elections, and—surprise—drinking eight glasses of water a day has never actually been shown to do a thing for your health. Conventional wisdom is often shoddily formed and devilishly difficult to see through, but it can be done.

Dramatic effects often have distant, even subtle, causes. The answer to a given riddle is not always right in front of you. Norma McCorvey had a far greater impact on crime than did the combined forces of gun control, a strong economy, and innovative police strategies. So did, as we shall see, a man named Oscar Danilo Blandon, aka the Johnny Appleseed of Crack.

"Experts"—from criminologists to real-estate agents—use their informational advantage to serve their own agenda. However, they can be beat at their own game. And in the face of the Internet, their informational advantage is shrinking every day—as evidenced by,

among other things, the falling price of coffins and life-insurance premiums.

Knowing what to measure and how to measure it makes a complicated world much less so. If you learn to look at data in the right way, you can explain riddles that otherwise might have seemed impossible. Because there is nothing like the sheer power of numbers to scrub away layers of confusion and contradiction.

So the aim of this book is to explore the hidden side of . . . everything. This may occasionally be a frustrating exercise. It may sometimes feel as if we are peering at the world through a straw or even staring into a funhouse mirror; but the idea is to look at many different scenarios and examine them in a way they have rarely been examined. In some regards, this is a strange concept for a book. Most books put forth a single theme, crisply expressed in a sentence or two, and then tell the entire story of that theme: the history of salt; the fragility of democracy; the use and misuse of punctuation. This book has no such unifying theme. We did consider, for about six minutes, writing a book that would revolve around a single theme—the theory and practice of applied microeconomics, anyone?—but opted instead for a sort of treasure-hunt approach. Yes, this approach employs the best analytical tools that economics can offer, but it also allows us to follow whatever freakish curiosities may occur to us. Thus our invented field of study: Freakonomics. The sort of stories told in this book are not often covered in Econ 101, but that may change. Since the science of economics is primarily a set of tools, as opposed to a subject matter, then no subject, however offbeat, need be beyond its reach.

It is worth remembering that Adam Smith, the founder of classical economics, was first and foremost a philosopher. He strove to be a moralist and, in doing so, became an economist. When he published *The Theory of Moral Sentiments* in 1759, modern capitalism was just getting under way. Smith was entranced by the sweeping changes wrought by this new force, but it wasn't just the numbers that interested him. It was the human effect, the fact that economic forces were vastly changing the way a person thought and behaved in a given situation. What might lead one person to cheat or steal while another didn't? How would one person's seemingly innocuous choice, good or bad, affect a great number of people down the line? In Smith's era, cause and effect had begun to wildly accelerate; incentives were magnified tenfold. The gravity and shock of these changes were as overwhelming to the citizens of his time as the gravity and shock of modern life may seem to us today.

Smith's true subject was the friction between individual desire and societal norms. The economic historian Robert Heilbroner, writing in *The Worldly Philosophers*, wondered how Smith was able to separate the doings of man, a creature of self-interest, from the greater moral plane in which man operated. "Smith held that the answer lay in our ability to put ourselves in the position of a third person, an impartial observer," Heilbroner wrote, "and in this way to form a notion of the objective . . . merits of a case."

Consider yourself, then, in the company of a third person—or, if you will, a pair of third people—eager to explore the objective merits of interesting cases. These explorations generally begin with the asking of a simple unasked question. Such as: what do schoolteachers and sumo wrestlers have in common?

Chapter 1

WHAT DO SCHOOLTEACHERS AND
SUMO WRESTLERS HAVE IN COMMON?

Imagine for a moment that you are the manager of a day-care center. You have a clearly stated policy that children are supposed to be picked up by 4 p.m. But very often parents are late. The result: at day's end, you have some anxious children and at least one teacher who must wait around for the parents to arrive. What to do?

A pair of economists who heard of this dilemma—it turned out to be a rather common one—offered a solution: fine the tardy parents. Why, after all, should the day-care center take care of these kids for free?

The economists decided to test their solution by conducting a study of ten day-care centers in Haifa, Israel. The study lasted twenty weeks, but the fine was not introduced immediately. For the first four weeks, the economists simply kept track of the number of parents who came late; there were, on average, eight late pickups per week per day-care center. In the fifth week, the fine was enacted. It was announced that any parent arriving more than ten minutes late would pay $3 per child for each incident. The fee would be added to the parents' monthly bill, which was roughly $380.

After the fine was enacted, the number of late pickups promptly went . . . up. Before long there were twenty late pickups per week, more than double the original average. The incentive had plainly backfired.

Economics is, at root, the study of incentives: how people get what they want, or need, especially when other people want or need the same thing. Economists love incentives. They love to dream them up and enact them, study them and tinker with them. The typical economist believes the world has not yet invented a problem that he cannot fix if given a free hand to design the proper incentive scheme. His solution may not always be pretty—it may involve coercion or exorbitant penalties or the violation of civil liberties—but the original problem, rest assured, will be fixed. An incentive is a bullet, a lever, a key: an often tiny object with astonishing power to change a situation.

We all learn to respond to incentives, negative and positive, from the outset of life. If you toddle over to the hot stove and touch it, you burn a finger. But if you bring home straight A's from school, you get a new bike. If you are spotted picking your nose in class, you get ridiculed. But if you make the basketball team, you move up the social ladder. If you break curfew, you get grounded. But if you ace your SATs, you get to go to a good college. If you flunk out of law school, you have to go to work at your father's insurance company. But if you perform so well that a rival company comes calling, you become a vice president and no longer have to work for your father. If you become so excited about your new vice president job that you drive home at eighty mph, you get pulled over by the police and fined $100. But if you hit your sales projections and collect a year-end bonus, you not only aren't worried about the $100 ticket but can also afford to buy that Viking range you've always wanted—and on which your toddler can now burn her own finger.

An incentive is simply a means of urging people to do more of a good thing and less of a bad thing. But most incentives don't come about organically. Someone—an economist or a politician or a parent—has to invent them. Your three-year-old eats all her vegetables for a week? She wins a trip to the toy store. A big steelmaker belches too much smoke into the air? The company is fined for each metric ton of pollutants over the legal limit. Too many Americans aren't paying their share of income tax? It was the economist Milton Friedman who helped come up with a solution to this one: automatic tax withholding from employees' paychecks.

There are three basic flavors of incentive: economic, social, and moral. Very often a single incentive scheme will include all three varieties. Think about the anti-smoking campaign of recent years. The addition of a $3-per-pack "sin tax" is a strong economic incentive against buying cigarettes. The banning of cigarettes in restaurants and bars is a powerful social incentive. And when the U.S. government asserts that terrorists raise money by selling black-market cigarettes, that acts as a rather jarring moral incentive.

Some of the most compelling incentives yet invented have been put in place to deter crime. Considering this fact, it might be worthwhile to take a familiar question—why is there so much crime in modern society?—and stand it on its head: why isn't there a lot *more* crime?

After all, every one of us regularly passes up opportunities to maim, steal, and defraud. The chance of going to jail—thereby losing your job, your house, and your freedom, all of which are essentially economic penalties—is certainly a strong incentive. But when it comes to crime, people also respond to moral incentives (they don't want to do something they consider wrong) and social incentives (they don't want to be seen by others as doing something wrong). For certain types of misbehavior, social incentives are terribly powerful. In an echo of Hester Prynne's scarlet letter, many American cities now fight prostitution with a "shaming" offensive, posting pictures of convicted johns (and prostitutes) on websites or on local-access television. Which is a more horrifying deterrent: a $500 fine for soliciting a prostitute or the thought of your friends and family ogling you on www.HookersAndJohns.com?

So through a complicated, haphazard, and constantly readjusted web of economic, social, and moral incentives, modern society does its best to militate against crime. Some people would argue that we don't do a very good job. But taking the long view, that is clearly not true. Consider the historical trend in homicide (not including wars), which is both the most reliably measured crime and the best barometer of a society's overall crime rate. These statistics, compiled by the criminologist Manuel Eisner, track the historical homicide levels in five European regions.

HOMICIDES

(PER 100,000 PEOPLE)

	ENGLAND	NETHERLANDS & BELGIUM	SCANDINAVIA	GERMANY & SWITZERLAND	ITALY
13TH&14TH C.	23.0	47.0	N.A.	37.0	56.0
15TH C.	N.A.	45.0	46.0	16.0	73.0
16TH C.	7.0	25.0	21.0	11.0	47.0
17TH C.	5.0	7.5	18.0	7.0	32.0
18TH C.	1.5	5.5	1.9	7.5	10.5
19TH C.	1.7	1.6	1.1	2.8	12.6
1900–1949	0.8	1.5	0.7	1.7	3.2
1950–1994	0.9	0.9	0.9	1.0	1.5

The steep decline of these numbers over the centuries suggests that, for one of the gravest human concerns—getting murdered— the incentives that we collectively cook up are working better and better.

So what was wrong with the incentive at the Israeli day-care centers?

You have probably already guessed that the $3 fine was simply too small. For that price, a parent with one child could afford to be late every day and only pay an extra $60 each month—just one-sixth of the base fee. As babysitting goes, that's pretty cheap. What if the fine had been set at $100 instead of $3? That would have likely put an end to the late pickups, though it would have also engendered plenty of ill will. (Any incentive is inherently a trade-off; the trick is to balance the extremes.)

But there was another problem with the day-care center fine. It substituted an economic incentive (the $3 penalty) for a moral incentive (the guilt that parents were supposed to feel when they came late). For just a few dollars each day, parents could buy off their guilt. Furthermore, the small size of the fine sent a signal to the parents that late pickups weren't such a big problem. If the day-care center suffers only $3 worth of pain for each late pickup, why bother to cut short your tennis game? Indeed, when the economists eliminated the $3 fine in the seventeenth week of their study, the number of late-arriving parents didn't change. Now they could arrive late, pay no fine, *and* feel no guilt.

Such is the strange and powerful nature of incentives. A slight tweak can produce drastic and often unforeseen results. Thomas Jefferson noted this while reflecting on the tiny incentive that led to the Boston Tea Party and, in turn, the American Revolution: "So inscrutable is the arrangement of causes and consequences in this world that a two-penny duty on tea, unjustly imposed in a sequestered part of it, changes the condition of all its inhabitants."

In the 1970s, researchers conducted a study that, like the Israeli day-care study, pitted a moral incentive against an economic incentive. In this case, they wanted to learn about the motivation behind blood donations. Their discovery: when people are given a small stipend for donating blood rather than simply being praised for their altruism, they tend to donate *less* blood. The stipend turned a noble act of charity into a painful way to make a few dollars, and it wasn't worth it.

What if the blood donors had been offered an incentive of $50, or $500, or $5,000? Surely the number of donors would have changed dramatically.

But something else would have changed dramatically as well, for every incentive has its dark side. If a pint of blood were suddenly worth $5,000, you can be sure that plenty of people would take note. They might literally steal blood at knifepoint. They might pass off pig blood as their own. They might circumvent donation limits by using fake IDs. Whatever the incentive, whatever the situation, dishonest people will try to gain an advantage by whatever means necessary.

Or, as W. C. Fields once said: a thing worth having is a thing worth cheating for.

Who cheats?

Well, just about anyone, if the stakes are right. You might say to yourself, *I* don't cheat, regardless of the stakes. And then you might remember the time you cheated on, say, a board game. Last week. Or the golf ball you nudged out of its bad lie. Or the time you really wanted a bagel in the office break room but couldn't come up with the dollar you were supposed to drop in the coffee can. And then took the bagel anyway. And told yourself you'd pay double the next time. And didn't.

For every clever person who goes to the trouble of creating an incentive scheme, there is an army of people, clever and otherwise, who will inevitably spend even more time trying to beat it. Cheating may or may not be human nature, but it is certainly a prominent feature in just about every human endeavor. Cheating is a primordial economic act: getting more for less. So it isn't just the boldface names—inside-trading CEOs and pill-popping ballplayers and perk-abusing politicians—who cheat. It is the waitress who pockets her tips instead of pooling them. It is the Wal-Mart payroll manager who goes into the computer and shaves his employees' hours to make his own performance look better. It is the third grader who, worried about not making it to the fourth grade, copies test answers from the kid sitting next to him.

Some cheating leaves barely a shadow of evidence. In other cases, the evidence is massive. Consider what happened one spring evening at midnight in 1987: seven million American children suddenly disappeared. The worst kidnapping wave in history? Hardly. It was the night of April 15, and the Internal Revenue Service had just changed a rule. Instead of merely listing the name of each dependent child, tax filers were now required to provide a Social Security number. Suddenly, seven million children—children who had existed only as phantom exemptions on the previous year's 1040 forms—vanished, representing about one in ten of all dependent children in the United States.

The incentive for those cheating taxpayers was quite clear. The same for the waitress, the payroll manager, and the third grader. But what about that third grader's *teacher*? Might she have an incentive to cheat? And if so, how would she do it?

Imagine now that instead of running a day-care center in Haifa, you are running the Chicago Public Schools, a system that educates 400,000 students each year.

The most volatile current debate among American school administrators, teachers, parents, and students concerns "high-stakes" testing. The stakes are considered high because instead of simply testing students to measure their progress, schools are increasingly held accountable for the results.

The federal government mandated high-stakes testing as part of the No Child Left Behind law, signed by President Bush in 2002. But even before that law, most states gave annual standardized tests to students in elementary and secondary school. Twenty states rewarded individual schools for good test scores or dramatic improvement; thirty-two states sanctioned the schools that didn't do well.

The Chicago Public School system embraced high-stakes testing in 1996. Under the new policy, a school with low reading scores would be placed on probation and face the threat of being shut down, its staff to be dismissed or reassigned. The CPS also did away with what is known as social promotion. In the past, only a dramatically inept or difficult student was held back a grade. Now, in order to be promoted, every student in third, sixth, and eighth grade had to manage a minimum score on the standardized, multiple-choice exam known as the Iowa Test of Basic Skills.

Advocates of high-stakes testing argue that it raises the standards of learning and gives students more incentive to study. Also, if the test prevents poor students from advancing without merit, they won't clog up the higher grades and slow down good students. Opponents, meanwhile, worry that certain students will be unfairly penalized if they don't happen to test well, and that teachers may concentrate on the test topics at the exclusion of more important lessons.

Schoolchildren, of course, have had incentive to cheat for as long as there have been tests. But high-stakes testing has so radically changed the incentives for teachers that they too now have added reason to cheat. With high-stakes testing, a teacher whose students test poorly can be censured or passed over for a raise or promotion. If the entire school does poorly, federal funding can be withheld; if the school is put on probation, the teacher stands to be fired. High-stakes testing also presents teachers with some positive incentives. If her students do well enough, she might find herself praised, promoted, and even richer: the state of California at one point introduced bonuses of $25,000 for teachers who produced big test-score gains.

And if a teacher were to survey this newly incentivized landscape and consider somehow inflating her students' scores, she just might be persuaded by one final incentive: teacher cheating is rarely looked for, hardly ever detected, and just about never punished.

How might a teacher go about cheating? There are any number of possibilities, from brazen to subtle. A fifth-grade student in Oakland recently came home from school and gaily told her mother that her super-nice teacher had written the answers to the state exam right there on the chalkboard. Such instances are certainly rare, for placing your fate in the hands of thirty prepubescent witnesses doesn't seem like a risk that even the worst teacher would take. (The Oakland teacher was duly fired.) There are more nuanced ways to inflate students' scores. A teacher can simply give students extra time to complete the test. If she obtains a copy of the exam early—that is, illegitimately—she can prepare them for specific questions. More broadly, she can "teach to the test," basing her lesson plans on questions from past years' exams, which isn't considered cheating but may well violate the spirit of the test. Since these tests all have multiple-choice answers, with no penalty for wrong guesses, a teacher might instruct her students to randomly fill in every blank as the clock is winding down, perhaps inserting a long string of Bs or an alternating pattern of Bs and Cs. She might even fill in the blanks for them after they've left the room.

But if a teacher *really* wanted to cheat—and make it worth her while—she might collect her students' answer sheets and, in the hour or so before turning them in to be read by an electronic scanner, erase the wrong answers and fill in correct ones. (And you always thought that no. 2 pencil was for the *children* to change their answers.) If this kind of teacher cheating is truly going on, how might it be detected?

To catch a cheater, it helps to think like one. If you were willing to erase your students' wrong answers and fill in correct ones, you probably wouldn't want to change too many wrong answers. That would clearly be a tip-off. You probably wouldn't even want to change answers on every student's test—another tip-off. Nor, in all likelihood, would you have enough time, because the answer sheets have to be turned in soon after the test is over. So what you might do is select a string of eight or ten consecutive questions and fill in the correct answers for, say, one-half or two-thirds of your students. You could easily memorize a short pattern of correct answers, and it would be a lot faster to erase and change that pattern than to go through each student's answer sheet individually. You might even think to focus your activity toward the end of the test, where the questions tend to be harder than the earlier questions. In that way, you'd be most likely to substitute correct answers for wrong ones.

If economics is a science primarily concerned with incentives, it is also—fortunately—a science with statistical tools to measure how people respond to those incentives. All you need are some data.

In this case, the Chicago Public School system obliged. It made available a database of the test answers for every CPS student from third grade through seventh grade from 1993 to 2000. This amounts to roughly 30,000 students per grade per year, more than 700,000 sets of test answers, and nearly 100 million individual answers. The data, organized by classroom, included each student's question-by-question answer strings for reading and math tests. (The actual paper answer sheets were not included; they were habitually shredded soon after a test.) The data also included some information about each teacher and demographic information for every student, as well as his or her past and future test scores—which would prove a key element in detecting the teacher cheating.

Now it was time to construct an algorithm that could tease some conclusions from this mass of data. What might a cheating teacher's classroom look like?

The first thing to search for would be unusual answer patterns in a given classroom: blocks of identical answers, for instance, especially among the harder questions. If ten very bright students (as indicated by past and future test scores) gave correct answers to the exam's first five questions (typically the easiest ones), such an identical block shouldn't be considered suspicious. But if ten poor students gave correct answers to the *last* five questions on the exam (the hardest ones), that's worth looking into. Another red flag would be a strange pattern within any one student's exam—such as getting the hard questions right while missing the easy ones—especially when measured against the thousands of students in other classrooms who scored similarly on the same test. Furthermore, the algorithm would seek out a classroom full of students who performed far better than their past scores would have predicted and who then went on to score significantly lower the following year. A dramatic one-year spike in test scores might initially be attributed to a *good* teacher; but with a dramatic fall to follow, there's a strong likelihood that the spike was brought about by artificial means.

Consider now the answer strings from the students in two sixth-grade Chicago classrooms who took the identical math test. Each horizontal row represents one student's answers. The letter a, b, c, or d indicates a correct answer; a number indicates a wrong answer, with 1 corresponding to a, 2 corresponding to b, and so on. A zero represents an answer that was left blank. One of these classrooms almost certainly had a cheating teacher and the other did not. Try to tell the difference—although be forewarned that it's not easy with the naked eye.

CLASSROOM A

```
112a4a342cb214d0001acd24a3a12dadbcb4a0000000
d4a2341cacbddad3142a2344a2ac23421c00adb4b3cb
1b2a34d4ac42d23b141acd24a3a12dadbcb4a2134141
dbaab3dcacb1dadbc42ac2cc31012dadbcb4adb40000
d12443d43232d32323c213c22d2c23234c332db4b300
db2abad1acbdda212b1acd24a3a12dadbcb400000000
d4aab2124cbddadbcb1a42cca3412dadbcb423134bc1
1b33b4d4a2b1dadbc3ca22c00000000000000000000
d43a3a24acb1d32b412acd24a3a12dadbcb422143bc0
313a3ad1ac3d2a23431223c000012dadbcb400000000
db2a33dcacbd32d313c21142323cc300000000000000
d43ab4d1ac3dd43421240d24a3a12dadbcb400000000
db223a24acb11a3b24cacd12a241cdadbcb4adb4b300
db4abadcacb1dad3141ac212a3a1c3a144ba2db41b43
1142340c2cbddadb4b1acd24a3a12dadbcb43d133bc4
214ab4dc4cbdd31b1b2213c4ad412dadbcb4adb00000
1423b4d4a23d24131413234123a243a2413a21441343
3b3ab4d14c3d2ad4cbcac1c003a12dadbcb4adb40000
```

```
dba2ba21ac3d2ad3c4c4cd40a3a12dadbcb400000000
d122ba2cacbd1a13211a2d02a2412d0dbcb4adb4b3c0
144a3adc4cbddadbcbc2c2cc43a12dadbcb4211ab343
d43aba3cacbddadbcbca42c2a3212dadbcb42344b3cb
```

CLASSROOM B

```
db3a431422bd131b4413cd422a1acda332342d3ab4c4
d1aa1a11acb2d3dbc1ca22c23242c3a142b3adb243c1
d42a12d2a4b1d32b21ca2312a3411d000000000000000
3b2a34344c32d21b1123cdc00000000000000000000000
34aabad12cbdd3d4c1ca112cad2ccd00000000000000
d33a3431a2b2d2d44b2acd2cad2c2223b40000000000
23aa32d2a1bd2431141342c13d212d233c34a3b3b000
d32234d4a1bdd23b242a22c2a1a1cda2b1baa33a0000
d3aab23c4cbddadb23c322c2a222223232b443b24bc3
d13a14313c31d42b14c421c42332cd2242b3433a3343
d13a3ad122b1da2b11242dc1a3a12100000000000000
d12a3ad1a13d23d3cb2a21ccada24d2131b440000000
314a133c4cbd142141ca424cad34c122413223ba4b40
d42a3adcacbddadbc42ac2c2ada2cda341baa3b24321
db1134dc2cb2dadb24c412c1ada2c3a341ba20000000
d1341431acbddad3c4c213412da22d3d1132a1344b1b
1ba41a21a1b2dadb24ca22c1ada2cd32413200000000
dbaa33d2a2bddadbcbca11c2a2accda1b2ba20000000
```

If you guessed that classroom A was the cheating classroom,
congratulations. Here again are the answer strings from classroom
A, now reordered by a computer that has been asked to apply the
cheating algorithm and seek out suspicious patterns.

CLASSROOM A   (WITH CHEATING ALGORITHM APPLIED)

1   112a4a342cb214d0001**acd24a3a12dadbcb4**a0000000
2   1b2a34d4ac42d23b141**acd24a3a12dadbcb4**a2134141
3   db2abad1acbdda212b1**acd24a3a12dadbcb4**00000000
4   d43a3a24acb1d32b412**acd24a3a12dadbcb4**22143bc0
5   1142340c2cbddadb4b1**acd24a3a12dadbcb4**3d133bc4
6   d43ab4d1ac3dd43421240d24**a3a12dadbcb4**00000000
7   dba2ba21ac3d2ad3c4c4cd40**a3a12dadbcb4**00000000
8   144a3adc4cbddadbcbc2c2cc4**3a12dadbcb4**211ab343
9   3b3ab4d14c3d2ad4cbcac1c00**3a12dadbcb4**adb40000
10 d43aba3cacbddadbcbca42c2a32**12dadbcb4**2344b3cb
11 214ab4dc4cbdd31b1b2213c4ad4**12dadbcb4**adb00000
12 313a3ad1ac3d2a23431223c0000**12dadbcb4**00000000
13 d4aab2124cbddadbcb1a42cca34**12dadbcb4**23134bc1
14 dbaab3dcacb1dadbc42ac2cc310**12dadbcb4**adb40000
15 db223a24acb11a3b24cacd12a241c**dadbcb4**adb4b300
16 d122ba2cacbd1a13211a2d02a2412d0dbcb4adb4b3c0
17 1423b4d4a23d24131413234123a243a2413a21441343
18 db4abadcacb1dad3141ac212a3a1c3a144ba2db41b43
19 db2a33dcacbd32d313c21142323cc300000000000000
20 1b33b4d4a2b1dadbc3ca22c0000000000000000000000
21 d12443d43232d32323c213c22d2c23234c332db4b300
22 d4a2341cacbddad3142a2344a2ac23421c00adb4b3cb

Take a look at the answers in bold. Did fifteen out of twenty-two students somehow manage to reel off the same six consecutive correct answers (the d-a-d-b-c-b string) all by themselves?

There are at least four reasons this is unlikely. One: those questions, coming near the end of the test, were harder than the earlier questions. Two: these were mainly subpar students to begin with, few of whom got six consecutive right answers elsewhere on the test, making it all the more unlikely they would get right the same six hard questions. Three: up to this point in the test, the fifteen students' answers were virtually uncorrelated. Four: three of the students (numbers 1, 9, and 12) left more than one answer blank *before* the suspicious string and then ended the test with another string of blanks. This suggests that a long, unbroken string of blank answers was broken not by the student but by the teacher.

There is another oddity about the suspicious answer string. On nine of the fifteen tests, the six correct answers are preceded by another identical string, 3-a-1-2, which includes three of four *incorrect* answers. And on all fifteen tests, the six correct answers are followed by the same incorrect answer, a 4. Why on earth would a cheating teacher go to the trouble of erasing a student's test sheet and then fill in the *wrong* answer?

Perhaps she is merely being strategic. In case she is caught and hauled into the principal's office, she could point to the wrong answers as proof that she didn't cheat. Or perhaps—and this is a less charitable but just as likely answer—she doesn't know the right answers herself. (With standardized tests, the teacher is typically not given an answer key.) If this is the case, then we have a pretty good clue as to why her students are in need of inflated grades in the first place: they have a bad teacher.

Another indication of teacher cheating in classroom A is the class's overall performance. As sixth graders who were taking the test in the eighth month of the academic year, these students needed to achieve an average score of 6.8 to be considered up to national standards. (Fifth graders taking the test in the eighth month of the year needed to score 5.8, seventh graders 7.8, and so on.) The students in classroom A averaged 5.8 on their sixth-grade tests, which is a full grade level below where they should be. So plainly these are poor students. A year earlier, however, these students did even worse, averaging just 4.1 on their fifth-grade tests. Instead of improving by one full point between fifth and sixth grade, as would be expected, they improved by 1.7 points, nearly two grades' worth. But this miraculous improvement was short-lived. When these sixth-grade students reached seventh grade, they averaged 5.5—more than two grade levels below standard and even *worse* than they did in sixth grade. Consider the erratic year-to-year scores of three particular students from classroom A:

	5TH GRADE SCORE	6TH GRADE SCORE	7TH GRADE SCORE
STUDENT 3	3.0	6.5	5.1
STUDENT 5	3.6	6.3	4.9
STUDENT 14	3.8	7.1	5.6

The three-year scores from classroom B, meanwhile, are also poor but at least indicate an honest effort: 4.2, 5.1, and 6.0. So an entire roomful of children in classroom A suddenly got very smart one year and very dim the next, or more likely, their sixth-grade teacher worked some magic with her pencil.

There are two noteworthy points to be made about the children in classroom A, tangential to the cheating itself. The first is that they are obviously in poor academic shape, which makes them the very children whom high-stakes testing is promoted as helping the most. The second point is that these students (and their parents) would be in for a terrible shock once they reached the seventh grade. All they knew was that they had been successfully promoted due to their test scores. (No child left behind, indeed.) *They* weren't the ones who artificially jacked up their scores; they probably expected to do great in the seventh grade—and then they failed miserably. This may be the cruelest twist yet in high-stakes testing. A cheating teacher may tell herself that she is helping her students, but the fact is that she would appear far more concerned with helping herself.

An analysis of the entire Chicago data reveals evidence of teacher cheating in more than two hundred classrooms per year, roughly 5 percent of the total. This is a conservative estimate, since the algorithm was able to identify only the most egregious form of cheating—in which teachers systematically changed students' answers—and not the many subtler ways a teacher might cheat. In a recent study among North Carolina schoolteachers, some 35 percent of the respondents said they had witnessed their colleagues cheating in some fashion, whether by giving students extra time, suggesting answers, or manually changing students' answers.

What are the characteristics of a cheating teacher? The Chicago data shows that male and female teachers are equally prone to cheating. A cheating teacher tends to be younger and less qualified than average. She is also more likely to cheat after her incentives change. Because the Chicago data ran from 1993 to 2000, it bracketed the introduction of high-stakes testing in 1996. Sure enough, there was a pronounced spike in cheating in 1996. Nor was the cheating random. It was the teachers in the lowest-scoring classrooms who were most likely to cheat. It should also be noted that the $25,000 bonus for California teachers was eventually revoked, in part because of suspicions that too much of the money was going to cheaters.

Not every result of the Chicago cheating analysis was so dour. In addition to detecting cheaters, the algorithm could also identify the best teachers in the school system. A good teacher's impact was nearly as distinctive as a cheater's. Instead of getting random answers correct, her students would show real improvement on the easier types of questions they had previously missed, an indication of actual learning. And a good teacher's students carried over all their gains into the next grade.

Most academic analyses of this sort tend to languish, unread, on a dusty library shelf. But in early 2002, the new CEO of the Chicago Public Schools, Arne Duncan, contacted the study's authors. He didn't want to protest or hush up their findings. Rather, he wanted to make sure that the teachers identified by the algorithm as cheaters were truly cheating—and then do something about it.

Duncan was an unlikely candidate to hold such a powerful job. He was only thirty-six when appointed, a onetime academic all-American at Harvard who later played pro basketball in Australia. He had spent just three years with the CPS—and never in a job important enough to have his own secretary—before becoming its CEO. It didn't hurt that Duncan had grown up in Chicago. His father taught psychology at the University of Chicago; his mother ran an afterschool program for forty years, without pay, in a poor neighborhood. When Duncan was a boy, his afterschool playmates were the underprivileged kids his mother cared for. So when he took over the public schools, his allegiance lay more with schoolchildren and their families than with teachers and their union.

The best way to get rid of cheating teachers, Duncan had decided, was to readminister the standardized exam. He only had the resources to retest 120 classrooms, however, so he asked the creators of the cheating algorithm to help choose which classrooms to test.

How could those 120 retests be used most effectively? It might have seemed sensible to retest only the classrooms that likely had a cheating teacher. But even if their retest scores were lower, the teachers could argue that the students did worse merely because they were told that the scores wouldn't count in their official record—which, in fact, all retested students would be told. To make the retest results convincing, some non-cheaters were needed as a control group. The best control group? The classrooms shown by the algorithm to have the best teachers, in which big gains were thought to have been legitimately attained. If those classrooms held their gains while the classrooms with a suspected cheater lost ground, the cheating teachers could hardly argue that their students did worse only because the scores wouldn't count.

So a blend was settled upon. More than half of the 120 retested classrooms were those suspected of having a cheating teacher. The remainder were divided between the supposedly excellent teachers (high scores but no suspicious answer patterns) and, as a further control, classrooms with mediocre scores and no suspicious answers.

The retest was given a few weeks after the original exam. The children were not told the reason for the retest. Neither were the teachers. But they may have gotten the idea when it was announced that CPS officials, not the teachers, would administer the test. The teachers were asked to stay in the classroom with their students, but they would not be allowed to even touch the answer sheets.

The results were as compelling as the cheating algorithm had predicted. In the classrooms chosen as controls, where no cheating was suspected, scores stayed about the same or even rose. In contrast, the students with the teachers identified as cheaters scored far worse, by an average of more than a full grade level.

As a result, the Chicago Public School system began to fire its cheating teachers. The evidence was only strong enough to get rid of a dozen of them, but the many other cheaters had been duly warned. The final outcome of the Chicago study is further testament to the power of incentives: the following year, cheating by teachers fell more than 30 percent.

You might think that the sophistication of teachers who cheat would increase along with the level of schooling. But an exam given at the University of Georgia in the fall of 2001 disputes that idea. The course was called Coaching Principles and Strategies of Basketball, and the final grade was based on a single exam that had twenty questions. Among the questions:

How many halves are in a college basketball game?

a. 1   b. 2   c. 3   d. 4

How many points does a 3-pt. field goal account for in a basketball game?

a. 1   b. 2   c. 3   d. 4

What is the name of the exam which all high school seniors in the state of Georgia must pass?

a. Eye Exam
b. How Do the Grits Taste Exam
c. Bug Control Exam
d. Georgia Exit Exam

In your opinion, who is the best Division I assistant coach in the country?

a. Ron Jirsa
b. John Pelphrey
c. Jim Harrick Jr.
d. Steve Wojciechowski

If you are stumped by the final question, it might help to know that Coaching Principles was taught by Jim Harrick Jr., an assistant coach with the university's basketball team. It might also help to know that his father, Jim Harrick Sr., was the head basketball coach. Not surprisingly, Coaching Principles was a favorite course among players on the Harricks' team. Every student in the class received an A. Not long afterward, both Harricks were relieved of their coaching duties.

If it strikes you as disgraceful that Chicago schoolteachers and University of Georgia professors will cheat—a teacher, after all, is meant to instill values along with the facts—then the thought of cheating among sumo wrestlers may also be deeply disturbing. In Japan, sumo is not only the national sport but also a repository of the country's religious, military, and historical emotion. With its purification rituals and its imperial roots, sumo is sacrosanct in a way that American sports will never be. Indeed, sumo is said to be less about competition than about honor itself.

It is true that sports and cheating go hand in hand. That's because cheating is more common in the face of a bright-line incentive (the line between winning and losing, for instance) than with a murky incentive. Olympic sprinters and weightlifters, cyclists in the Tour de France, football linemen and baseball sluggers: they have all been shown to swallow whatever pill or powder may give them an edge. It is not only the participants who cheat. Cagey baseball managers try to steal an opponent's signs. In the 2002 Winter Olympic figure-skating competition, a French judge and a Russian judge were caught trying to swap votes to make sure their skaters medaled. (The man accused of orchestrating the vote swap, a reputed Russian mob boss named Alimzhan Tokhtakhounov, was also suspected of rigging beauty pageants in Moscow.)

An athlete who gets caught cheating is generally condemned, but most fans at least appreciate his motive: he wanted so badly to win that he bent the rules. (As the baseball player Mark Grace once said, "If you're not cheating, you're not trying.") An athlete who cheats to *lose*, meanwhile, is consigned to a deep circle of sporting hell. The 1919 Chicago White Sox, who conspired with gamblers to throw the World Series (and are therefore known forever as the Black Sox), retain a stench of iniquity among even casual baseball fans. The City College of New York's championship basketball team, once beloved for its smart and scrappy play, was instantly reviled when it was discovered in 1951 that several players had taken mob money to shave points—intentionally missing baskets to help gamblers beat the point spread. Remember Terry

Malloy, the tormented former boxer played by Marlon Brando in *On the Waterfront*? As Malloy saw it, all his troubles stemmed from the one fight in which he took a dive. Otherwise, he could have had class; he could have been a contender.

If cheating to lose is sport's premier sin, and if sumo wrestling is the premier sport of a great nation, cheating to lose couldn't possibly exist in sumo. Could it?

Once again, the data can tell the story. As with the Chicago school tests, the data set under consideration here is surpassingly large: the results from nearly every official match among the top rank of Japanese sumo wrestlers between January 1989 and January 2000, a total of 32,000 bouts fought by 281 different wrestlers.

The incentive scheme that rules sumo is intricate and extraordinarily powerful. Each wrestler maintains a ranking that affects every slice of his life: how much money he makes, how large an entourage he carries, how much he gets to eat, sleep, and otherwise take advantage of his success. The sixty-six highest-ranked wrestlers in Japan, comprising the *makuuchi* and *juryo* divisions, make up the sumo elite. A wrestler near the top of this elite pyramid may earn millions and is treated like royalty. Any wrestler in the top forty earns at least $170,000 a year. The seventieth-ranked wrestler in Japan, meanwhile, earns only $15,000 a year. Life isn't very sweet outside the elite. Low-ranked wrestlers must tend to their superiors, preparing their meals, cleaning their quarters, and even soaping up their hardest-to-reach body parts. So ranking is everything.

A wrestler's ranking is based on his performance in the elite tournaments that are held six times a year. Each wrestler has fifteen bouts per tournament, one per day over fifteen consecutive days. If he finishes the tournament with a winning record (eight victories or better), his ranking will rise. If he has a losing record, his ranking falls. If it falls far enough, he is booted from the elite rank entirely. The eighth victory in any tournament is therefore critical, the difference between promotion and demotion; it is roughly four times as valuable in the rankings as the typical victory.

So a wrestler entering the final day of a tournament on the bubble, with a 7–7 record, has far more to gain from a victory than an opponent with a record of 8–6 has to lose.

Is it possible, then, that an 8–6 wrestler might allow a 7–7 wrestler to beat him? A sumo bout is a concentrated flurry of force and speed and leverage, often lasting only a few seconds. It wouldn't be very hard to let yourself be tossed. Let's imagine for a moment that sumo wrestling *is* rigged. How might we measure the data to prove it?

The first step would be to isolate the bouts in question: those fought on a tournament's final day between a wrestler on the bubble and a wrestler who has already secured his eighth win. (Because more than half of all wrestlers end a tournament with either seven, eight, or nine victories, hundreds of bouts fit these criteria.) A final-day match between two 7–7 wrestlers isn't likely to be fixed, since both fighters badly need the victory. A wrestler with ten or more victories probably wouldn't throw a match either, since he has his own strong incentive to win: the $100,000 prize for overall tournament champion and a series of $20,000 prizes for the "outstanding technique" award, "fighting spirit" award, and others.

Let's now consider the following statistic, which represents the hundreds of matches in which a 7–7 wrestler faced an 8–6 wrestler on a tournament's final day. The left column tallies the probability, based on all past meetings between the two wrestlers fighting that day, that the 7–7 wrestler will win. The right column shows how often the 7–7 wrestler actually did win.

7–7 WRESTLER'S PREDICTED WIN PERCENTAGE AGAINST 8–6 OPPONENT	7–7 WRESTLER'S ACTUAL WIN PERCENTAGE AGAINST 8–6 OPPONENT
48.7	79.6

So the 7–7 wrestler, based on past outcomes, was expected to win just less than half the time. This makes sense; their records in this tournament indicate that the 8–6 wrestler is slightly better. But in actuality, the wrestler on the bubble won *almost eight out of ten* matches against his 8–6 opponent. Wrestlers on the bubble also do astonishingly well against 9–5 opponents:

7–7 WRESTLER'S PREDICTED WIN PERCENTAGE AGAINST 9–5 OPPONENT	7–7 WRESTLER'S ACTUAL WIN PERCENTAGE AGAINST 9–5 OPPONENT
47.2	73.4

As suspicious as this looks, a high winning percentage alone isn't enough to prove that a match is rigged. Since so much depends on a wrestler's eighth win, he should be expected to fight harder in a crucial bout. But perhaps there are further clues in the data that prove collusion.

It's worth thinking about the incentive a wrestler might have to throw a match. Maybe he accepts a bribe (which would obviously not be recorded in the data). Or perhaps some other arrangement is made between the two wrestlers. Keep in mind that the pool of elite sumo wrestlers is extraordinarily tight-knit. Each of the sixty-six elite wrestlers fights fifteen of the others in a tournament every two months. Furthermore, each wrestler belongs to a stable that is typically managed by a former sumo champion, so even the rival stables have close ties. (Wrestlers from the same stable do not wrestle one another.)

Now let's look at the win-loss percentage between the 7–7 wrestlers and the 8–6 wrestlers the *next* time they meet, when neither one is on the bubble. In this case, there is no great pressure on the individual match. So you might expect the wrestlers who won their 7–7 matches in the previous tournament to do about as well as they had in earlier matches against these same opponents—that is, winning roughly 50 percent of the time. You certainly wouldn't expect them to uphold their 80 percent clip.

As it turns out, the data show that the 7–7 wrestlers win only 40 percent of the rematches. Eighty percent in one match and 40 percent in the next? How do you make sense of that?

The most logical explanation is that the wrestlers made a quid pro quo agreement: you let me win today, when I really need the victory, and I'll let you win the next time. (Such an arrangement wouldn't preclude a cash bribe.) It's especially interesting to note that by the two wrestlers' *second* subsequent meeting, the win percentages revert to the expected level of about 50 percent, suggesting that the collusion spans only two matches.

And it isn't only the individual wrestlers whose records are suspect. The collective records of the various sumo stables are similarly aberrational. When one stable's wrestlers fare well on the bubble against wrestlers from a second stable, they tend to do especially *poorly* when the second stable's wrestlers are on the bubble. This indicates that some match rigging may be choreographed at the highest level of the sport—much like the Olympic skating judges' vote swapping.

No formal disciplinary action has ever been taken against a Japanese sumo wrestler for match rigging. Officials from the Japanese Sumo Association typically dismiss any such charges as fabrications by disgruntled former wrestlers. In fact, the mere utterance of the words "sumo" and "rigged" in the same sentence can cause a national furor. People tend to get defensive when the integrity of their national sport is impugned.

Still, allegations of match rigging do occasionally find their way into the Japanese media. These occasional media storms offer one more chance to measure possible corruption in sumo. Media scrutiny, after all, creates a powerful incentive: if two sumo wrestlers or their stables *have* been rigging matches, they might be leery to continue when a swarm of journalists and TV cameras descend upon them.

So what happens in such cases? The data show that in the sumo tournaments held immediately after allegations of match rigging, 7–7 wrestlers win only 50 percent of their final-day matches against 8–6 opponents instead of the typical 80 percent. No matter how the data are sliced, they inevitably suggest one thing: it is hard to argue that sumo wrestling isn't rigged.

Several years ago, two former sumo wrestlers came forward with extensive allegations of match rigging—and more. Aside from the crooked matches, they said, sumo was rife with drug use and sexcapades, bribes and tax evasion, and close ties to the *yakuza*, the Japanese mafia. The two men began to receive threatening phone calls; one of them told friends he was afraid he would be killed by the *yakuza*. Still, they went forward with plans to hold a press conference at the Foreign Correspondents' Club in Tokyo. But shortly beforehand, the two men died—hours apart, in the same hospital, of a similar respiratory ailment. The police declared there had been no foul play but did not conduct an investigation. "It seems very strange for these two people to die on the same day at the same hospital," said Mitsuru Miyake, the editor of a sumo magazine. "But no one has seen them poisoned, so you can't prove the skepticism."

Whether or not their deaths were intentional, these two men had done what no other sumo insider had previously done: named names. Of the 281 wrestlers covered in the data cited above, they identified 29 crooked wrestlers and 11 who were said to be incorruptible.

What happens when the whistle-blowers' corroborating evidence is factored into the analysis of the match data? In matches between two supposedly corrupt wrestlers, the wrestler who was on the bubble won about 80 percent of the time. In bubble matches against a supposedly clean opponent, meanwhile, the bubble wrestler was no more likely to win than his record would predict. Furthermore, when a supposedly corrupt wrestler faced an opponent whom the whistle-blowers did not name as either corrupt or clean, the results were nearly as skewed as when two corrupt wrestlers met—suggesting that most wrestlers who *weren't* specifically named were also corrupt.

So if sumo wrestlers, schoolteachers, and day-care parents all cheat, are we to assume that mankind is innately and universally corrupt? And if so, how corrupt?

The answer may lie in . . . bagels. Consider this story about a man named Paul Feldman.

Once upon a time, Feldman dreamed big dreams. With early training in agricultural economics, he wanted to tackle world hunger. Instead, he took a job in Washington, analyzing weapons expenditures for the U.S. Navy. This was in 1962. For the next twenty-odd years, he did further analytic work in Washington. He held senior-level jobs and earned good money, but he wasn't always recognized for his best work. At the office Christmas party, colleagues would introduce him to their wives not as "the head of the public research group" (which he was) but as "the guy who brings in the bagels."

The bagels had begun as a casual gesture: a boss treating his employees whenever they won a research contract. Then he made it a habit. Every Friday, he would bring in some bagels, a serrated knife, and cream cheese. When employees from neighboring floors heard about the bagels, they wanted some too. Eventually he was bringing in fifteen dozen bagels a week. In order to recoup his costs, he set out a cash basket and a sign with the suggested price. His collection rate was about 95 percent; he attributed the underpayment to oversight, not fraud.

In 1984, when his research institute fell under new management, Feldman took a look at his future and grimaced. He decided to quit his job and sell bagels. His economist friends thought he had lost his mind, but his wife supported him. The last of their three children was finishing college, and they had retired their mortgage.

Driving around the office parks that encircle Washington, he solicited customers with a simple pitch: early in the morning, he would deliver some bagels and a cash basket to a company's snack room; he would return before lunch to pick up the money and the leftovers. It was an honor-system commerce scheme, and it worked. Within a few years, Feldman was delivering 8,400 bagels a week to 140 companies and earning as much as he had ever made as a research analyst. He had thrown off the shackles of cubicle life and made himself happy.

He had also—quite without meaning to—designed a beautiful economic experiment. From the beginning, Feldman kept rigorous data on his bagel business. So by measuring the money collected against the bagels taken, he found it possible to tell, down to the penny, just how honest his customers were. Did they steal from him? If so, what were the characteristics of a company that stole versus a company that did not? Under what circumstances did people tend to steal more, or less?

As it happens, Feldman's accidental study provides a window onto a form of cheating that has long stymied academics: white-collar crime. (Yes, shorting the bagel man is white-collar crime, writ however small.) It might seem ludicrous to address as large and intractable a problem as white-collar crime through the life of a bagel man. But often a small and simple question can help chisel away at the biggest problems.

Despite all the attention paid to rogue companies like Enron, academics know very little about the practicalities of white-collar crime. The reason? There are no good data. A key fact of white-collar crime is that we hear about only the very slim fraction of people who are *caught* cheating. Most embezzlers lead quiet and theoretically happy lives; employees who steal company property are rarely detected.

With street crime, meanwhile, that is not the case. A mugging or a burglary or a murder is usually tallied whether or not the criminal is caught. A street crime has a victim, who typically reports the crime to the police, who generate data, which in turn generate thousands of academic papers by criminologists, sociologists, and economists. But white-collar crime presents no obvious victim. From whom, exactly, did the masters of Enron steal? And how can you measure something if you don't know to whom it happened, or with what frequency, or in what magnitude?

Paul Feldman's bagel business was different. It did present a victim. The victim was Paul Feldman.

When he started his business, he expected a 95 percent payment rate, based on the experience at his own office. But just as crime tends to be low on a street where a police car is parked, the 95 percent rate was artificially high: Feldman's presence had deterred theft. Not only that, but those bagel eaters knew the provider and had feelings (presumably good ones) about him. A broad swath of psychological and economic research has shown that people will pay different amounts for the same item depending on who is providing it. The economist Richard Thaler, in his 1985 "Beer on the Beach" study, showed that a thirsty sunbather would pay $2.65 for a beer delivered from a resort hotel but only $1.50 for the same beer if it came from a shabby grocery store.

In the real world, Feldman learned to settle for less than 95 percent. He came to consider a company "honest" if its payment rate was above 90 percent. He considered a rate between 80 and 90 percent "annoying but tolerable." If a company habitually paid below 80 percent, Feldman might post a hectoring note, like this one:

The cost of bagels has gone up dramatically since the beginning of the year. Unfortunately, the number of bagels that disappear without being paid for has also gone up. Don't let that continue. I don't imagine that you would teach your children to cheat, so why do it yourselves?

In the beginning, Feldman left behind an open basket for the cash, but too often the money vanished. Then he tried a coffee can with a money slot in its plastic lid, which also proved too tempting. In the end, he resorted to making small plywood boxes with a slot cut into the top. The wooden box has worked well. Each year he drops off about seven thousand boxes and loses, on average, just one to theft. This is an intriguing statistic: the same people who routinely steal more than 10 percent of his bagels almost never stoop to stealing his money box—a tribute to the nuanced social calculus of theft. From Feldman's perspective, an office worker who eats a bagel without paying is committing a crime; the office worker probably doesn't think so. This distinction probably has less to do with the admittedly small amount of money involved (Feldman's bagels cost one dollar each, cream cheese included) than with the context of the "crime." The same office worker who fails to pay for his bagel might also help himself to a long slurp of soda while filling a glass in a self-serve restaurant, but he is very unlikely to leave the restaurant without paying.

So what do the bagel data have to say? In recent years, there have been two noteworthy trends in the overall payment rate. The first was a long, slow decline that began in 1992. By the summer of 2001, the overall rate had slipped to about 87 percent. But immediately after September 11 of that year, the rate spiked a full 2 percent and hasn't slipped much since. (If a 2 percent gain in payment doesn't sound like much, think of it this way: the nonpayment rate fell from 13 to 11 percent, which amounts to a 15 percent decline in theft.) Because many of Feldman's customers are affiliated with national security, there may have been a patriotic element to this 9/11 Effect. Or it may have represented a more general surge in empathy.

The data also show that smaller offices are more honest than big ones. An office with a few dozen employees generally outpays by 3 to 5 percent an office with a few hundred employees. This may seem counterintuitive. In a bigger office, a bigger crowd is bound to convene around the bagel table, providing more witnesses to make sure you drop your money in the box. But in the big-office/small-office comparison, bagel crime seems to mirror street crime. There is far less street crime per capita in rural areas than in cities, in large part because a rural criminal is more likely to be known (and therefore caught). Also, a smaller community tends to exert greater social incentives against crime, the main one being shame.

The bagel data also reflect how much personal mood seems to affect honesty. Weather, for instance, is a major factor. Unseasonably pleasant weather inspires people to pay at a higher rate. Unseasonably cold weather, meanwhile, makes people cheat prolifically; so do heavy rain and wind. Worst are the holidays. The week of Christmas produces a 2 percent drop in payment rates—again, a 15 percent increase in theft, an effect on the same magnitude, in reverse, as that of 9/11. Thanksgiving is nearly as bad; the week of Valentine's Day is also lousy, as is the week straddling April 15. There are, however, several good holidays: the weeks that include the Fourth of July, Labor Day, and Columbus Day. The difference in the two sets of holidays? The low-cheating holidays represent little more than an extra day off from work. The high-cheating holidays are fraught with miscellaneous anxieties and the high expectations of loved ones.

Feldman has also reached some of his own conclusions about honesty, based more on his experience than the data. He has come to believe that morale is a big factor—that an office is more honest when the employees like their boss and their work. He also believes that employees further up the corporate ladder cheat more than those down below. He got this idea after delivering for years to one company spread out over three floors—an executive floor on top and two lower floors with sales, service, and administrative employees. (Feldman wondered if perhaps the executives cheated out of an overdeveloped sense of entitlement. What he didn't consider is that perhaps cheating was how they got to *be* executives.)

If morality represents the way we would like the world to work and economics represents how it actually does work, then the story of Feldman's bagel business lies at the very intersection of morality and economics. Yes, a lot of people steal from him, but the vast majority, even though no one is watching over them, do not. This outcome may surprise some people—including Feldman's economist friends, who counseled him twenty years ago that his honor-system scheme would never work. But it would not have surprised Adam Smith. In fact, the theme of Smith's first book, *The Theory of Moral Sentiments*, was the innate honesty of mankind. "How selfish soever man may be supposed," Smith wrote, "there are evidently some principles in his nature, which interest him in the fortune of others, and render their happiness necessary to him, though he derives nothing from it, except the pleasure of seeing it."

There is a tale, "The Ring of Gyges," that Feldman sometimes tells his economist friends. It comes from Plato's *Republic*. A student named Glaucon offered the story in response to a lesson by Socrates—who, like Adam Smith, argued that people are generally good even without enforcement. Glaucon, like Feldman's economist friends, disagreed. He told of a shepherd named Gyges who stumbled upon a secret cavern with a corpse inside that wore a ring. When Gyges put on the ring, he found that it made him invisible. With no one able to monitor his behavior, Gyges proceeded to do woeful things—seduce the queen, murder the king, and so on. Glaucon's story posed a moral question: could any man resist the temptation of evil if he knew his acts could not be witnessed? Glaucon seemed to think the answer was no. But Paul Feldman sides with Socrates and Adam Smith—for he knows that the answer, at least 87 percent of the time, is yes.

Chapter 2

HOW IS THE KU KLUX KLAN LIKE A GROUP OF REAL-ESTATE AGENTS?

As institutions go, the Ku Klux Klan has had a markedly up-and-down history. It was founded in the immediate aftermath of the Civil War by six former Confederate soldiers in Pulaski, Tennessee. The six young men, four of whom were budding lawyers, saw themselves as merely a circle of like-minded friends. Thus the name they chose, "kuklux," a slight mangling of *kuklos*, the Greek word for "circle." In the beginning, their activities were said to be harmless midnight pranks—for instance, riding horses through the countryside while draped in white sheets and pillow-case hoods. But soon the Klan evolved into a multistate terror-ist organization designed to frighten and kill emancipated slaves. Among its regional leaders were five former Confederate generals; its staunchest supporters were the plantation owners for whom Reconstruction posed an economic and political nightmare. In 1872, President Ulysses S. Grant spelled out for the House of

Representatives the true aims of the Ku Klux Klan: "By force and terror, to prevent all political action not in accord with the views of the members, to deprive colored citizens of the right to bear arms and of the right of a free ballot, to suppress the schools in which colored children were taught, and to reduce the colored people to a condition closely allied to that of slavery."

The early Klan did its work through pamphleteering, lynching, shooting, burning, castrating, pistol-whipping, and a thousand forms of intimidation. They targeted former slaves and any whites who supported the blacks' rights to vote, acquire land, or gain an education. But within barely a decade, the Klan had been extinguished, largely by legal and military interventions out of Washington, D.C.

If the Klan itself was defeated, however, its aims had largely been achieved through the establishment of Jim Crow laws. Congress, which during Reconstruction had been quick to enact measures of legal, social, and economic freedom for blacks, just as quickly began to roll them back. The federal government agreed to withdraw its occupation troops from the South, allowing the restoration of white rule. In *Plessy v. Ferguson*, the U.S. Supreme Court gave the go-ahead to full-scale racial segregation.

The Ku Klux Klan lay largely dormant until 1915, when D. W. Griffith's film *The Birth of a Nation* (originally titled *The Clansman*) helped spark its rebirth. Griffith presented the Klan as crusaders for white civilization itself, and as one of the noblest forces in American history. The film quoted a line from *A History of the American People*, written by a renowned historian: "At last there had sprung into existence a great Ku Klux Klan, a veritable empire of the South, to protect the Southern country." The historian in question was U.S. president Woodrow Wilson, one-time scholar and president of Princeton University.

By the 1920s, a revived Klan claimed eight million members. This time around, the Klan was not confined to the South but ranged throughout the country; this time, it concerned itself not only with blacks but also with Catholics, Jews, communists, unionists, immigrants, agitators, and other disrupters of the status quo. In 1933, with Hitler ascendant in Germany, Will Rogers was the first to draw a line between the new Klan and the new threat in Europe: "Papers all state Hitler is trying to copy Mussolini," he wrote. "Looks to me like it's the Ku Klux that he is copying."

The onset of World War II and a number of internal scandals once again laid the Klan low. Public sentiment turned against the Klan as the unity of a country at war trumped its message of separatism.

But within a few years, there were already signs of a massive revival. As wartime anxiety gave way to postwar uncertainty, Klan membership flourished. Barely two months after V-J Day, the Klan in Atlanta burned a 300-foot cross on the face of Stone Mountain, site of a storied rock carving of Robert E. Lee. The extravagant cross burning, one Klansman later said, was intended "just to let the niggers know the war is over and that the Klan is back on the market."

Atlanta had by now become Klan headquarters. The Klan was thought to hold great sway with key Georgia politicians, and its Georgia chapters were said to include many policemen and sheriff's deputies. Yes, the Klan was a secret society, reveling in passwords and cloak-and-dagger ploys, but its real power lay in the very public fear that it fostered, exemplified by the open secret that the Ku Klux Klan and the law-enforcement establishment were brothers in arms.

Atlanta—the Imperial City of the KKK's Invisible Empire, in Klan jargon—was also home to Stetson Kennedy, a thirty-year-old man with the bloodlines of a Klansman but a temperament that ran opposite. He came from a good southern family which claimed ancestors including two signers of the Declaration of Independence, an officer in the Confederate Army, and John B. Stetson, founder of the famed hat company and the man for whom Stetson University was named.

Stetson Kennedy grew up in a fourteen-room house in Jacksonville, Florida, the youngest of five children. His uncle Brady was a Klansman. But Kennedy would go on to become a self-described "dissident at large," writing numberless articles and several books that railed against bigotry. He first worked as a folklorist, traveling around Florida to collect old native tales and songs. Years later, when he served as a rare white correspondent for the *Pittsburgh Courier*, the country's largest black newspaper, he wrote under the pseudonym Daddy Mention—after a black folk hero who, as myth told it, could outrun the blast of a sheriff's shotgun.

What drove Kennedy was a hatred of small-mindedness, ignorance, obstructionism, and intimidation—which, in his view, were displayed by no organization more proudly than the Ku Klux Klan. Kennedy saw the Klan as the terrorist arm of the white establishment itself. This struck him as an intractable problem, for a variety of reasons. The Klan was in cahoots with political, business, and law-enforcement leaders. The public was frightened and felt powerless to act against the Klan. And the few anti-hate groups that existed at the time had little leverage or even information about the Klan. "Almost all of the things writ-ten on the subject were editorials, not exposés," Kennedy would later explain. "The writers were *against* the Klan, all right, but they had precious few inside facts *about* it."

So Kennedy set out to gather those facts. He would spend years interviewing Klan leaders and sympathizers, sometimes taking advantage of his own background and lineage to pretend that he was on their side of the issues. He also attended public Klan events and, as he would later write, he even set about to infiltrate the Klan in Atlanta.

The Klan Unmasked, Kennedy's memoir of his exploits "inside" the Klan, is in fact more of a novelization than a straight nonfic-tion account. Kennedy, a folklorist at heart, apparently wanted to put across the most dramatic story possible, and therefore in-cluded not only his own anti-Klan activities but those of another man, code-named John Brown. Brown was a union worker and a former Klan official who had changed his ways and offered to infiltrate the Klan. It was John Brown who apparently performed many of the most dramatic and dangerous episodes portrayed in *The Klan Unmasked*—physically attending Klan meetings and other functions in Atlanta—but since Stetson Kennedy was the man who later wrote the book, he rendered Brown's actions as his own.

Regardless, there was a great deal of information to be gleaned from this Brown/Kennedy collaboration. Brown divulged what he was learning at the weekly Klan meetings: the identities of the Klan's local and regional leaders; their upcoming plans; the Klan's current rituals, passwords, and language. It was Klan custom, for instance, to append a *Kl* to many words. (Thus would two Klans-men hold a Klonversation in the local Klavern.) The secret Klan handshake was a left-handed, limp-wristed fish wiggle. When a traveling Klansman wanted to locate brethren in a strange town, he would ask for a "Mr. Ayak"—"Ayak" being code for "Are You a Klansman?" He would hope to hear this response: "Yes, and I also know a Mr. Akai"—code for "A Klansman Am I."

Before long, John Brown was invited to join the Klavaliers, the Klan's secret police and "flog squad." For an infiltrator, this posed a particularly sticky problem: What would happen if he were called upon to inflict violence?

But as it happened, a central tenet of life in the Klan—and of terrorism in general—is that most of the threatened violence never goes beyond the threat stage.

Consider lynching, the Klan's hallmark sign of violence. Here, compiled by the Tuskegee Institute, are the decade-by-decade statistics on the lynching of blacks in the United States:

YEARS	LYNCHINGS OF BLACKS
1890–1899	1,111
1900–1909	791
1910–1919	569
1920–1929	281
1930–1939	119
1940–1949	31
1950–1959	6
1960–1969	3

Bear in mind that these figures represent not only lynchings attributed to the Ku Klux Klan but the total number of reported lynchings. The statistics reveal at least three noteworthy facts. The first is the obvious decrease in lynchings over time. The second is the absence of a correlation between lynchings and Klan membership: there were actually *more* lynchings of blacks between 1900 and 1909, when the Klan was dormant, than during the 1920s, when the Klan had millions of members—which suggests that the Ku Klux Klan carried out far fewer lynchings than is generally thought.

Third, relative to the size of the black population, lynchings were exceedingly rare. To be sure, one lynching is one too many. But by the turn of the century, lynchings were hardly the everyday occurrence that they are often considered in the public recollection. Compare the 281 victims of lynchings in the 1920s to the number of black infants who were dying at that time as a result of malnutrition, pneumonia, diarrhea, and the like. As of 1920, about 13 out of every 100 black children died in infancy, or roughly 20,000 children each year—compared to 28 people who were lynched in a year. As late as 1940, about 10,000 black infants died each year.

What larger truths do these lynching figures suggest? What does it mean that lynchings were relatively rare and that they fell precipitously over time, even in the face of a boom in Klan membership?

The most compelling explanation is that all those early lynchings *worked*. White racists—whether or not they belonged to the Ku Klux Klan—had through their actions and their rhetoric developed a strong incentive scheme that was terribly clear and terribly frightening. If a black person violated the accepted code of behavior, whether by talking back to a bus driver or daring to try to vote, he knew he might well be punished, perhaps by death.

So it may be that by the mid-1940s, when Stetson Kennedy was trying to bust up the Klan, it didn't really *need* to use as much violence. Many blacks, having long been told to behave like second-class citizens—or else—simply obliged. One or two lynchings went a long way toward inducing docility among even a large group of people, for people respond strongly to strong incentives. And there are few incentives more powerful than the fear of random violence—which, in essence, is why terrorism is so effective.

But if the Ku Klux Klan of the 1940s wasn't uniformly violent, what was it? The Klan that Stetson Kennedy wrote about was in fact a sorry fraternity of men, most of them poorly educated and with poor prospects, who needed a place to vent—and an excuse for occasionally staying out all night. That their fraternity engaged in quasi-religious chanting and oath taking and hosanna hailing, all of it top secret, made it that much more appealing.

Kennedy also found the Klan to be a slick money-making operation, at least for those near the top of the organization. Klan leaders had any number of revenue sources: thousands of dues-paying rank-and-file members; business owners who hired the Klan to scare off the unions or who paid the Klan protection money; Klan rallies that generated huge cash donations; even the occasional gunrunning or moonshine operation. Then there were rackets like the Klan's Death Benefit Association, which sold insurance policies to Klan members and accepted only cash or personal checks made out to the Grand Dragon himself.

And, even though the Klan may not have been as deadly as generally thought, it was plenty violent and, perhaps worse, had ever greater designs on political influence. Kennedy was therefore eager to damage the Klan in any way he could. When he heard about Klan plans for a union-busting rally, he fed the information to a union friend. He passed along Klan information to the assistant attorney general of Georgia, an established Klan buster. After researching the Klan's corporate charter, Kennedy wrote to the governor of Georgia suggesting the grounds upon which the charter should be revoked: the Klan had been designated a non-profit, non-political organization, but Kennedy had proof that it was clearly devoted to both profits and politics.

The problem was that most of Kennedy's efforts weren't producing the desired effect. The Klan was so entrenched and broad-based that Kennedy felt as if he were tossing pebbles at a giant. And even if he could somehow damage the Klan in Atlanta, the hundreds of other chapters around the country would go untouched.

Kennedy was supremely frustrated, and out of this frustration was born a new strategy. He had noticed one day a group of young boys playing some kind of spy game in which they exchanged silly secret passwords. It reminded him of the Klan. Wouldn't it be nice, he thought, to get the Klan's passwords and the rest of its secrets into the hands of kids all across the country—and their parents too? What better way to defang a secret society than to make public its most secret information? Instead of futilely attacking the Klan from the outside, what if he could somehow unleash all the secret inside information that John Brown was gathering from the Klan's weekly meetings? Between Brown's inside dope and everything that Kennedy had learned via his own investigations, he probably knew more Klan secrets than the average Klansman.

Kennedy turned to the most powerful mass medium of his day: radio. He began feeding Klan reports to the journalist Drew

Pearson, whose *Washington Merry-Go-Round* program was heard by millions of adults every day, and to the producers of the *Adventures of Superman* show, which reached millions of children each night. He told them about Mr. Ayak and Mr. Akai, and he passed along overheated passages from the Klan's bible, which was called the Kloran. (Kennedy never did learn why a white Christian supremacist group would give its bible essentially the same name as the most holy book of Islam.) He explained the role of Klan officers in any local Klavern: the Klaliff (vice president), Klokard (lecturer), Kludd (chaplain), Kligrapp (secretary), Klabee (treasurer), Kladd (conductor), Klarogo (inner guard), Klexter (outer guard), the Klokann (a five-man investigative committee), and the Klavaliers (whose leader was called Chief Ass Tearer). He spelled out the Klan hierarchy as it proceeded from the local to the national level: an Exalted Cyclops and his twelve Terrors; a Great Titan and his twelve Furies; a Grand Dragon and his nine Hydras; and the Imperial Wizard and his fifteen Genii. And Kennedy passed along all the information and gossip that John Brown gleaned by infiltrating the main Klan chapter, Nathan Bedford Forrest Klavern No. 1, Atlanta, Realm of Georgia.

During the war, the *Adventures of Superman* program had portrayed its hero fighting Hitler and Mussolini and Hirohito. But now he was in need of fresh villains. The Klan was a perfect target, and Superman turned his powers against them. Drew Pearson, an avowed Klan hater, now began giving regular Klan updates on his radio show, and then gave further updates, based on John Brown's inside reports, to show how the original updates were infuriating Klan officials. Pearson's work created an echo chamber that seemed to be driving Grand Dragon Samuel Green crazy. Here is Pearson's radio report from November 17, 1948:

Speaking at Klavern No. 1, Atlanta, Ga., the week after elections, the Grand Dragon wrung his hands and once again cautioned Klansmen to be careful about leaks.

"I have to talk frankly at these meetings," he said, "but I might as well call Drew Pearson before I come to the meeting and give him the information, for {the} next day he gives it out to everybody from coast to coast. The A.P. and U.P. are both calling me about it next morning while I am eating breakfast." . . .

The Grand Dragon spoke about plans for a big cross-burning to be held in Macon, Ga., on Dec. 10. It would be the biggest in Klan history, he said, and he expected 10,000 Klansmen to be there—in their robes. . . .

He added that the Klavalier Klub—the Klan's whipping and flogging department—was now on the job and had plenty of friends on the Atlanta police force.

As the Pearson and *Superman* radio shows played on, and as Stetson Kennedy continued to relay the Klan secrets obtained by John Brown to other broadcast and print outlets, a funny thing happened: attendance at Klan meetings began to fall, as did applications for new membership. Of all the ideas that Kennedy had thought up to fight bigotry, this campaign was easily the cleverest. He turned the Klan's secrecy against itself by making its private information public; he converted heretofore precious knowledge into ammunition for mockery.

Americans who might have been philosophically inclined to oppose the Klan had now been given enough specific information to oppose them more actively, and public sentiment began to shift. Americans who might have been philosophically inclined to *embrace* the Klan had now been given all sorts of caution against doing so. Although the Klan would never quite die, especially down south—David Duke, a smooth-talking Klan leader from Louisiana, mounted substantive bids for the U.S. Senate and other offices—it was certainly handicapped, at least in the short term, by Kennedy's brazen dissemination of inside information. While it is impossible to tease out the exact impact that his work had on the Klan, many people have given him a great deal of credit for damaging an institution that was in grave need of being damaged.

This did not come about because Stetson Kennedy was courageous or resolute or unflappable, even though he was all of these. It happened because he understood the raw power of information. The Ku Klux Klan—much like politicians or real-estate agents or stockbrokers—was a group whose power was derived in large part from the fact that it hoarded information. Once that information falls into the wrong hands (or, depending on your point of view, the *right* hands), much of the group's advantage disappears.

In the late 1990s, the price of term life insurance fell dramatically. This posed something of a mystery, for the decline had no obvious cause. Other types of insurance, including health and automobile and homeowners' coverage, were certainly not falling in price. Nor had there been any radical changes among insurance companies, insurance brokers, or the people who buy term life insurance. So what happened?

The Internet happened. In the spring of 1996, Quotesmith.com became the first of several websites that enabled a customer to compare, within seconds, the price of term life insurance sold by dozens of different companies. For such websites, term life insurance was a perfect product. Unlike other forms of insurance—

especially whole life insurance, which is a far more complicated financial instrument—term life policies are fairly homogeneous: any given thirty-year, guaranteed policy for $1 million is essentially identical to the next. So what really matters is the price. Shopping around for the cheapest policy, a process that had been convoluted and time-consuming, was suddenly made simple. With customers able to instantaneously find the cheapest policy, the more expensive companies had no choice but to lower their prices. Suddenly customers were paying $1 billion less a year for term life insurance.

It is worth noting that these websites only listed prices; they didn't even sell the policies. So it wasn't really insurance they were peddling. Like Stetson Kennedy, they were dealing in information. (Had the Internet been around when Kennedy was attacking the Klan, he probably would have been blogging his brains out.) To be sure, there are differences between exposing the Ku Klux Klan and exposing insurance companies' high premiums. The Klan trafficked in secret information whose secrecy engendered fear, while insurance prices were less a secret than a set of facts dispensed in a way that made comparisons difficult. But in both instances, the dissemination of the information diluted its power. As Supreme Court Justice Louis D. Brandeis once wrote, "Sunlight is said to be the best of disinfectants."

Information is a beacon, a cudgel, an olive branch, a deterrent—all depending on who wields it and how. Information is so powerful that the *assumption* of information, even if the information does not actually exist, can have a sobering effect. Consider the case of a one-day-old car.

The day that a car is driven off the lot is the worst day in its life, for it instantly loses as much as a quarter of its value. This might seem absurd, but we know it to be true. A new car that was bought for $20,000 cannot be resold for more than perhaps $15,000. Why? Because the only person who might logically want to resell a brand-new car is someone who found the car to be a lemon. So even if the car isn't a lemon, a potential buyer assumes that it is. He assumes that the seller has some information about the car that he, the buyer, does not have—and the seller is punished for this assumed information.

And if the car *is* a lemon? The seller would do well to wait a year to sell it. By then, the suspicion of lemonness will have faded; by then, some people will be selling their perfectly good year-old cars, and the lemon can blend in with them, likely selling for more than it is truly worth.

It is common for one party to a transaction to have better information than another party. In the parlance of economists, such a case is known as an information asymmetry. We accept as a verity of capitalism that someone (usually an expert) knows more than someone else (usually a consumer). But information asymmetries everywhere have in fact been gravely wounded by the Internet.

Information is the currency of the Internet. As a medium, the Internet is brilliantly efficient at shifting information from the hands of those who have it into the hands of those who do not. Often, as in the case of term life insurance prices, the information existed but in a woefully scattered way. (In such instances, the Internet acts like a gigantic horseshoe magnet waved over an endless sea of haystacks, plucking the needle out of each one.) The Internet has accomplished what even the most fervent consumer advocates usually cannot: it has vastly shrunk the gap between the experts and the public.

The Internet has proven particularly fruitful for situations in which a face-to-face encounter with an expert might actually *exacerbate* the problem of asymmetrical information—situations in which an expert uses his informational advantage to make us feel stupid or rushed or cheap or ignoble. Consider a scenario in which your loved one has just died and now the funeral director (who knows that you know next to nothing about his business and are under emotional duress to boot) steers you to the $8,000 mahogany casket. Or consider the automobile dealership: a salesman does his best to obscure the car's base price under a mountain of add-ons and incentives. Later, however, in the cool-headed calm of your home, you can use the Internet to find out exactly how much the dealer paid the manufacturer for that car. Or you might just log on to www.TributeDirect.com and buy that mahogany casket yourself for only $3,595, delivered overnight. Unless you decide to spend $2,300 for "The Last Hole" (a casket with golf scenes) or "Memories of the Hunt" (featuring big-racked bucks and other prey) or one of the much cheaper models that the funeral director somehow failed even to mention.

The Internet, powerful as it is, has hardly slain the beast that is information asymmetry. Consider the corporate scandals of the early 2000s. The crimes committed by Enron included hidden partnerships, disguised debt, and the manipulation of energy markets. Henry Blodget of Merrill Lynch and Jack Grubman of Salomon Smith Barney wrote glowing research reports of companies they knew to be junk. Sam Waksal dumped his ImClone stock when he got early word of a damaging report from the Food and Drug Administration; his friend Martha Stewart also dumped her shares, then lied about the reason. WorldCom and Global Crossing fabricated billions of dollars in revenues to pump up their stock prices. One group of mutual fund companies let preferred customers trade at preferred prices, and another group was charged with hiding management fees.

Though extraordinarily diverse, these crimes all have a common trait: they were sins of information. Most of them involved an expert, or a gang of experts, promoting false information or hiding true information; in each case the experts were trying to keep the information asymmetry as asymmetrical as possible.

The practitioners of such acts, especially in the realm of high finance, inevitably offer this defense: "Everybody else was doing it." Which may be largely true. One characteristic of information crimes is that very few of them are detected. Unlike street crimes, they do not leave behind a corpse or a broken window. Unlike a bagel criminal—that is, someone who eats one of Paul Feldman's bagels but doesn't pay—an information criminal typically doesn't have someone like Feldman tallying every nickel. For an information crime to reach the surface, something drastic must happen. When it does, the results tend to be pretty revealing. The perpetrators, after all, weren't thinking about their private actions being made public. Consider the "Enron tapes," the secretly recorded conversations of Enron employees that surfaced after the company imploded. During a phone conversation on August 5, 2000, two traders chatted about how a wildfire in California would allow Enron to jack up its electricity prices. "The magical word of the day," one trader said, "is 'Burn, Baby, Burn.' " A few months later, a pair of Enron traders named Kevin and Bob talked about how California officials wanted to make Enron refund the profits of its price gouging.

KEVIN: *They're fucking taking all the money back from you guys? All the money you guys stole from those poor grandmas in California?*

BOB: *Yeah, Grandma Millie, man.*

KEVIN: *Yeah, now she wants her fucking money back for all the power you jammed right up her ass for fucking $250 a megawatt hour.*

If you were to assume that many experts use their information to your detriment, you'd be right. Experts depend on the fact that you don't have the information they do. Or that you are so befuddled by the complexity of their operation that you wouldn't know what to do with the information if you had it. Or that you are so in awe of their expertise that you wouldn't dare challenge them. If your doctor suggests that you have angioplasty—even though some current research suggests that angioplasty often does little to prevent heart attacks—you aren't likely to think that the doctor is using his informational advantage to make a few thousand dollars for himself or his buddy. But as David Hillis, an interventional cardiologist at the University of Texas Southwestern Medical Center in Dallas, explained to *The New York Times*, a doctor may have the same economic incentives as a car salesman or a funeral director or a mutual fund manager: "If you're an invasive cardiologist and Joe Smith, the local internist, is sending you patients, and if you tell them they don't need the procedure, pretty soon Joe Smith doesn't send patients anymore."

Armed with information, experts can exert a gigantic, if unspoken, leverage: fear. Fear that your children will find you dead on the bathroom floor of a heart attack if you do not have angioplasty

67

surgery. Fear that a cheap casket will expose your grandmother to a terrible underground fate. Fear that a $25,000 car will crumple like a toy in an accident, whereas a $50,000 car will wrap your loved ones in a cocoon of impregnable steel. The fear created by commercial experts may not quite rival the fear created by terrorists like the Ku Klux Klan, but the principle is the same.

Consider a transaction that wouldn't seem, on the surface, to create much fear: selling your house. What's so scary about that? Aside from the fact that selling a house is typically the largest financial transaction in your life, and that you probably have scant experience in real estate, and that you may have an enormous emotional attachment to your house, there are at least two pressing fears: that you will sell the house for far less than it is worth and that you will not be able to sell it at all.

In the first case, you fear setting the price too low; in the second, you fear setting it too high. It is the job of your real-estate agent, of course, to find the golden mean. She is the one with all the information: the inventory of similar houses, the recent sales trends, the tremors of the mortgage market, perhaps even a lead on an interested buyer. You feel fortunate to have such a knowledgeable expert as an ally in this most confounding enterprise.

Too bad she sees things differently. A real-estate agent may see you not so much as an ally but as a mark. Think back to the study cited at the beginning of this book, which measured the difference between the sale prices of homes that belonged to real-estate agents themselves and the houses they sold for their clients. The study found that an agent keeps her own house on the market an average ten extra days, waiting for a better offer, and sells it for over 3 percent more than your house—or $10,000 on the sale of a $300,000 house. That's $10,000 going into her pocket that does not go into yours, a nifty profit produced by the abuse of information and a keen understanding of incentives. The problem is that the agent only stands to personally gain an additional $150 by selling your house for $10,000 more, which isn't much reward for a lot of extra work. So her job is to convince you that a $300,000 offer is in fact a very good offer, even a generous one, and that only a fool would refuse it.

This can be tricky. The agent does not want to come right out and call you a fool. So she merely implies it—perhaps by telling you about the much bigger, nicer, newer house down the block that has sat unsold for six months. Here is the agent's main weapon: the conversion of information into fear. Consider this true story, related by John Donohue, a law professor who in 2001 was teaching at Stanford University: "I was just about to buy a house on the Stanford campus," he recalls, "and the seller's agent kept telling me what a good deal I was getting because the market was about to zoom. As soon as I signed the purchase contract, he asked me if I would need an agent to sell my previous Stanford house. I told him that I would probably try to sell without an agent, and he replied, 'John, that might work under normal conditions, but with the market tanking now, you really need the help of a broker.' "

Within five minutes, a zooming market had tanked. Such are the marvels that can be conjured by an agent in search of the next deal.

Consider now another true story of a real-estate agent's information abuse. The tale involves K., a close friend of one of this book's authors. K. wanted to buy a house that was listed at $469,000. He was prepared to offer $450,000 but he first called the seller's agent and asked her to name the lowest price that she thought the homeowner might accept. The agent promptly scolded K. "You ought to be ashamed of yourself," she said. "That is clearly a violation of real-estate ethics."

K. apologized. The conversation turned to other, more mundane issues. After ten minutes, as the conversation was ending, the agent told K., "Let me say one last thing. My client is willing to sell this house for a lot less than you might think."

Based on this conversation, K. then offered $425,000 for the house instead of the $450,000 he had planned to offer. In the end, the seller accepted $430,000. Thanks to *his own agent's* intervention, the seller lost at least $20,000. The agent, meanwhile, only lost $300—a small price to pay to ensure that she would quickly and easily lock up the sale, which netted her a commission of $6,450.

So a big part of a real-estate agent's job, it would seem, is to persuade the homeowner to sell for less than he would like while at the same time letting potential buyers know that a house can be bought for less than its listing price. To be sure, there are more subtle means of doing so than coming right out and telling the buyer to bid low. The study of real-estate agents cited above also includes data that reveals how agents convey information through the for-sale ads they write. A phrase like "well maintained," for instance, is as full of meaning to an agent as "Mr. Ayak" was to a Klansman; it means that a house is old but not quite falling down. A savvy buyer will know this (or find out for himself once he sees the house), but to the sixty-five-year-old retiree who is selling his house, "well maintained" might sound like a compliment, which is just what the agent intends.

An analysis of the language used in real-estate ads shows that certain words are powerfully correlated with the final sale price of

THE KU KLUX KLAN AND REAL-ESTATE AGENTS

a house. This doesn't necessarily mean that labeling a house "well maintained" *causes* it to sell for less than an equivalent house. It does, however, indicate that when a real-estate agent labels a house "well maintained," she may be subtly encouraging a buyer to bid low.

Listed below are ten terms commonly used in real-estate ads. Five of them have a strong positive correlation to the ultimate sale price, and five have a strong negative correlation. Guess which are which.

TEN COMMON REAL-ESTATE AD TERMS

Fantastic

Granite

Spacious

State-of-the-Art

!

Corian

Charming

Maple

Great Neighborhood

Gourmet

A "fantastic" house is surely fantastic enough to warrant a high price, isn't it? What about a "charming" and "spacious" house in a "great neighborhood!"? No, no, no, and no. Here's the breakdown:

FIVE TERMS CORRELATED TO A HIGHER SALE PRICE

Granite

State-of-the-Art

71

Corian

Maple

Gourmet

FIVE TERMS CORRELATED TO A LOWER SALE PRICE

Fantastic

Spacious

!

Charming

Great Neighborhood

Three of the five terms correlated with a higher sale price are physical descriptions of the house itself: granite, Corian, and maple. As information goes, such terms are specific and straightforward—and therefore pretty useful. If you like granite, you might like the house; but even if you don't, "granite" certainly doesn't connote a fixer-upper. Nor does "gourmet" or "state-of-the-art," both of which seem to tell a buyer that a house is, on some level, truly fantastic.

"Fantastic," meanwhile, is a dangerously ambiguous adjective, as is "charming." Both these words seem to be real-estate agent code for a house that doesn't have many specific attributes worth describing. "Spacious" homes, meanwhile, are often decrepit or impractical. "Great neighborhood" signals a buyer that, well, *this* house isn't very nice but others nearby may be. And an exclamation point in a real-estate ad is bad news for sure, a bid to paper over real shortcomings with false enthusiasm.

If you study the words in ads for a real-estate agent's *own* home, meanwhile, you see that she indeed emphasizes descriptive terms (especially "new," "granite," "maple," and "move-in condition") and avoids empty adjectives (including "wonderful," "immaculate," and the telltale "!"). Then she patiently waits for the best buyer to come along. She might tell this buyer about a house nearby that just sold for $25,000 *above* the asking price, or another house that is currently the subject of a bidding war. She is careful to exercise every advantage of the information asymmetry she enjoys.

Does this make her a bad person? That's hard to say, at least hard for *us* to say. The point here is not that real-estate agents are bad people, but that they simply *are* people—and people inevitably respond to incentives. The incentives of the real-estate business, as currently configured, plainly encourage some agents to act against the best interests of their customers.

But like the funeral director and the car salesman and the life-insurance company, the real-estate agent has also seen her advantage eroded by the Internet. After all, anyone selling a home can now get online and gather her own information about sales trends and housing inventory and mortgage rates. The information has been set loose. And recent sales data show the results. Real-estate agents still get a higher price for their own homes than comparable homes owned by their clients, but since the proliferation of real-estate websites, the gap between the two prices has shrunk by a third.

It would be naïve to suppose that people abuse information only when they are acting as experts or as agents of commerce. After all, agents and experts are people too—which suggests that we are likely to abuse information in our personal lives as well, whether by withholding true information or editing the information we choose to put forth. A real-estate agent may wink and nod when she lists a "well-maintained" house, but we each have our equivalent hedges.

Think about how you describe yourself during a job interview versus how you might describe yourself on a first date. (For even more fun, compare that first-date conversation to a conversation with the same person during your tenth year of marriage.) Or think about how you might present yourself if you were going on national television for the first time. What sort of image would you want to project? Perhaps you want to seem clever or kind or good-looking; presumably you *don't* want to come off as cruel or bigoted. During the heyday of the Ku Klux Klan, its members took pride in publicly disparaging anybody who wasn't a conservative white Christian. But public bigotry has since been vastly curtailed. Even subtle displays of bigotry, if they become public, are now costly. Trent Lott, the majority leader of the U.S. Senate, learned this in 2002 after making a toast at a one hundredth birthday party for Strom Thurmond, his fellow senator and fellow southerner. Lott made a reference in his toast to Thurmond's 1948 campaign for president, which was built on a platform of segregation; Mississippi—Lott's home state—was one of just four states that Thurmond carried. "We're proud of it," Lott told the partygoers. "And if the rest of the country had followed our lead, we wouldn't have had all these problems over all these years either." The implication that Lott was a fan of segregation raised enough of a fury that he was forced to quit his Senate leadership post.

Even if you are a private citizen, you surely wouldn't want to seem bigoted while appearing in public. Might there be a way to test for discrimination in a public setting?

Unlikely as it may seem, the television game show *The Weakest*

Link provides a unique laboratory to study discrimination. An import from the United Kingdom, *The Weakest Link* for a short time became wildly popular in the United States. The game includes eight contestants (or, in a later daytime version, six) who each answer trivia questions and compete for a single cash jackpot. But the player who answers the most questions correctly isn't necessarily the player who advances. After each round, every contestant votes to eliminate one other contestant. A player's trivia-answering ability is presumably the only worthwhile factor to consider; race, gender, and age wouldn't seem to matter. But do they? By measuring a contestant's actual votes against the votes that would truly best serve his self-interest, it's possible to tell if discrimination is at play.

The voting strategy changes as the game progresses. In the first several rounds, it makes sense to eliminate bad players since the jackpot grows only when correct answers are given. In later rounds, the strategic incentives are flipped. The value of building the jackpot is now outweighed by each contestant's desire to win the jackpot. It's easier to do that if you eliminate the other good players. So, roughly speaking, the typical contestant will vote to eliminate the worse players in the early rounds and the better players in the later rounds.

The key to measuring the *Weakest Link* voting data is to tease out a contestant's playing ability from his race, gender, and age. If a young black man answers a lot of questions correctly but is voted off early, discrimination would seem to be a factor. Meanwhile, if an elderly white woman doesn't answer a single question correctly and is still not voted off, some sort of discriminatory favoritism would seem to be at play.

Again, keep in mind that all of this is happening on camera. A contestant knows that his friends, family, and co-workers—along with a few million strangers—are watching. So who, if anyone, is discriminated against on *The Weakest Link*?

Not, as it turns out, blacks. An analysis of more than 160 episodes reveals that black contestants, in both the early and late rounds of the game, are eliminated at a rate commensurate with their trivia-answering abilities. The same is true for female contestants. In a way, neither of these findings is so surprising. Two of the most potent social campaigns of the past half-century were the civil rights movement and the feminist movement, which demonized discrimination against blacks and women, respectively.

So perhaps, you say hopefully, discrimination was practically eradicated during the twentieth century, like polio.

Or more likely, it has become so unfashionable to discriminate against certain groups that all but the most insensitive people take pains to at least *appear* fair-minded, at least in public. This hardly means that discrimination itself has ended—only that people are embarrassed to show it. How might you determine whether the lack of discrimination against blacks and women represents a true absence or just a charade? The answer can be found by looking at other groups that society doesn't protect as well. Indeed, the *Weakest Link* voting data do indicate two kinds of contestants who *are* consistently discriminated against: the elderly and Latinos.

Among economists, there are two leading theories of discrimination. Interestingly, elderly *Weakest Link* contestants seem to suffer from one type, while Latinos suffer the other. The first type is called taste-based discrimination, which means that one person discriminates simply because he prefers to not interact with a particular type of other person. In the second type, known as information-based discrimination, one person believes that another type of person has poor skills, and acts accordingly.

On *The Weakest Link*, Latinos suffer information-based discrimination. Other contestants seem to view the Latinos as poor players, even when they are not. This perception translates into Latinos' being eliminated in the early rounds even if they are doing well and *not* being eliminated in the later rounds, when other contestants want to keep the Latinos around to weaken the field.

Elderly players, meanwhile, are victims of taste-based discrimination: in the early rounds *and* late rounds, they are eliminated far out of proportion to their skills. It seems as if the other contestants—this is a show on which the average age is thirty-four—simply don't want the older players around.

It's quite possible that a typical *Weakest Link* contestant isn't even cognizant of his discrimination toward Latinos and the elderly (or, in the case of blacks and women, his *lack* of discrimination). He is bound to be nervous, after all, and excited, playing a fast-moving game under the glare of television lights. Which naturally suggests another question: how might that same person express his preferences—and reveal information about himself—in the privacy of his home?

In a given year, some forty million Americans swap intimate truths about themselves with complete strangers. It all happens on Internet dating sites. Some of them, like Match.com, eHarmony .com, and Yahoo! Personals, appeal to a broad audience. Others cater to more specific tastes: ChristianSingles.com, JDate.com, Latin Matcher.com, BlackSinglesConnection.com, CountryWestern Singles.com, USMilitarySingles.com, OverweightDate.com, and

Gay.com. Dating websites are the most successful subscription-based business on the Internet.

Each site operates a bit differently, but the gist is this: You compose a personal ad about yourself that typically includes a photo, vital statistics, your income range, level of education, likes and dislikes, and so on. If the ad catches someone's fancy, that someone will e-mail you and perhaps arrange a date. On many sites, you also specify your dating aims: "long-term relationship," "a casual lover," or "just looking."

So there are two massive layers of data to be mined here: the information that people include in their ads and the level of response gleaned by any particular ad. Each layer of the data can be asked its own question. In the case of the ads, how forthright (and honest) are people when it comes to sharing their personal information? And in the case of the responses, what kind of information in personal ads is considered the most (and least) desirable?

Two economists and a psychologist recently banded together to address these questions. Günter J. Hitsch, Ali Hortaçsu, and Dan Ariely analyzed the data from one of the mainstream dating sites, focusing on more than 20,000 active users, half in Boston and half in San Diego. Fifty-six percent of the users were men, and the median age range for all users was twenty-one to thirty-five. Although they represented an adequate racial mix to reach some conclusions about race, they were predominantly white.

They were also a lot richer, taller, skinnier, and better-looking than average. That, at least, is what they wrote about themselves. More than 4 percent of the online daters claimed to earn more than $200,000 a year, whereas fewer than 1 percent of typical Internet users actually earn that much, suggesting that three of the four big earners were exaggerating. Male and female users typically reported that they are about an inch taller than the national average. As for weight, the men were in line with the national average, but the women typically said they weighed about twenty pounds less than the national average.

Most impressively, fully 72 percent of the women claimed "above average" looks, including 24 percent claiming "very good looks." The online men too were gorgeous: 68 percent called themselves "above average," including 19 percent with "very good looks." This leaves only about 30 percent of the users with "average" looks, including a paltry 1 percent with "less than average" looks—which suggests that the typical online dater is either a fabulist, a narcissist, or simply resistant to the meaning of "average." (Or perhaps they are all just pragmatists: as any real-estate agent knows, the typical house isn't "charming" or "fantastic," but unless you say it is, no one will even bother to take a look.) Twenty-eight percent of the women on the site said they were blond, a number far beyond the national average, which indicates a lot of dyeing, or lying, or both.

Some users, meanwhile, were bracingly honest. Seven percent of the men conceded that they were married, with a significant minority of these men reporting that they were "happily married." But the fact that they were honest doesn't mean they were rash. Of the 243 "happily married" men in the sample, only 12 chose to post a picture of themselves. The reward of gaining a mistress was evidently outweighed by the risk of having your wife discover your personal ad. ("And what were *you* doing on that website?" the husband might bluster, undoubtedly to little avail.)

Of the many ways to fail on a dating website, not posting a photo of yourself is perhaps the most certain. (Not that the photo necessarily *is* a photo of yourself; it may well be some better-looking stranger, but such deception would obviously backfire in time.) A man who does not include his photo gets only 60 percent of the volume of e-mail response of a man who does; a woman who doesn't include her photo gets only 24 percent as much. A low-income, poorly educated, unhappily employed, not very attractive, slightly overweight, and balding man who posts his photo stands a better chance of gleaning some e-mails than a man who says he makes $200,000 and is deadly handsome but doesn't post a photo. There are plenty of reasons someone might not post a photo—he's technically challenged or is ashamed of being spotted by friends or is just plain unattractive—but as in the case of a brand-new car with a For Sale sign, prospective customers will assume he's got something seriously wrong under the hood.

Getting a date is hard enough as it is. Fifty-six percent of the men who post ads don't receive even one e-mail; 21 percent of the women don't get a single response. The traits that do draw a big response, meanwhile, will not be a big surprise to anyone with even a passing knowledge of the sexes. In fact, the preferences expressed by online daters fit snugly with the most common stereotypes about men and women.

For instance, men who say they want a long-term relationship do much better than men looking for an occasional lover. But women looking for an occasional lover do great. For men, a woman's looks are of paramount importance. For women, a man's income is terribly important. The richer a man is, the more e-mails he receives. But a woman's income appeal is a bell-shaped curve: men do not want to date *low*-earning women, but once a woman starts earning too much, they seem to be scared off. Women are eager to date military men, policemen, and firemen (possibly the result of a 9/11 Effect, like the higher payments to Paul Feldman's bagel business), along with lawyers and doctors; they generally avoid men with manufacturing jobs. For men, being short is a big disadvantage (which is probably why so many lie about it), but weight doesn't much matter. For women, being overweight is deadly (which is probably why *they* lie). For a man, having red hair or curly hair is a downer, as is "bald with a fringe"—but a shaved head is okay. For a woman, salt-and-pepper hair is bad, while blond hair is, not surprisingly, very good.

In addition to all the information about income, education, and looks, men and women on the dating site listed their race. They were also asked to indicate a preference regarding the race of their potential dates. The two preferences were "the same as mine" or "it doesn't matter." Like the *Weakest Link* contestants, the website users were now publicly declaring how they felt about people who didn't look like them. They would reveal their *actual* preferences later, in confidential e-mails to the people they wanted to date.

Roughly half of the white women on the site and 80 percent of the white men declared that race didn't matter to them. But the response data tell a different story. The white men who said that race didn't matter sent 90 percent of their e-mail queries to white women. The white women who said race didn't matter sent about 97 percent of their e-mail queries to white men. This means that an Asian man who is good-looking, rich, and well educated will receive fewer than 25 percent as many e-mails from white women as a white man with the same qualifications would receive; similarly, black and Latino men receive about half as many e-mails from white women as they would if they were white.

Is it possible that race really didn't matter for these white women and men and that they simply never happened to browse a non-white date that interested them? Or, more likely, did they say that race didn't matter because they wanted to come across—especially to potential mates of their own race—as open-minded?

The gulf between the information we publicly proclaim and the information we know to be true is often vast. (Or, put a more familiar way: we say one thing and do another.) This can be seen in personal relationships, in commercial transactions, and of course in politics.

By now we are fully accustomed to the false public proclamations of politicians themselves. But voters lie too. Consider an election between a black candidate and a white candidate. Might white voters lie to pollsters, claiming they will vote for the black candidate in order to appear more color-blind than they actually are? Apparently so. In New York City's 1989 mayoral race between David Dinkins (a black candidate) and Rudolph Giuliani (who is white), Dinkins won by only a few points. Although Dinkins became the city's first black mayor, his slender margin of victory came as a surprise, for pre-election polls showed Dinkins winning by nearly 15 points. When the white supremacist David Duke ran for the U.S. Senate in 1990, he garnered nearly 20 percent more of the vote than pre-election polls had projected, an indication that thousands of Louisiana voters did not want to admit their preference for a candidate with racist views.

Duke, though he never won the high political office he often sought, proved himself a master of information abuse. As Grand Wizard of the Knights of the Ku Klux Klan, he was able to compile a mailing list of thousands of rank-and-file Klansmen and other supporters who would eventually become his political base. Not content to use the list only for himself, he sold it for $150,000 to the governor of Louisiana. Years later, Duke would once again use the list himself, letting his supporters know that he'd fallen on hard times and needed their donations. In this way Duke was able to raise hundreds of thousands of dollars for his continuing work in the field of white supremacy. He had explained to his supporters in a letter that he was so broke that the bank was trying to repossess his house.

In truth, Duke had already sold his house for a solid profit. (It isn't known whether he used a real-estate agent.) And most of the money he raised from his supporters was being used not to promote any white supremacist cause but rather to satisfy Duke's gambling habit. It was a sweet little scam he was running—until he was arrested and sent to federal prison in Big Spring, Texas.

Chapter 3

WHY DO DRUG DEALERS STILL LIVE WITH THEIR MOMS?

The two previous chapters were built around a pair of admittedly freakish questions: *What do schoolteachers and sumo wrestlers have in common?* and *How is the Ku Klux Klan like a group of real-estate agents?* But if you ask enough questions, strange as they seem at the time, you may eventually learn something worthwhile.

The first trick of asking questions is to determine if your question is a good one. Just because a question has never been asked does not make it good. Smart people have been asking questions for quite a few centuries now, so many of the questions that *haven't* been asked are bound to yield uninteresting answers.

But if you can question something that people really care about and find an answer that may surprise them—that is, if you can overturn the conventional wisdom—then you may have some luck.

It was John Kenneth Galbraith, the hyperliterate economic

sage, who coined the phrase "conventional wisdom." He did not consider it a compliment. "We associate truth with convenience," he wrote, "with what most closely accords with self-interest and personal well-being or promises best to avoid awkward effort or unwelcome dislocation of life. We also find highly acceptable what contributes most to self-esteem." Economic and social behaviors, Galbraith continued, "are complex, and to comprehend their character is mentally tiring. Therefore we adhere, as though to a raft, to those ideas which represent our understanding."

So the conventional wisdom in Galbraith's view must be simple, convenient, comfortable, and comforting—though not necessarily true. It would be silly to argue that the conventional wisdom is *never* true. But noticing where the conventional wisdom may be false—noticing, perhaps, the contrails of sloppy or self-interested thinking—is a nice place to start asking questions.

Consider the recent history of homelessness in the United States. In the early 1980s, an advocate for the homeless named Mitch Snyder took to saying that there were about 3 million homeless Americans. The public duly sat up and took notice. More than 1 of every 100 people were homeless? That sure seemed high, but . . . well, the expert said it. A heretofore quiescent problem was suddenly catapulted into the national consciousness. Snyder even testified before Congress about the magnitude of the problem. He also reportedly told a college audience that 45 homeless people die each second—which would mean a whopping 1.4 billion dead homeless every year. (The U.S. population at the time was about 225 million.) Assuming that Snyder misspoke or was misquoted and meant to say that *one* homeless person died *every forty-five seconds*, that's still 701,000 dead homeless people every year—roughly one-third of all deaths in the United States. Hmm.

Ultimately, when Snyder was pressed on his figure of 3 million homeless, he admitted that it was a fabrication. Journalists had been hounding him for a specific number, he said, and he hadn't wanted them to walk away empty-handed.

It may be sad but not surprising to learn that experts like Snyder can be self-interested to the point of deceit. But they cannot deceive on their own. Journalists need experts as badly as experts need journalists. Every day there are newspaper pages and television newscasts to be filled, and an expert who can deliver a jarring piece of wisdom is always welcome. Working together, journalists and experts are the architects of much conventional wisdom.

Advertising too is a brilliant tool for creating conventional wisdom. Listerine, for instance, was invented in the nineteenth century as a powerful surgical antiseptic. It was later sold, in distilled form, as a floor cleaner and a cure for gonorrhea. But it wasn't a runaway success until the 1920s, when it was pitched as a solution for "chronic halitosis"—a then obscure medical term for bad breath. Listerine's new ads featured forlorn young women and men, eager for marriage but turned off by their mate's rotten breath. "Can I be happy with him in spite of *that?*" one maiden asked herself. Until that time, bad breath was not conventionally considered such a catastrophe. But Listerine changed that. As the advertising scholar James B. Twitchell writes, "Listerine did not make mouthwash as much as it made halitosis." In just seven years, the company's revenues rose from $115,000 to more than $8 million.

However created, the conventional wisdom can be hard to budge. The economist Paul Krugman, a *New York Times* columnist and devout critic of George W. Bush, bemoaned this fact as the President's reelection campaign got under way in early 2004:

"The approved story line about Mr. Bush is that he's a bluff, honest, plainspoken guy, and anecdotes that fit that story get reported. But if the conventional wisdom were instead that he's a phony, a silver-spoon baby who pretends to be a cowboy, journalists would have plenty of material to work with."

In the months leading up to the U.S. invasion of Iraq in 2003, dueling experts floated diametrically opposite forecasts about Iraq's weapons of mass destruction. But more often, as with Mitch Snyder's homeless "statistics," one side wins the war of conventional wisdom. Women's rights advocates, for instance, have hyped the incidence of sexual assault, claiming that one in three American women will in her lifetime be a victim of rape or attempted rape. (The actual figure is more like one in eight—but the advocates know it would take a callous person to publicly dispute their claims.) Advocates working for the cures of various tragic diseases regularly do the same. Why not? A little creative lying can draw attention, indignation, and—perhaps most important—the money and political capital to address the actual problem.

Of course an expert, whether a women's health advocate or a political advisor or an advertising executive, tends to have different incentives than the rest of us. And an expert's incentives may shift 180 degrees, depending on the situation.

Consider the police. A recent audit discovered that the police in Atlanta were radically underreporting crime since the early 1990s. The practice apparently began when Atlanta was working to land the 1996 Olympics. The city needed to shed its violent image, and fast. So each year thousands of crime reports were either downgraded from violent to nonviolent or simply thrown away. (Despite these continuing efforts—there were more than

22,000 missing police reports in 2002 alone—Atlanta regularly ranks among the most violent American cities.)

Police in other cities, meanwhile, were spinning a different story during the 1990s. The sudden, violent appearance of crack cocaine had police departments across the country scrapping for resources. They made it known that it wasn't a fair fight: the drug dealers were armed with state-of-the-art weapons and a bottomless supply of cash. This emphasis on illicit cash proved to be a winning effort, for nothing infuriated the law-abiding populace more than the image of the millionaire crack dealer. The media eagerly glommed on to this story, portraying crack dealing as one of the most profitable jobs in America.

But if you were to have spent a little time around the housing projects where crack was so often sold, you might have noticed something strange: not only did most of the crack dealers still live in the projects, but most of them still lived at home with their moms. And then you may have scratched your head and said, "Why is that?"

The answer lies in finding the right data, and the secret to finding the right data usually means finding the right person—which is more easily said than done. Drug dealers are rarely trained in economics, and economists rarely hang out with crack dealers. So the answer to this question begins with finding someone who *did* live among the drug dealers and managed to walk away with the secrets of their trade.

Sudhir Venkatesh—his boyhood friends called him Sid, but he has since reverted to Sudhir—was born in India, raised in the suburbs of upstate New York and southern California, and graduated from the University of California at San Diego with a degree in mathematics. In 1989 he began to pursue his PhD in sociology at the University of Chicago. He was interested in understanding how young people form their identities; to that end, he had just spent three months following the Grateful Dead around the country. What he was not interested in was the grueling fieldwork that typifies sociology.

But his graduate advisor, the eminent poverty scholar William Julius Wilson, promptly sent Venkatesh into the field. His assignment: to visit Chicago's poorest black neighborhoods with a clipboard and a seventy-question, multiple-choice survey. This was the first question on the survey:

How do you feel about being black and poor?

a. Very bad
b. Bad
c. Neither bad nor good
d. Somewhat good
e. Very good

One day Venkatesh walked twenty blocks from the university to a housing project on the shore of Lake Michigan to administer his survey. The project comprised three sixteen-story buildings made of yellow-gray brick. Venkatesh soon discovered that the names and addresses he had been given were badly outdated. These buildings were condemned, practically abandoned. Some families lived on the lower floors, pirating water and electricity, but the elevators didn't work. Neither did the lights in the stairwell. It was late afternoon in early winter, nearly dark outside.

Venkatesh, who is a thoughtful, handsome, and well-built but not aberrationally brave person, had made his way up to the sixth floor, trying to find someone willing to take his survey. Suddenly, on the stairwell landing, he startled a group of teenagers shooting dice. They turned out to be a gang of junior-level crack dealers who operated out of the building, and they were not happy to see him.

"I'm a student at the University of Chicago," Venkatesh sputtered, sticking to his survey script, "and I am administering—"

"Fuck you, nigger, what are you doing in our stairwell?"

There was an ongoing gang war in Chicago. Things had been violent lately, with shootings nearly every day. This gang, a branch of the Black Gangster Disciple Nation, was plainly on edge. They didn't know what to make of Venkatesh. He didn't *seem* to be a member of a rival gang. But maybe he was some kind of spy? He certainly wasn't a cop. He wasn't black, wasn't white. He wasn't exactly threatening—he was armed only with his clipboard—but he didn't seem quite harmless either. Thanks to his three months trailing the Grateful Dead, he still looked, as he would later put it, "like a genuine freak, with hair down to my ass."

The gang members started arguing over what should be done with Venkatesh. Let him go? But if he *did* tell the rival gang about this stairwell hangout, they'd be susceptible to a surprise attack. One jittery kid kept wagging something back and forth in his hands—in the dimming light, Venkatesh eventually realized it was a gun—and muttering, "Let me have him, let me have him." Venkatesh was very, very scared.

The crowd grew bigger and louder. Then an older gang member appeared. He snatched the clipboard from Venkatesh's hands and, when he saw that it was a written questionnaire, looked puzzled.

"I can't read any of this shit," he said.

"That's because you can't *read*," said one of the teenagers, and everyone laughed at the older gangster.

He told Venkatesh to go ahead and ask him a question from the survey. Venkatesh led with the how-does-it-feel-to-be-black-and-poor question. It was met with a round of guffaws, some angrier than others. As Venkatesh would later tell his university colleagues, he realized that the multiple-choice answers A through E were insufficient. In reality, he now knew, the answers should have looked like this:

a. Very bad
b. Bad
c. Neither bad nor good
d. Somewhat good
e. Very good
f. Fuck you

Just as things were looking their bleakest for Venkatesh, another man appeared. This was J. T., the gang's leader. J. T. wanted to know what was going on. Then he told Venkatesh to read him the survey question. He listened but then said he couldn't answer the question because he wasn't black.

"Well then," Venkatesh said, "how does it feel to be *African American* and poor?"

"I ain't no African American either, you idiot. I'm a *nigger*." J. T. then administered a lively though not unfriendly taxonomical lesson in "nigger" versus "African American" versus "black." When he was through, there was an awkward silence. Still nobody seemed to know what to do with Venkatesh. J. T., who was in his late twenties, had cooled down his subordinates, but he didn't seem to want to interfere directly with their catch. Darkness fell and J. T. left. "People don't come out of here alive," the jittery teenager with the gun told Venkatesh. "You know that, don't you?"

As night deepened, his captors eased up. They gave Venkatesh one of their beers, and then another and another. When he had to pee, he went where they went—on the stairwell landing one floor up. J. T. stopped by a few times during the night but didn't have much to say. Daybreak came and then noon. Venkatesh would occasionally try to discuss his survey, but the young crack dealers just laughed and told him how stupid his questions were. Finally, nearly twenty-four hours after Venkatesh stumbled upon them, they set him free.

He went home and took a shower. He was relieved but he was also curious. It struck Venkatesh that most people, including himself, had never given much thought to the daily life of ghetto criminals. He was now eager to learn how the Black Disciples worked, from top to bottom.

After a few hours, he decided to walk back to the housing project. By now he had thought of some better questions to ask.

Having seen firsthand that the conventional method of data gathering was in this case absurd, Venkatesh vowed to scrap his questionnaire and embed himself with the gang. He tracked down J. T. and sketched out his proposal. J. T. thought Venkatesh was crazy, literally—a university student wanting to cozy up to a crack gang? But he also admired what Venkatesh was after. As it happened, J. T. was a college graduate himself, a business major. After college, he had taken a job in the Loop, working in the marketing department of a company that sold office equipment. But he felt so out of place there—like a white man working at Afro Sheen headquarters, he liked to say—that he quit. Still, he never forgot what he learned. He knew the importance of collecting data and finding new markets; he was always on the lookout for better management strategies. It was no coincidence, in other words, that J. T. was the leader of this crack gang. He was bred to be a boss.

After some wrangling, J. T. promised Venkatesh unfettered access to the gang's operations as long as J. T. retained veto power over any information that, if published, might prove harmful.

When the yellow-gray buildings on the lakefront were demolished, shortly after Venkatesh's first visit, the gang relocated to another housing project even deeper in Chicago's south side. For the next six years, Venkatesh practically lived there. Under J. T.'s protection he watched the gang members up close, at work and at home. He asked endless questions. Sometimes the gangsters were annoyed by his curiosity; more often they took advantage of his willingness to listen. "It's a war out here, man," one dealer told him. "I mean, every day people struggling to survive, so you know, we just do what we can. We ain't got no choice, and if that means getting killed, well, shit, it's what niggers do around here to feed their family."

Venkatesh would move from one family to the next, washing their dinner dishes and sleeping on the floor. He bought toys for their children; he once watched a woman use her baby's bib to sop up the blood of a teenaged drug dealer who was shot to death in front of Venkatesh. William Julius Wilson, back at the U. of C., was having regular nightmares on Venkatesh's behalf.

Over the years the gang endured bloody turf wars and, eventually, a federal indictment. A member named Booty, who was one rank beneath J. T., came to Venkatesh with a story. Booty was being blamed by the rest of the gang for bringing about the indictment, he told Venkatesh, and therefore suspected that he would soon be killed. (He was right.) But first Booty wanted to do a little atoning. For all the gang's talk about how crack dealing didn't do any harm—they even liked to brag that it kept black money in the black community—Booty was feeling guilty. He wanted to leave behind something that might somehow benefit the next generation. He handed Venkatesh a stack of wellworn spiral notebooks—blue and black, the gang's colors. They represented a complete record of four years' worth of the gang's financial transactions. At J. T.'s direction, the ledgers had been rigorously compiled: sales, wages, dues, even the death benefits paid out to the families of murdered members.

At first Venkatesh didn't even want the notebooks. What if the Feds found out he had them—perhaps he'd be indicted too? Besides, what was he supposed to do with the data? Despite his math background, he had long ago stopped thinking in numbers.

Upon completing his graduate work at the University of Chicago, Venkatesh was awarded a three-year stay at Harvard's Society of Fellows. Its environment of sharp thinking and bonhomie—the walnut paneling, the sherry cart once owned by Oliver Wendell Holmes—delighted Venkatesh. He went so far as to become the society's wine steward. And yet he regularly left Cambridge, returning again and again to the crack gang in Chicago. This street-level research made Venkatesh something of an anomaly. Most of the other young Fellows were dyed-in-the-tweed intellectuals who liked to pun in Greek.

One of the society's aims was to bring together scholars from various fields who might not otherwise have occasion to meet. Venkatesh soon encountered another anomalous young Fellow, one who also failed the society stereotype. This one happened to be an economist who, instead of thinking grand macro thoughts, favored his own list of offbeat micro curiosities. At the very top of his list was crime. And so, within ten minutes of their meeting, Sudhir Venkatesh told Steven Levitt about the spiral notebooks from Chicago and they decided to collaborate on a paper. It would be the first time that such priceless financial data had fallen into an economist's hands, affording an analysis of a heretofore uncharted criminal enterprise.

So how *did* the gang work? An awful lot like most American businesses, actually, though perhaps none more so than McDonald's. In fact, if you were to hold a McDonald's organizational chart and a Black Disciples org chart side by side, you could hardly tell the difference.

The gang that Venkatesh had fallen in with was one of about a hundred branches—franchises, really—of a larger Black Disciples organization. J. T., the college-educated leader of his franchise, reported to a central leadership of about twenty men that was called, without irony, the board of directors. (At the same time that white suburbanites were studiously mimicking black rappers' ghetto culture, black ghetto criminals were studiously mimicking the suburbanites' dads' corp-think.) J. T. paid the board of directors nearly 20 percent of his revenues for the right to sell crack in a designated twelve-square-block area. The rest of the money was his to distribute as he saw fit.

Three officers reported directly to J. T.: an enforcer (who ensured the gang members' safety), a treasurer (who watched over the gang's liquid assets), and a runner (who transported large quantities of drugs and money to and from the supplier). Beneath the officers were the street-level salesmen known as foot soldiers. The goal of a foot soldier was to someday become an officer. J. T. had anywhere from twenty-five to seventy-five foot soldiers on his payroll at any given time, depending on the time of year (autumn was the best crack-selling season; summer and Christmastime were slow) and the size of the gang's territory (which doubled at one point when the Black Disciples engineered a hostile takeover of a rival gang's turf). At the very bottom of J. T.'s organization were as many as two hundred members known as the rank and file. They were not employees at all. They did, however, pay dues to the gang—some for protection from rival gangs, others for the chance to eventually earn a job as a foot soldier.

The four years recorded in the gang's notebooks coincided with the peak years of the crack boom, and business was excellent. J. T.'s franchise quadrupled its revenues during this period. In the first year, it took in an average of $18,500 each month; by the final year, it was collecting $68,400 a month. Here's a look at the monthly revenues in the third year:

DRUG SALES	$ 24,800
DUES	$ 5,100
EXTORTIONARY TAXES	$ 2,100
TOTAL MONTHLY REVENUES	**$ 32,000**

"Drug sales" represents only the money from dealing crack co-caine. The gang did allow some rank-and-file members to sell heroin on its turf but accepted a fixed licensing fee in lieu of a share of profits. (This was off-the-books money and went straight into J. T.'s pocket; he probably skimmed from other sources as well.) The $5,100 in dues came from rank-and-file members only, since full gang members didn't pay dues. The extortionary taxes were paid by other businesses that operated on the gang's turf, including grocery stores, gypsy cabs, pimps, and people selling stolen goods or repairing cars on the street.

Now, here's what it cost J. T., excluding wages, to bring in that $32,000 per month:

WHOLESALE COST OF DRUGS	$ 5,000
BOARD OF DIRECTORS FEE	$ 5,000
MERCENARY FIGHTERS	$ 1,300
WEAPONS	$ 300
MISCELLANEOUS	$ 2,400
TOTAL MONTHLY NONWAGE COSTS	**$14,000**

Mercenary fighters were nonmembers hired on short-term contracts to help the gang fight turf wars. The cost of weapons is small here because the Black Disciples had a side deal with local gunrunners, helping them navigate the neighborhood in exchange for free or steeply discounted guns. The miscellaneous expenses include legal fees, parties, bribes, and gang-sponsored "community events." (The Black Disciples worked hard to be seen as a pillar rather than a scourge of the housing-project community.) The miscellaneous expenses also include the costs associated with a gang member's murder. The gang not only paid for the funeral but often gave a stipend of up to three years' wages to the victim's family. Venkatesh had once asked why the gang was so generous in this regard. "That's a fucking stupid question," he was told, " 'cause as long as you been with us, you still don't understand that their families is our families. We can't just leave 'em out. We been knowing these folks our whole lives, man, so we grieve when they grieve. You got to respect the family." There was another reason for the death benefits: the gang feared community backlash (its enterprise was plainly a destructive one) and figured it could buy some goodwill for a few hundred dollars here and there.

The rest of the money the gang took in went to its members, starting with J. T. Here is the single line item in the gang's budget that made J. T. the happiest:

NET MONTHLY PROFIT ACCRUING TO LEADER.... $8,500

At $8,500 per month, J. T.'s annual salary was about $100,000—tax-free, of course, and not including the various off-the-books money he pocketed. This was a lot more than he earned at his short-lived office job in the Loop. And J. T. was just one of roughly 100 leaders at this level within the Black Disciples network. So there were indeed some drug dealers who could afford to live large—or, in the case of the gang's board of directors, *extremely* large. Each of those top 20 bosses stood to earn about $500,000 a year. (A third of them, however, were typically imprisoned at any time, a significant downside of an up position in an illicit industry.)

So the top 120 men on the Black Disciples' pyramid were paid very well. But the pyramid they sat atop was gigantic. Using J. T.'s franchise as a yardstick—3 officers and roughly 50 foot soldiers—there were some 5,300 other men working for those 120 bosses. Then there were another 20,000 unpaid rank-and-file members, many of whom wanted nothing more than an opportunity to become a foot soldier. They were even willing to pay gang dues to have their chance.

And how well did that dream job pay? Here are the monthly totals for the wages that J. T. paid his gang members:

COMBINED WAGES PAID TO ALL THREE OFFICERS	**$2,100**
COMBINED WAGES PAID TO ALL FOOT SOLDIERS	**$7,400**
TOTAL MONTHLY GANG WAGES (EXCLUDING LEADER)	**$9,500**

So J. T. paid his employees $9,500, a *combined* monthly salary that was only $1,000 more than his own official salary. J. T.'s hourly wage was $66. His three officers, meanwhile, each took home $700 a month, which works out to about $7 an hour. And the foot soldiers earned just $3.30 an hour, less than the minimum wage. So the answer to the original question—if drug dealers make so much money, why are they still living with their mothers?—is that, except for the top cats, they *don't* make much money. They had no choice but to live with their mothers. For every big earner, there were hundreds more just scraping along. The top 120 men in the Black Disciples gang represented just 2.2 percent of the full-fledged gang membership but took home well more than half the money.

In other words, a crack gang works pretty much like the standard capitalist enterprise: you have to be near the top of the pyramid to make a big wage. Notwithstanding the leadership's rhetoric about the family nature of the business, the gang's wages are about as skewed as wages in corporate America. A foot soldier had plenty in common with a McDonald's burger flipper or a Wal-Mart shelf stocker. In fact, most of J. T.'s foot soldiers also held minimum-wage jobs in the legitimate sector to supplement their skimpy illicit earnings. The leader of another crack gang once told Venkatesh that he could easily afford to pay his foot soldiers more, but it wouldn't be prudent. "You got all these niggers below you who want your job, you dig?" he said. "So, you know, you try to take care of them, but you know, you also have to show them you the boss. You always have to get yours first, or else you really ain't no leader. If you start taking losses, they see you as weak and shit."

Along with the bad pay, the foot soldiers faced terrible job conditions. For starters, they had to stand on a street corner all day and do business with crackheads. (The gang members were strongly advised against using the product themselves, advice that was enforced by beatings if necessary.) Foot soldiers also risked arrest and, more worrisome, violence. Using the gang's financial documents and the rest of Venkatesh's research, it is possible to construct an adverse-events index of J. T.'s gang during the four years in question. The results are astonishingly bleak. If you were a member of J. T.'s gang for all four years, here is the typical fate you would have faced during that period:

NUMBER OF TIMES ARRESTED	5.9
NUMBER OF NONFATAL WOUNDS OR INJURIES	2.4
(NOT INCLUDING INJURIES METED OUT BY THE GANG ITSELF FOR RULES VIOLATIONS)	
CHANCE OF BEING KILLED	1 IN 4

A 1-in-4 chance of being killed! Compare these odds with those for a timber cutter, which the Bureau of Labor Statistics calls the most dangerous job in the United States. Over four years' time, a timber cutter would stand only a 1-in-200 chance of being killed. Or compare the crack dealer's odds to those of a death-row inmate in Texas, which executes more prisoners than any other state. In 2003, Texas put to death twenty-four inmates—or just 5 percent of the nearly 500 inmates on its death row during that time. Which means that you stand a greater chance of dying while dealing crack in a Chicago housing project than you do while sitting on death row in Texas.

So if crack dealing is the most dangerous job in America, and if the salary was only $3.30 an hour, why on earth would anyone take such a job?

Well, for the same reason that a pretty Wisconsin farm girl moves to Hollywood. For the same reason that a high-school quarterback wakes up at 5 a.m. to lift weights. They all want to succeed in an extremely competitive field in which, if you reach the top, you are paid a fortune (to say nothing of the attendant glory and power).

To the kids growing up in a housing project on Chicago's south side, crack dealing seemed like a glamour profession. For many of them, the job of gang boss—highly visible and highly lucrative—was easily the best job they thought they had access to. Had they grown up under different circumstances, they might have thought about becoming economists or writers. But in the neighborhood where J. T.'s gang operated, the path to a decent legitimate job was practically invisible. Fifty-six percent of the neighborhood's children lived below the poverty line (compared to a national average of 18 percent). Seventy-eight percent came from single-parent homes. Fewer than 5 percent of the neighborhood's adults had a college degree; barely one in three adult men worked at all. The neighborhood's median income was about $15,000 a year, well less than half the U.S. average. During the years that Venkatesh lived with J. T.'s gang, foot soldiers often asked his help in landing what they called "a good job": working as a janitor at the University of Chicago.

The problem with crack dealing is the same as in every other glamour profession: a lot of people are competing for a very few prizes. Earning big money in the crack gang wasn't much more likely than the Wisconsin farm girl becoming a movie star or the high-school quarterback playing in the NFL. But criminals, like everyone else, respond to incentives. So if the prize is big enough, they will form a line down the block just hoping for a chance. On the south side of Chicago, people wanting to sell crack vastly outnumbered the available street corners.

These budding drug lords bumped up against an immutable law of labor: when there are a lot of people willing and able to do a job, that job generally doesn't pay well. This is one of four meaningful factors that determine a wage. The others are the specialized skills a job requires, the unpleasantness of a job, and the demand for services that the job fulfills.

The delicate balance between these factors helps explain why, for instance, the typical prostitute earns more than the typical architect. It may not seem as though she should. The architect would appear to be more skilled (as the word is usually defined) and better educated (again, as usually defined). But little girls don't grow up dreaming of becoming prostitutes, so the supply of potential prostitutes is relatively small. Their skills, while not necessarily "specialized," are practiced in a very specialized context. The job is unpleasant and forbidding in at least two significant ways: the likelihood of violence and the lost opportunity of having a stable family life. As for demand? Let's just say that an architect is more likely to hire a prostitute than vice versa.

In the glamour professions—movies, sports, music, fashion—there is a different dynamic at play. Even in second-tier glamour industries like publishing, advertising, and media, swarms of bright young people throw themselves at grunt jobs that pay poorly and demand unstinting devotion. An editorial assistant earning $22,000 at a Manhattan publishing house, an unpaid high-school quarterback, and a teenage crack dealer earning $3.30 an hour are all playing the same game, a game that is best viewed as a tournament.

The rules of a tournament are straightforward. You must start at the bottom to have a shot at the top. (Just as a Major League shortstop probably played Little League and just as a Grand Dragon of the Ku Klux Klan probably started out as a lowly spear-carrier, a drug lord typically began by selling drugs on a street corner.) You must be willing to work long and hard at substandard wages. In order to advance in the tournament, you must prove yourself not merely above average but spectacular. (The way to distinguish yourself differs from profession to profession, of course; while J. T. certainly monitored his foot soldiers' sales performance, it was their force of personality that really counted—more than it would for, say, a shortstop.) And finally, once you come to the sad realization that you will never make it to the top, you will quit the tournament. (Some people hang on longer than others—witness the graying "actors" who wait tables in New York—but people generally get the message quite early.)

Most of J. T.'s foot soldiers were unwilling to stay foot soldiers for long after they realized they weren't advancing. Especially once the shooting started. After several relatively peaceful years, J. T.'s gang got involved in a turf war with a neighboring gang. Drive-by shootings became a daily event. For a foot soldier—the gang's man on the street—this development was particularly dangerous. The nature of the business demanded that customers be able to find him easily and quickly; if he hid from the other gang, he couldn't sell his crack.

Until the gang war, J. T.'s foot soldiers had been willing to balance the risky, low-paying job with the reward of advancement. But as one foot soldier told Venkatesh, he now wanted to be compensated for the added risk: "Would you stand around here when all this shit is going on? No, right? So if I gonna be asked to put my life on the line, then front me the cash, man. Pay me more 'cause it ain't worth my time to be here when they're warring."

J. T. hadn't wanted this war. For one thing, he was forced to pay his foot soldiers higher wages because of the added risk. Far worse, gang warfare was bad for business. If Burger King and McDonald's launch a price war to gain market share, they partly make up in volume what they lose in price. (Nor is anyone getting shot.) But with a gang war, sales plummet because customers are so scared of the violence that they won't come out in the open to buy their crack. In every way, war was expensive for J. T.

So why did he start the war? As a matter of fact, he didn't. It was his foot soldiers who started it. It turns out that a crack boss didn't have as much control over his subordinates as he would have liked. That's because they had different incentives.

For J. T., violence was a distraction from the business at hand; he would have preferred that his members never fired a single gunshot. For a foot soldier, however, violence served a purpose. One of the few ways that a foot soldier could distinguish himself—and advance in the tournament—was by proving his mettle for violence. A killer was respected, feared, talked about. A foot soldier's incentive was to make a name for himself; J. T.'s incentive was, in effect, to keep the foot soldiers from doing so. "We try to tell these shorties that they belong to a serious organization," he once told Venkatesh. "It ain't all about killing. They see these movies and shit, they think it's all about running around tearing shit up. But it's not. You've got to learn to be part of an organization; you can't be fighting all the time. It's bad for business."

In the end, J. T. prevailed. He oversaw the gang's expansion and ushered in a new era of prosperity and relative peace. J. T. was a winner. He was paid well because so few people could do what he did. He was a tall, good-looking, smart, tough man who knew how to motivate people. He was shrewd too, never tempting arrest by carrying guns or cash. While the rest of his gang lived in poverty with their mothers, J. T. had several homes, several women, several cars. He also had his business education, of course. He constantly worked to extend this advantage. That was why he ordered the corporate-style bookkeeping that eventually found its way into Sudhir Venkatesh's hands. No other franchise leader had ever done such a thing. J. T. once showed his ledgers to the board of directors to prove, as if proof were needed, the extent of his business acumen.

And it worked. After six years running his local gang, J. T. was promoted to the board of directors. He was now thirty-four years old. He had won the tournament. But this tournament had a catch that publishing and pro sports and even Hollywood don't have. Selling drugs, after all, is illegal. Not long after he made the board of directors, the Black Disciples were essentially shut down by a federal indictment—the same indictment that led the gangster named Booty to turn over his notebooks to Venkatesh—and J. T. was sent to prison.

• • •

Now for another unlikely question: what did crack cocaine have in common with nylon stockings?

In 1939, when DuPont introduced nylons, countless American women felt as if a miracle had been performed in their honor. Until then, stockings were made of silk, and silk was delicate, expensive, and in ever shorter supply. By 1941, some sixty-four million pairs of nylon stockings had been sold—more stockings than there were adult women in the United States. They were easily affordable, immensely appealing, practically addictive.

DuPont had pulled off the feat that every marketer dreams of: it brought class to the masses. In this regard, the invention of nylon stockings was markedly similar to the invention of crack cocaine.

In the 1970s, if you were the sort of person who did drugs, there was no classier drug than cocaine. Beloved by rock stars and movie stars, ballplayers and even the occasional politician, cocaine was a drug of power and panache. It was clean, it was white, it was pretty. Heroin was droopy and pot was foggy but cocaine provided a beautiful high.

Alas, it was also very expensive. Nor did the high last long. This led cocaine users to try jacking up the drug's potency. They did this primarily by freebasing—adding ammonia and ethyl ether to cocaine hydrochloride, or powdered cocaine, and burning it to free up the "base" cocaine. But this could be dangerous. As more than a few flame-scarred drug users could attest, chemistry is best left to chemists.

Meanwhile, cocaine dealers and aficionados across the country, and perhaps also in the Caribbean and South America, were working on a safer version of distilled cocaine. They found that mixing powdered cocaine in a saucepan with baking soda and water, and then cooking off the liquid, produced tiny rocks of smokeable cocaine. It came to be called crack for the crackling sound the baking soda made when it was burned. More affectionate nicknames would soon follow: Rock, Kryptonite, Kibbles 'n Bits, Scrabble, and Love. By the early 1980s, the class drug was ready for the masses. Now only two things were needed to turn crack into a phenomenon: an abundant supply of raw cocaine and a way to get the new product to a mass market.

The cocaine was easy to come by, for the invention of crack coincided with a Colombian cocaine glut. During the late 1970s, the wholesale price of cocaine in the United States fell dramatically, even as its purity was rising. One man, a Nicaraguan émigré named Oscar Danilo Blandon, was suspected of importing far more Colombian cocaine than anyone else. Blandon did so much business with the budding crack dealers of South Central Los Angeles that he came to be known as the Johnny Appleseed of Crack. Blandon would later claim that he was selling the cocaine to raise money for the CIA-sponsored Contras back home in Nicaragua. He liked to say that the CIA was in turn watching his back in the United States, allowing him to sell cocaine with impunity. This claim would spark a belief that still seethes to this day, especially among urban blacks, that the CIA itself was the chief sponsor of the American crack trade.

Verifying that claim is beyond the purview of this book. What *is* demonstrably true is that Oscar Danilo Blandon helped establish a link—between Colombian cocaine cartels and inner-city crack merchants—that would alter American history. By putting massive amounts of cocaine into the hands of street gangs, Blandon and others like him gave rise to a devastating crack boom. And gangs like the Black Gangster Disciple Nation were given new reason to exist.

As long as there have been cities, there have been gangs of one sort or another. In the United States, gangs have traditionally been a sort of halfway house for recent immigrants. In the 1920s, Chicago alone had more than 1,300 street gangs, catering to every ethnic, political, and criminal leaning imaginable. As a rule, gangs would prove much better at making mayhem than money. Some fancied themselves commercial enterprises, and a few—the Mafia, most notably—actually did make money (at least for the higher-ups). But most gangsters were, as the cliché assures us, two-bit gangsters.

Black street gangs in particular flourished in Chicago, with membership in the tens of thousands by the 1970s. They constituted the sort of criminals, petty and otherwise, who sucked the life out of urban areas. Part of the problem was that these criminals never seemed to get locked up. The 1960s and 1970s were, in retrospect, a great time to be a street criminal in most American cities. The likelihood of punishment was so low—this was the heyday of a liberal justice system and the criminals' rights movement—that it simply didn't cost very much to commit a crime.

By the 1980s, however, the courts had begun to radically reverse that trend. Criminals' rights were curtailed and stricter sentencing guidelines put in place. More and more of Chicago's black gangsters were getting sent to federal prisons. By happy coincidence, some of their fellow inmates were Mexican gang members with close ties to Colombian drug dealers. In the past, the black gangsters had bought their drugs from a middleman, the

Mafia—which, as it happened, was then being pummeled by the federal government's new anti-racketeering laws. But by the time crack came to Chicago, the black gangsters had made the connections to buy their cocaine directly from Colombian dealers.

Cocaine had never been a big seller in the ghetto: it was too expensive. But that was before the invention of crack. This new product was ideal for a low-income, street-level customer. Because it required such a tiny amount of pure cocaine, one hit of crack cost only a few dollars. Its powerful high reached the brain in just a few seconds—and then faded fast, sending the user back for more. From the outset, crack was bound to be a huge success.

And who better to sell it than the thousands of junior members of all those street gangs like the Black Gangster Disciple Nation? The gangs already owned the territory—real estate was, in essence, their core business—and they were suitably menacing to keep customers from even thinking about ripping them off. Suddenly the urban street gang evolved from a club for wayward teenagers into a true commercial enterprise.

The gang also presented an opportunity for longtime employment. Before crack, it was just about impossible to earn a living in a street gang. When it was time for a gangster to start supporting a family, he would have to quit. There was no such thing as a thirty-year-old gangster: he was either working a legitimate job, dead, or in prison. But with crack, there was real money to be made. Instead of moving on and making way for the younger gangsters to ascend, the veterans stayed put. This was happening just as the old-fashioned sort of lifetime jobs—factory jobs especially—were disappearing. In the past, a semi-skilled black man in Chicago could earn a decent wage working in a factory. With that option narrowing, crack dealing looked even better.

How hard could it be? The stuff was so addictive that a fool could sell it.

Who cared if the crack game was a tournament that only a few of them could possibly win? Who cared if it was so dangerous—standing out there on a corner, selling it as fast and anonymously as McDonald's sells hamburgers, not knowing any of your customers, wondering who might be coming to arrest or rob or kill you? Who cared if your product got twelve-year-olds and grandmothers and preachers so addicted that they stopped thinking about anything except their next hit? Who cared if crack killed the neighborhood?

For black Americans, the four decades between World War II and the crack boom had been marked by steady and often dramatic improvement. Particularly since the civil rights legislation of the mid-1960s, the telltale signs of societal progress had finally taken root among black Americans. The black-white income gap was shrinking. So was the gap between black children's test scores and those of white children. Perhaps the most heartening gain had been in infant mortality. As late as 1964, a black infant was twice as likely to die as a white infant, often of a cause as basic as diarrhea or pneumonia. With segregated hospitals, many black patients received what amounted to Third World care. But that changed when the federal government ordered the hospitals to be desegregated: within just seven years, the black infant mortality rate had been cut in half. By the 1980s, virtually every facet of life was improving for black Americans, and the progress showed no sign of stopping.

Then came crack cocaine.

While crack use was hardly a black-only phenomenon, it hit black neighborhoods much harder than most. The evidence can be seen by measuring the same indicators of societal progress cited above. After decades of decline, black infant mortality began to soar in the 1980s, as did the rate of low-birthweight babies and parent abandonment. The gap between black and white school-children widened. The number of blacks sent to prison tripled. Crack was so dramatically destructive that if its effect is averaged for all black Americans, not just crack users and their families, you will see that the group's postwar progress was not only stopped cold but was often knocked as much as ten years backward. Black Americans were hurt more by crack cocaine than by any other single cause since Jim Crow.

And then there was the crime. Within a five-year period, the homicide rate among young urban blacks *quadrupled*. Suddenly it was just as dangerous to live in parts of Chicago or St. Louis or Los Angeles as it was to live in Bogotá.

The violence associated with the crack boom was various and relentless. It coincided with an even broader American crime wave that had been building for two decades. Although the rise of this crime wave long predated crack, the trend was so exacerbated by crack that criminologists got downright apocalyptic in their predictions. James Alan Fox, perhaps the most widely quoted crime expert in the popular press, warned of a coming "bloodbath" of youth violence.

But Fox and the other purveyors of conventional wisdom turned out to be wrong. The bloodbath did not materialize. The crime rate in fact began to fall—so unexpectedly and dramatically and thoroughly that now, from the distance of several years, it is almost hard to recall the crushing grip of that crime wave.

Why did it fall?

For a few reasons, but one of them more surprising than the

rest. Oscar Danilo Blandon, the so-called Johnny Appleseed of Crack, may have been the instigator of one ripple effect, in which by his actions a single person inadvertently causes an ocean of despair. But unbeknownst to just about everybody, another remarkably powerful ripple effect—this one moving in the opposite direction—had just come into play.

Chapter 4

WHERE HAVE ALL THE CRIMINALS GONE?

In 1966, one year after Nicolae Ceauşescu became the Communist dictator of Romania, he made abortion illegal. "The fetus is the property of the entire society," he proclaimed. "Anyone who avoids having children is a deserter who abandons the laws of national continuity."

Such grandiose declarations were commonplace during Ceauşescu's reign, for his master plan—to create a nation worthy of the New Socialist Man—was an exercise in grandiosity. He built palaces for himself while alternately brutalizing and neglecting his citizens. Abandoning agriculture in favor of manufacturing, he forced many of the nation's rural dwellers into unheated apartment buildings. He gave government positions to forty family members including his wife, Elena, who required forty homes and a commensurate supply of fur and jewels. Madame Ceauşescu, known officially as the Best Mother Romania Could

Have, was not particularly maternal. "The worms never get satisfied, regardless of how much food you give them," she said when Romanians complained about the food shortages brought on by her husband's mismanagement. She had her own children bugged to ensure their loyalty.

Ceauşescu's ban on abortion was designed to achieve one of his major aims: to rapidly strengthen Romania by boosting its population. Until 1966, Romania had had one of the most liberal abortion policies in the world. Abortion was in fact the main form of birth control, with four abortions for every live birth. Now, virtually overnight, abortion was forbidden. The only exemptions were mothers who already had four children or women with significant standing in the Communist Party. At the same time, all contraception and sex education were banned. Government agents sardonically known as the Menstrual Police regularly rounded up women in their workplaces to administer pregnancy tests. If a woman repeatedly failed to conceive, she was forced to pay a steep "celibacy tax."

Ceauşescu's incentives produced the desired effect. Within one year of the abortion ban, the Romanian birth rate had doubled. These babies were born into a country where, unless you belonged to the Ceauşescu clan or the Communist elite, life was miserable. But these children would turn out to have particularly miserable lives. Compared to Romanian children born just a year earlier, the cohort of children born after the abortion ban would do worse in every measurable way: they would test lower in school, they would have less success in the labor market, and they would also prove much more likely to become criminals.

The abortion ban stayed in effect until Ceauşescu finally lost his grip on Romania. On December 16, 1989, thousands of people took to the streets of Timisoara to protest his corrosive regime. Many of the protestors were teenagers and college students. The police killed dozens of them. One of the opposition leaders, a forty-one-year-old professor, later said it was his thirteen-year-old daughter who insisted he attend the protest, despite his fear. "What is most interesting is that we learned not to be afraid from our children," he said. "Most were aged thirteen to twenty." A few days after the massacre in Timisoara, Ceauşescu gave a speech in Bucharest before one hundred thousand people. Again the young people were out in force. They shouted down Ceauşescu with cries of "Timisoara!" and "Down with the murderers!" His time had come. He and Elena tried to escape the country with $1 billion, but they were captured, given a crude trial, and, on Christmas Day, executed by firing squad.

Of all the Communist leaders deposed in the years bracketing the collapse of the Soviet Union, only Nicolae Ceauşescu met a violent death. It should not be overlooked that his demise was precipitated in large measure by the youth of Romania—a great number of whom, were it not for his abortion ban, would never have been born at all.

The story of abortion in Romania might seem an odd way to begin telling the story of American crime in the 1990s. But it's not. In one important way, the Romanian abortion story is a reverse image of the American crime story. The point of overlap was on that Christmas Day of 1989, when Nicolae Ceauşescu learned the hard way—with a bullet to the head—that his abortion ban had much deeper implications than he knew.

On that day, crime was just about at its peak in the United States. In the previous fifteen years, violent crime had risen

80 percent. It was crime that led the nightly news and the national conversation.

When the crime rate began falling in the early 1990s, it did so with such speed and suddenness that it surprised everyone. It took some experts many years to even recognize that crime was falling, so confident had they been of its continuing rise. Long after crime had peaked, in fact, some of them continued to predict ever darker scenarios. But the evidence was irrefutable: the long and brutal spike in crime was moving in the opposite direction, and it wouldn't stop until the crime rate had fallen back to the levels of forty years earlier.

Now the experts hustled to explain their faulty forecasting. The criminologist James Alan Fox explained that his warning of a "bloodbath" was in fact an intentional overstatement. "I never said there would be blood flowing in the streets," he said, "but I used strong terms like 'bloodbath' to get people's attention. And it did. I don't apologize for using alarmist terms." (If Fox seems to be offering a distinction without a difference—"bloodbath" versus "blood flowing in the streets"—we should remember that even in retreat mode, experts can be self-serving.)

After the relief had settled in, after people remembered how to go about their lives without the pressing fear of crime, there arose a natural question: just where did all those criminals go?

At one level, the answer seemed puzzling. After all, if none of the criminologists, police officials, economists, politicians, or others who traffic in such matters had foreseen the crime decline, how could they suddenly identify its causes?

But this diverse army of experts now marched out a phalanx of hypotheses to explain the drop in crime. A great many newspaper articles would be written on the subject. Their conclusions often hinged on which expert had most recently spoken to which reporter. Here, ranked by frequency of mention, are the crime-drop explanations cited in articles published from 1991 to 2001 in the ten largest-circulation papers in the LexisNexis database:

CRIME–DROP EXPLANATION	NUMBER OF CITATIONS
1. INNOVATIVE POLICING STRATEGIES	52
2. INCREASED RELIANCE ON PRISONS	47
3. CHANGES IN CRACK AND OTHER DRUG MARKETS	33
4. AGING OF THE POPULATION	32
5. TOUGHER GUN–CONTROL LAWS	32
6. STRONG ECONOMY	28
7. INCREASED NUMBER OF POLICE	26
8. ALL OTHER EXPLANATIONS (INCREASED USE OF CAPITAL PUNISHMENT, CONCEALED–WEAPONS LAWS, GUN BUYBACKS, AND OTHERS)	34

If you are the sort of person who likes guessing games, you may wish to spend the next few moments pondering which of the preceding explanations seem to have merit and which don't. Hint: of the seven major explanations on the list, only three can be shown to have contributed to the drop in crime. The others are, for the most part, figments of someone's imagination, self-interest, or wishful thinking. Further hint: one of the greatest measurable causes of the crime drop does not appear on the list at all, for it didn't receive a single newspaper mention.

Let's begin with a fairly uncontroversial one: *the strong economy*. The decline in crime that began in the early 1990s was accompanied by a blistering national economy and a significant drop in unemployment. It might seem to follow that the economy was a hammer that helped beat down crime. But a closer look at the data destroys this theory. It is true that a stronger job market may make certain crimes relatively less attractive. But that is only the case for crimes with a direct financial motivation—burglary, robbery, and auto theft—as opposed to violent crimes like homicide, assault, and rape. Moreover, studies have shown that an unemployment decline of 1 percentage point accounts for a 1 percent drop in nonviolent crime. During the 1990s, the unemployment rate fell by 2 percentage points; nonviolent crime, meanwhile, fell by roughly 40 percent. But an even bigger flaw in the strong-economy theory concerns violent crime. Homicide fell at a greater rate during the 1990s than any other sort of crime, and a number of reliable studies have shown virtually *no* link between the economy and violent crime. This weak link is made even weaker by glancing back to a recent decade, the 1960s, when the economy went on a wild growth spurt—as did violent crime. So while a strong 1990s economy might have seemed, on the surface, a likely explanation for the drop in crime, it almost certainly didn't affect criminal behavior in any significant way.

Unless, that is, "the economy" is construed in a broader sense—as a means to build and maintain hundreds of prisons. Let's now consider another crime-drop explanation: *increased reliance on prisons*. It might help to start by flipping the crime question around. Instead of wondering what made crime fall, think about this: why had it risen so dramatically in the first place?

During the first half of the twentieth century, the incidence of violent crime in the United States was, for the most part, fairly steady. But in the early 1960s, it began to climb. In retrospect, it is clear that one of the major factors pushing this trend was a more lenient justice system. Conviction rates declined during the 1960s, and criminals who were convicted served shorter sentences. This trend was driven in part by an expansion in the rights of people accused of crimes—a long overdue expansion, some would argue. (Others would argue that the expansion went too far.) At the same time, politicians were growing increasingly softer on crime—"for fear of sounding racist," as the economist Gary Becker has written, "since African-Americans and Hispanics commit a disproportionate share of felonies." So if you were the kind of person who might want to commit a crime, the incentives were lining up in your favor: a slimmer likelihood of being convicted and, if convicted, a shorter prison term. Because criminals respond to incentives as readily as anyone, the result was a surge in crime.

It took some time, and a great deal of political turmoil, but these incentives were eventually curtailed. Criminals who would have previously been set free—for drug-related offenses and parole revocation in particular—were instead locked up. Between 1980 and 2000, there was a fifteenfold increase in the number of people sent to prison on drug charges. Many other sentences, especially for violent crime, were lengthened. The total effect was dramatic. By 2000, more than two million people were in prison, roughly four times the number as of 1972. Fully half of that increase took place during the 1990s.

The evidence linking increased punishment with lower crime rates is very strong. Harsh prison terms have been shown to act as both deterrent (for the would-be criminal on the street) and prophylactic (for the would-be criminal who is already locked up). Logical as this may sound, some criminologists have fought the logic. A 1977 academic study called "On Behalf of a Moratorium on Prison Construction" noted that crime rates tend to be high when imprisonment rates are high, and concluded that crime would fall if imprisonment rates could only be lowered. (Fortunately, jailers did not suddenly turn loose their wards and sit back waiting for crime to fall. As the political scientist John J. DiIulio Jr. later commented, "Apparently, it takes a Ph.D. in criminology to doubt that keeping dangerous criminals incarcerated cuts crime.")

The "Moratorium" argument rests on a fundamental confusion of correlation and causality. Consider a parallel argument. The mayor of a city sees that his citizens celebrate wildly when their team wins the World Series. He is intrigued by this correlation but, like the "Moratorium" author, fails to see the direction in which the correlation runs. So the following year, the mayor decrees that his citizens start celebrating the World Series *before the first pitch is thrown*—an act that, in his confused mind, will ensure a victory.

There are certainly plenty of reasons to dislike the huge surge in the prison population. Not everyone is pleased that such a significant fraction of Americans, especially black Americans, live behind bars. Nor does prison even begin to address the root causes of crime, which are diverse and complex. Lastly, prison is hardly a cheap solution: it costs about $25,000 a year to keep someone incarcerated. But if the goal here is to explain the drop in crime in the 1990s, imprisonment is certainly one of the key answers. It accounts for roughly one-third of the drop in crime.

Another crime-drop explanation is often cited in tandem with imprisonment: *the increased use of capital punishment.* The number of executions in the United States quadrupled between the 1980s and the 1990s, leading many people to conclude—in the context of a debate that has been going on for decades—that capital punishment helped drive down crime. Lost in the debate, however, are two important facts.

First, given the rarity with which executions are carried out in this country and the long delays in doing so, no reasonable criminal should be deterred by the threat of execution. Even though capital punishment quadrupled within a decade, there were still only 478 executions in the entire United States during the 1990s. Any parent who has ever said to a recalcitrant child, "Okay, I'm going to count to ten and this time I'm *really* going to punish you," knows the difference between deterrent and empty threat. New York State, for instance, has not as of this writing executed a single criminal since reinstituting its death penalty in 1995. Even among prisoners on death row, the annual execution rate is only 2 percent—compared with the 7 percent annual chance of dying faced by a member of the Black Gangster Disciple Nation crack gang. If life on death row is safer than life on the streets, it's hard to believe that the fear of execution is a driving force in a criminal's calculus. Like the $3 fine for late-arriving parents at the Israeli day-care centers, the negative incentive of capital punishment simply isn't serious enough for a criminal to change his behavior.

The second flaw in the capital punishment argument is even more obvious. Assume for a moment that the death penalty *is* a deterrent. How much crime does it actually deter? The economist Isaac Ehrlich, in an oft-cited 1975 paper, put forth an estimate that is generally considered optimistic: executing 1 criminal translates into 7 fewer homicides that the criminal might have committed. Now do the math. In 1991, there were 14 executions in the United States; in 2001, there were 66. According to Ehrlich's calculation, those 52 additional executions would have accounted for 364 fewer homicides in 2001—not a small drop, to be sure, but less than 4 percent of the actual decrease in homicides that year. So even in a death penalty advocate's best-case scenario, capital punishment could explain only one twenty-fifth of the drop in homicides in the 1990s. And because the death penalty is rarely given for crimes other than homicide, its deterrent effect cannot account for a speck of decline in other violent crimes.

It is extremely unlikely, therefore, that the death penalty, as currently practiced in the United States, exerts any real influence on crime rates. Even many of its onetime supporters have come to this conclusion. "I feel morally and intellectually obligated simply to concede that the death penalty experiment has failed," said U.S. Supreme Court Justice Harry A. Blackmun in 1994, nearly twenty years after he had voted for its reinstatement. "I no longer shall tinker with the machinery of death."

So it wasn't capital punishment that drove crime down, nor was it the booming economy. But higher rates of imprisonment did have a lot to do with it. All those criminals didn't march into jail by themselves, of course. Someone had to investigate the crime, catch the bad guy, and put together the case that would get him convicted. Which naturally leads to a related pair of crime-drop explanations:

Innovative policing strategies
Increased number of police

Let's address the second one first. The number of police officers per capita in the United States rose about 14 percent during the

1990s. Does merely increasing the number of police, however, reduce crime? The answer would seem obvious—yes—but proving that answer isn't so easy. That's because when crime is rising, people clamor for protection, and invariably more money is found for cops. So if you just look at raw correlations between police and crime, you will find that when there are more police, there tends to be more crime. That doesn't mean, of course, that the police are causing the crime, just as it doesn't mean, as some criminologists have argued, that crime will fall if criminals are released from prison.

To show causality, we need a scenario in which more police are hired for reasons completely unrelated to rising crime. If, for instance, police were randomly sprinkled in some cities and not in others, we could look to see whether crime declines in the cities where the police happen to land.

As it turns out, that exact scenario is often created by vote-hungry politicians. In the months leading up to Election Day, incumbent mayors routinely try to lock up the law-and-order vote by hiring more police—even when the crime rate is standing still. So by comparing the crime rate in one set of cities that have recently had an election (and which therefore hired extra police) with another set of cities that had no election (and therefore no extra police), it's possible to tease out the effect of the extra police on crime. The answer: yes indeed, additional police substantially lower the crime rate.

Again, it may help to look backward and see why crime had risen so much in the first place. From 1960 to 1985, the number of police officers *fell* more than 50 percent relative to the number of crimes. In some cases, hiring additional police was considered a violation of the era's liberal aesthetic; in others, it was simply deemed too expensive. This 50 percent decline in police translated into a roughly equal decline in the probability that a given criminal would be caught. Coupled with the above-cited leniency in the other half of the criminal justice system, the courtrooms, this decrease in policing created a strong positive incentive for criminals.

By the 1990s, philosophies—and necessities—had changed. The policing trend was put in reverse, with wide-scale hiring in cities across the country. Not only did all those police act as a deterrent, but they also provided the manpower to imprison criminals who might have otherwise gone uncaught. The hiring of additional police accounted for roughly 10 percent of the 1990s crime drop.

But it wasn't only the number of police that changed in the 1990s; consider the most commonly cited crime-drop explanation of all: *innovative policing strategies.*

There was perhaps no more attractive theory than the belief that smart policing stops crime. It offered a set of bona fide heroes rather than simply a dearth of villains. This theory rapidly became an article of faith because it appealed to the factors that, according to John Kenneth Galbraith, most contribute to the formation of conventional wisdom: the ease with which an idea may be understood and the degree to which it affects our personal well-being.

The story played out most dramatically in New York City, where newly elected mayor Rudolph Giuliani and his hand-picked police commissioner, William Bratton, vowed to fix the city's desperate crime situation. Bratton took a novel approach to policing. He ushered the NYPD into what one senior police official later called "our Athenian period," in which new ideas were given weight over calcified practices. Instead of coddling his precinct commanders, Bratton demanded accountability. Instead of relying solely on old-fashioned cop know-how, he introduced technological solutions like CompStat, a computerized method of addressing crime hot spots.

The most compelling new idea that Bratton brought to life stemmed from the broken window theory, which was conceived by the criminologists James Q. Wilson and George Kelling. The broken window theory argues that minor nuisances, if left unchecked, turn into major nuisances: that is, if someone breaks a window and sees it isn't fixed immediately, he gets the signal that it's all right to break the rest of the windows and maybe set the building afire too.

So with murder raging all around, Bill Bratton's cops began to police the sort of deeds that used to go unpoliced: jumping a subway turnstile, panhandling too aggressively, urinating in the streets, swabbing a filthy squeegee across a car's windshield unless the driver made an appropriate "donation."

Most New Yorkers loved this crackdown on its own merit. But they particularly loved the idea, as stoutly preached by Bratton and Giuliani, that choking off these small crimes was like choking off the criminal element's oxygen supply. Today's turnstile jumper might easily be wanted for yesterday's murder. That junkie peeing in an alley might have been on his way to a robbery.

As violent crime began to fall dramatically, New Yorkers were more than happy to heap laurels on their operatic, Brooklyn-bred mayor and his hatchet-faced police chief with the big Boston accent. But the two strong-willed men weren't very good at sharing the glory. Soon after the city's crime turnaround landed Bratton—and not Giuliani—on the cover of *Time*, Bratton was pushed to resign. He had been police commissioner for just twenty-seven months.

New York City was a clear innovator in police strategies during the 1990s crime drop, and it also enjoyed the greatest decline in crime of any large American city. Homicide rates fell from 30.7 per 100,000 people in 1990 to 8.4 per 100,000 people in 2000, a change of 73.6 percent. But a careful analysis of the facts shows that the innovative policing strategies probably had little effect on this huge decline.

First, the drop in crime in New York began in 1990. By the end of 1993, the rate of property crime and violent crime, including homicides, had already fallen nearly 20 percent. Rudolph Giuliani, however, did not become mayor—and install Bratton—until early 1994. Crime was well on its way down before either man arrived. And it would continue to fall long after Bratton was bumped from office.

Second, the new police strategies were accompanied by a much more significant change within the police force: a hiring binge. Between 1991 and 2001, the NYPD grew by 45 percent, more than three times the national average. As argued above, an increase in the number of police, regardless of new strategies, *has* been proven to reduce crime. By a conservative calculation, this huge expansion of New York's police force would be expected to reduce crime in New York by 18 percent relative to the national average. If you subtract that 18 percent from New York's homicide reduction, thereby discounting the effect of the police-hiring surge, New York no longer leads the nation with its 73.6 percent drop; it goes straight to the middle of the pack. Many of those new police were in fact hired by David Dinkins, the mayor whom

Giuliani defeated. Dinkins had been desperate to secure the law-and-order vote, having known all along that his opponent would be Giuliani, a former federal prosecutor. (The two men had run against each other four years earlier as well.) So those who wish to credit Giuliani with the crime drop may still do so, for it was his own law-and-order reputation that made Dinkins hire all those police. In the end, of course, the police increase helped everyone—but it helped Giuliani a lot more than Dinkins.

Most damaging to the claim that New York's police innovations radically lowered crime is one simple and often overlooked fact: crime went down *everywhere* during the 1990s, not only in New York. Few other cities tried the kind of strategies that New York did, and certainly none with the same zeal. But even in Los Angeles, a city notorious for bad policing, crime fell at about the same rate as it did in New York once the growth in New York's police force is accounted for.

It would be churlish to argue that smart policing isn't a good thing. Bill Bratton certainly deserves credit for invigorating New York's police force. But there is frighteningly little evidence that his strategy was the crime panacea that he and the media deemed it. The next step will be to continue measuring the impact of police innovations—in Los Angeles, for instance, where Bratton himself became police chief in late 2002. While he duly instituted some of the innovations that were his hallmark in New York, Bratton announced that his highest priority was a more basic one: finding the money to hire thousands of new police officers.

Now to explore another pair of common crime-drop explanations:

Tougher gun laws
Changes in crack and other drug markets

First, the guns. Debates on this subject are rarely coolheaded. Gun advocates believe that gun laws are too strict; opponents believe exactly the opposite. How can intelligent people view the world so differently? Because a gun raises a complex set of issues that change according to one factor: whose hand happens to be holding the gun.

It might be worthwhile to take a step back and ask a rudimentary question: what *is* a gun? It's a tool that can be used to kill someone, of course, but more significantly, a gun is a great disrupter of the natural order.

A gun scrambles the outcome of any dispute. Let's say that a tough guy and a not-so-tough guy exchange words in a bar, which leads to a fight. It's pretty obvious to the not-so-tough guy that he'll be beaten, so why bother fighting? The pecking order remains intact. But if the not-so-tough guy happens to have a gun, he stands a good chance of winning. In this scenario, the introduction of a gun may well lead to more violence.

Now instead of the tough guy and the not-so-tough guy, picture a high-school girl out for a nighttime stroll when she is suddenly set upon by a mugger. What if only the mugger is armed? What if only the girl is armed? What if *both* are armed? A gun opponent might argue that the gun has to be kept out of the mugger's hands in the first place. A gun advocate might argue that the high-school girl needs to have a gun to disrupt what has become the natural order: it's the bad guys that have the guns. (If the girl scares off the mugger, then the introduction of a gun in this case may lead to *less* violence.) Any mugger with even a little initiative is bound to be armed, for in a country like the United States, with a thriving black market in guns, anyone can get hold of one.

There are enough guns in the United States that if you gave one to every adult, you would run out of adults before you ran out of guns. Nearly two-thirds of U.S. homicides involve a gun, a far greater fraction than in other industrialized countries. Our homicide rate is also much higher than in those countries. It would therefore seem likely that our homicide rate is so high in part because guns are so easily available. Research indeed shows this to be true.

But guns are not the whole story. In Switzerland, every adult male is issued an assault rifle for militia duty and is allowed to keep the gun at home. On a per capita basis, Switzerland has more firearms than just about any other country, and yet it is one of the safest places in the world. In other words, guns do not cause crime. That said, the established U.S. methods of keeping guns away from the people who *do* cause crime are, at best, feeble. And since a gun—unlike a bag of cocaine or a car or a pair of pants—lasts pretty much forever, even turning off the spigot of new guns still leaves an ocean of available ones.

So bearing all this in mind, let's consider a variety of recent gun initiatives to see the impact they may have had on crime in the 1990s.

The most famous gun-control law is the Brady Act, passed in 1993, which requires a criminal check and a waiting period before a person can purchase a handgun. This solution may have seemed appealing to politicians, but to an economist it doesn't make much sense. Why? Because regulation of a legal market is bound to fail when a healthy black market exists for the same product. With guns so cheap and so easy to get, the standard criminal has no incentive to fill out a firearms application at his local gun shop and then wait a week. The Brady Act, accordingly, has proven to be practically impotent in lowering crime. (A study of imprisoned felons showed that even before the Brady Act, only about one-fifth of the criminals had bought their guns through a licensed dealer.) Various local gun-control laws have also failed. Washington, D.C., and Chicago both instituted handgun bans well before crime began to fall across the country in the 1990s, and yet those two cities were laggards, not leaders, in the national reduction in crime. One deterrent that *has* proven moderately effective is a stiff increase in prison time for anyone caught in possession of an illegal gun. But there is plenty of room for improvement. Not that this is likely, but if the death penalty were assessed to anyone carrying an illegal gun, and if the penalty were actually enforced, gun crimes would surely plunge.

Another staple of 1990s crime fighting—and of the evening news—was the gun buyback. You remember the image: a menacing, glistening heap of firearms surrounded by the mayor, the police chief, the neighborhood activists. It made for a nice photo op, but that's about as meaningful as a gun buyback gets. The guns that are turned in tend to be heirlooms or junk. The payoff to the gun seller—usually $50 or $100, but in one California buyback, three free hours of psychotherapy—isn't an adequate incentive for anyone who actually plans to use his gun. And the number of surrendered guns is no match for even the number of new guns simultaneously coming to market. Given the number of handguns in the United States and the number of homicides each year, the likelihood that a particular gun was used to kill someone that year is 1 in 10,000. The typical gun buyback program yields fewer than 1,000 guns—which translates into an expectation of less than one-tenth of one homicide per buyback. Not enough, that is, to make even a sliver of impact on the fall of crime.

Then there is an opposite argument—that we need *more* guns on the street, but in the hands of the right people (like the high-school girl above, instead of her mugger). The economist John R. Lott Jr. is the main champion of this idea. His calling card is the book *More Guns, Less Crime*, in which he argues that violent crime has decreased in areas where law-abiding citizens are allowed to carry concealed weapons. His theory might be surprising, but it is sensible. If a criminal thinks his potential victim may be armed, he may be deterred from committing the crime. Handgun opponents call Lott a pro-gun ideologue, and Lott let himself become a lightning rod for gun controversy. He exacerbated his trouble by creating a pseudonym, "Mary Rosh," to defend his theory in online debates. Rosh, identifying herself as a former student of Lott's, praised her teacher's intellect, his evenhandedness, his charisma. "I have to say that he was the best professor that I ever had," s/he wrote. "You wouldn't know that he was a 'right-wing' ideologue from the class. . . . There were a group of us students who would try to take any class that he taught. Lott finally had to tell us that it was best for us to try and take classes from other professors more to be exposed to other ways of teaching graduate material." Then there was the troubling allegation that Lott actually invented some of the survey data that support his more-guns/less-crime theory. Regardless of whether the data were faked, Lott's admittedly intriguing hypothesis doesn't seem to be true. When other scholars have tried to replicate his results, they found that right-to-carry laws simply don't bring down crime.

. . .

Consider the next crime-drop explanation: *the bursting of the crack bubble.* Crack cocaine was such a potent, addictive drug that a hugely profitable market had been created practically overnight. True, it was only the leaders of the crack gangs who were getting rich. But that only made the street-level dealers all the more desperate to advance. Many of them were willing to kill their rivals to do so, whether the rival belonged to the same gang or a different one. There were also gun battles over valuable drug-selling corners. The typical crack murder involved one crack dealer shooting another (or two of them, or three) and not, contrary to conventional wisdom, some bug-eyed crackhead shooting a shopkeeper over a few dollars. The result was a huge increase in violent crime. One study found that more than 25 percent of the homicides in New York City in 1988 were crack-related.

The violence associated with crack began to ebb in about 1991. This has led many people to think that crack itself went away. It didn't. Smoking crack remains much more popular today than most people realize. Nearly 5 percent of all arrests in the United States are still related to cocaine (as against 6 percent at crack's peak); nor have emergency room visits for crack users diminished all that much.

What *did* go away were the huge profits for selling crack. The price of cocaine had been falling for years, and it got only cheaper as crack grew more popular. Dealers began to underprice one another; profits vanished. The crack bubble burst as dramatically as the Nasdaq bubble would eventually burst. (Think of the first generation of crack dealers as the Microsoft millionaires; think of the second generation as Pets.com.) As veteran crack dealers were killed or sent to prison, younger dealers decided that the smaller profits didn't justify the risk. The tournament had lost its allure.

It was no longer worth killing someone to steal their crack turf, and certainly not worth being killed.

So the violence abated. From 1991 to 2001, the homicide rate among young black men—who were disproportionately represented among crack dealers—fell 48 percent, compared to 30 percent for older black men and older white men. (Another minor contributor to the falling homicide rate is the fact that some crack dealers took to shooting their enemies in the buttocks rather than murdering them; this method of violent insult was considered more degrading—and was obviously less severely punished—than murder.) All told, the crash of the crack market accounted for roughly 15 percent of the crime drop of the 1990s—a substantial factor, to be sure, though it should be noted that crack was responsible for far more than 15 percent of the crime *increase* of the 1980s. In other words, the net effect of crack is still being felt in the form of violent crime, to say nothing of the miseries the drug itself continues to cause.

The final pair of crime-drop explanations concern two demographic trends. The first one received many media citations: *aging of the population*.

Until crime fell so drastically, no one talked about this theory at all. In fact, the "bloodbath" school of criminology was touting exactly the opposite theory—that an increase in the teenage share of the population would produce a crop of superpredators who would lay the nation low. "Just beyond the horizon, there lurks a cloud that the winds will soon bring over us," James Q. Wilson wrote in 1995. "The population will start getting younger again. . . . Get ready."

But overall, the teenage share of the population *wasn't* getting much bigger. Criminologists like Wilson and James Alan Fox had badly misread the demographic data. The real population growth in the 1990s was in fact among the elderly. While this may have been scary news in terms of Medicare and Social Security, the average American had little to fear from the growing horde of oldsters. It shouldn't be surprising to learn that elderly people are not very criminally intent; the average sixty-five-year-old is about one-fiftieth as likely to be arrested as the average teenager. That is what makes this aging-of-the-population theory of crime reduction so appealingly tidy: since people mellow out as they get older, more older people must lead to less crime. But a thorough look at the data reveals that the graying of America did nothing to bring down crime in the 1990s. Demographic change is too slow and subtle a process—you don't graduate from teenage hoodlum to senior citizen in just a few years—to even begin to explain the suddenness of the crime decline.

There was another demographic change, however, unforeseen and long-gestating, that did drastically reduce crime in the 1990s.

Think back for a moment to Romania in 1966. Suddenly and without warning, Nicolae Ceauşescu declared abortion illegal. The children born in the wake of the abortion ban were much more likely to become criminals than children born earlier. Why was that? Studies in other parts of Eastern Europe and in Scandinavia from the 1930s through the 1960s reveal a similar trend. In most of these cases, abortion was not forbidden outright, but a woman had to receive permission from a judge in order to obtain one. Researchers found that in the instances where the woman was denied an abortion, she often resented her baby and failed to provide it with a good home. Even when controlling for the income, age, education, and health of the mother, the researchers found that these children too were more likely to become criminals.

The United States, meanwhile, has had a different abortion history than Europe. In the early days of the nation, it was permissible to have an abortion prior to "quickening"—that is, when the first movements of the fetus could be felt, usually around the sixteenth to eighteenth week of pregnancy. In 1828, New York became the first state to restrict abortion; by 1900 it had been made illegal throughout the country. Abortion in the twentieth century was often dangerous and usually expensive. Fewer poor women, therefore, had abortions. They also had less access to birth control. What they did have, accordingly, was a lot more babies.

In the late 1960s, several states began to allow abortion under extreme circumstances: rape, incest, or danger to the mother. By 1970 five states had made abortion entirely legal and broadly available: New York, California, Washington, Alaska, and Hawaii. On January 22, 1973, legalized abortion was suddenly extended to the entire country with the U.S. Supreme Court's ruling in *Roe v. Wade*. The majority opinion, written by Justice Harry Blackmun, spoke specifically to the would-be mother's predicament:

The detriment that the State would impose upon the pregnant woman by denying this choice altogether is apparent. . . . Maternity, or additional offspring, may force upon the woman a distressful life and future. Psychological harm may be imminent. Mental and physical health may be taxed by child care. There is also the distress, for all concerned, associated with the unwanted child, and there is the problem of bringing a child into a family already unable, psychologically and otherwise, to care for it.

The Supreme Court gave voice to what the mothers in Romania and Scandinavia—and elsewhere—had long known: when a woman does not want to have a child, she usually has good reason. She may be unmarried or in a bad marriage. She may consider herself too poor to raise a child. She may think her life is too unstable or unhappy, or she may think that her drinking or drug use will damage the baby's health. She may believe that she is too young or hasn't yet received enough education. She may want a child badly but in a few years, not now. For any of a hundred reasons, she may feel that she cannot provide a home environment that is conducive to raising a healthy and productive child.

In the first year after *Roe v. Wade*, some 750,000 women had abortions in the United States (representing one abortion for every 4 live births). By 1980 the number of abortions reached 1.6 million (one for every 2.25 live births), where it leveled off. In a country of 225 million people, 1.6 million abortions per year—one for every 140 Americans—may not have seemed so dramatic. In the first year after Nicolae Ceaușescu's death, when abortion was reinstated in Romania, there was one abortion for every *twenty-two* Romanians. But still: 1.6 million American women a year who got pregnant were suddenly not having those babies.

Before *Roe v. Wade*, it was predominantly the daughters of middle- or upper-class families who could arrange and afford a safe illegal abortion. Now, instead of an illegal procedure that might cost $500, any woman could easily obtain an abortion, often for less than $100.

What sort of woman was most likely to take advantage of *Roe v. Wade*? Very often she was unmarried or in her teens or poor, and sometimes all three. What sort of future might her child have had? One study has shown that the typical child who went unborn in the earliest years of legalized abortion would have been 50 percent more likely than average to live in poverty; he would have also been 60 percent more likely to grow up with just one parent. These two factors—childhood poverty and a single-parent household—are among the strongest predictors that a child will have a criminal future. Growing up in a single-parent home roughly doubles a child's propensity to commit crime. So does having a teenage mother. Another study has shown that low maternal education is the single most powerful factor leading to criminality.

In other words, the very factors that drove millions of American women to have an abortion also seemed to predict that their children, had they been born, would have led unhappy and possibly criminal lives.

To be sure, the legalization of abortion in the United States had myriad consequences. Infanticide fell dramatically. So did shotgun marriages, as well as the number of babies put up for adoption (which has led to the boom in the adoption of foreign babies). Conceptions rose by nearly 30 percent, but births actually *fell* by 6 percent, indicating that many women were using abortion as a method of birth control, a crude and drastic sort of insurance policy.

Perhaps the most dramatic effect of legalized abortion, however, and one that would take years to reveal itself, was its impact on crime. In the early 1990s, just as the first cohort of children born after *Roe v. Wade* was hitting its late teen years—the years during which young men enter their criminal prime—the rate of crime began to fall. What this cohort was missing, of course, were the children who stood the greatest chance of becoming criminals. And the crime rate continued to fall as an entire generation came of age minus the children whose mothers had not wanted to bring a child into the world. Legalized abortion led to less unwantedness; unwantedness leads to high crime; legalized abortion, therefore, led to less crime.

This theory is bound to provoke a variety of reactions, ranging from disbelief to revulsion, and a variety of objections, ranging from the quotidian to the moral. The likeliest first objection is the most straightforward one: is the theory true? Perhaps abortion and crime are merely correlated and not causal.

It may be more comforting to believe what the newspapers say, that the drop in crime was due to brilliant policing and clever gun control and a surging economy. We have evolved with a tendency to link causality to things we can touch or feel, not to some distant or difficult phenomenon. We believe especially in near-term causes: a snake bites your friend, he screams with pain, and he dies. The snakebite, you conclude, must have killed him. Most of the time, such a reckoning is correct. But when it comes to cause and effect, there is often a trap in such open-and-shut thinking. We smirk now when we think of ancient cultures that embraced faulty causes—the warriors who believed, for instance, that it was their raping of a virgin that brought them victory on the battlefield. But we too embrace faulty causes, usually at the urging of an expert proclaiming a truth in which he has a vested interest.

How, then, can we tell if the abortion-crime link is a case of causality rather than simply correlation?

One way to test the effect of abortion on crime would be to measure crime data in the five states where abortion was made legal before the Supreme Court extended abortion rights to the rest of the country. In New York, California, Washington, Alaska, and Hawaii, a woman had been able to obtain a legal abortion for at least two years before *Roe v. Wade*. And indeed, those early-legalizing states saw crime begin to fall earlier than the other forty-five states and the District of Columbia. Between 1988 and 1994, violent crime in the early-legalizing states fell 13 percent compared to the other states; between 1994 and 1997, their murder rates fell 23 percent more than those of the other states.

But what if those early legalizers simply got lucky? What else might we look for in the data to establish an abortion-crime link?

One factor to look for would be a correlation between each state's abortion rate and its crime rate. Sure enough, the states with the highest abortion rates in the 1970s experienced the greatest crime drops in the 1990s, while states with low abortion rates experienced smaller crime drops. (This correlation exists even when controlling for a variety of factors that influence crime: a state's level of incarceration, number of police, and its economic situation.) Since 1985, states with high abortion rates have experienced a roughly 30 percent drop in crime relative to low-abortion states. (New York City had high abortion rates *and* lay within an early-legalizing state, a pair of facts that further dampen the claim that innovative policing caused the crime drop.) Moreover, there was no link between a given state's abortion rate and its crime rate *before* the late 1980s—when the first cohort affected by legalized abortion was reaching its criminal prime—which is yet another indication that *Roe v. Wade* was indeed the event that tipped the crime scale.

There are even more correlations, positive and negative, that shore up the abortion-crime link. In states with high abortion rates, the entire decline in crime was among the post-*Roe* cohort as opposed to older criminals. Also, studies of Australia and Canada have since established a similar link between legalized abortion and crime. And the post-*Roe* cohort was not only missing thousands of young male criminals but also thousands of single, teenage mothers—for many of the aborted baby girls would have been the children most likely to replicate their *own* mothers' tendencies.

To discover that abortion was one of the greatest crime-lowering factors in American history is, needless to say, jarring. It feels less Darwinian than Swiftian; it calls to mind a long-ago dart attributed to G. K. Chesterton: when there aren't enough hats to go around, the problem isn't solved by lopping off some heads. The crime drop was, in the language of economists, an "unintended benefit" of legalized abortion. But one need not oppose abortion on moral or religious grounds to feel shaken by the notion of a private sadness being converted into a public good.

Indeed, there are plenty of people who consider abortion itself to be a violent crime. One legal scholar called legalized abortion worse than either slavery (since it routinely involves death) or the Holocaust (since the number of post-*Roe* abortions in the United States, roughly thirty-seven million as of 2004, outnumber the six million Jews killed in Europe). Whether or not one feels so strongly about abortion, it remains a singularly charged issue. Anthony V. Bouza, a former top police official in both the Bronx and Minneapolis, discovered this when he ran for Minnesota governor in 1994. A few years earlier, Bouza had written a book in which he called abortion "arguably the only effective crime-prevention device adopted in this nation since the late 1960s." When Bouza's opinion was publicized just before the election, he fell sharply in the polls. And then he lost.

However a person feels about abortion, a question is likely to come to mind: what are we to make of the trade-off of more abortion for less crime? Is it even possible to put a number on such a complicated transaction?

As it happens, economists have a curious habit of affixing numbers to complicated transactions. Consider the effort to save the northern spotted owl from extinction. One economic study found that in order to protect roughly five thousand owls, the opportunity costs—that is, the income surrendered by the logging industry and others—would be $46 billion, or just over $9 million per owl. After the *Exxon Valdez* oil spill in 1989, another study estimated the amount that the typical American household would be willing to pay to avoid another such disaster: $31. An economist can affix a value even to a particular body part. Consider the schedule that the state of Connecticut uses to compensate for work-related injuries.

LOST OR DAMAGED BODY PART	COMPENSATED WEEKS OF PAY
FINGER (FIRST)	36
FINGER (SECOND)	29
FINGER (THIRD)	21
FINGER (FOURTH)	17
THUMB (MASTER HAND)	63
THUMB (OTHER HAND)	54
HAND (MASTER)	168
HAND (OTHER)	155
ARM (MASTER)	208
ARM (OTHER)	194
TOE (GREAT)	28
TOE (ANY OTHER)	9
FOOT	125

LOST OR DAMAGED BODY PART	COMPENSATED WEEKS OF PAY
NOSE	35
EYE	157
KIDNEY	117
LIVER	347
PANCREAS	416
HEART	520
MAMMARY	35
OVARY	35
TESTIS	35
PENIS	35–104
VAGINA	35–104

Now, for the sake of argument, let's ask an outrageous question: what is the relative value of a fetus and a newborn? If faced with the Solomonic task of sacrificing the life of one newborn for an indeterminate number of fetuses, what number might you choose? This is nothing but a thought exercise—obviously there is no right answer—but it may help clarify the impact of abortion on crime.

For a person who is either resolutely pro-life or resolutely pro-choice, this is a simple calculation. The first, believing that life begins at conception, would likely consider the value of a fetus versus the value of a newborn to be 1:1. The second person, believing that a woman's right to an abortion trumps any other factor, would likely argue that no number of fetuses can equal even one newborn.

But let's consider a third person. (If you identify strongly with either person number one or person number two, the following exercise might strike you as offensive, and you may want to skip

WHERE HAVE ALL THE CRIMINALS GONE?

this paragraph and the next.) This third person does not believe that a fetus is the 1:1 equivalent of a newborn, yet neither does he believe that a fetus has no relative value. Let's say that he is forced, for the sake of argument, to affix a relative value, and he decides that 1 newborn is worth 100 fetuses.

There are roughly 1.5 million abortions in the United States every year. For a person who believes that 1 newborn is worth 100 fetuses, those 1.5 million abortions would translate—dividing 1.5 million by 100—into the equivalent of a loss of 15,000 human lives. Fifteen thousand lives: that happens to be about the same number of people who die in homicides in the United States every year. And it is far more than the number of homicides eliminated each year due to legalized abortion. So even for someone who considers a fetus to be worth only one one-hundredth of a human being, the trade-off between higher abortion and lower crime is, by an economist's reckoning, terribly inefficient.

What the link between abortion and crime does say is this: when the government gives a woman the opportunity to make her own decision about abortion, she generally does a good job of figuring out if she is in a position to raise the baby well. If she decides she can't, she often chooses the abortion.

But once a woman decides she *will* have her baby, a pressing question arises: what are parents supposed to do once a child is born?

**WHAT MAKES A
PERFECT PARENT?**

Has there ever been another art so devoutly converted into a science as the art of parenting?

Over the recent decades, a vast and diverse flock of parenting experts has arisen. Anyone who tries even casually to follow their advice may be stymied, for the conventional wisdom on parenting seems to shift by the hour. Sometimes it is a case of one expert differing from another. At other times the most vocal experts suddenly agree en masse that the old wisdom was wrong and that the new wisdom is, for a little while at least, irrefutably right. Breast feeding, for example, is the only way to guarantee a healthy and intellectually advanced child—unless bottle feeding is the answer. A baby should always be put to sleep on her back—until it is decreed that she should only be put to sleep on her stomach. Eating liver is either a) toxic or b) imperative for brain development. Spare the rod and spoil the child; spank the child and go to jail.

In her book *Raising America: Experts, Parents, and a Century of Advice About Children*, Ann Hulbert documented how parenting experts contradict one another and even themselves. Their banter might be hilarious were it not so confounding and, often, scary. Gary Ezzo, who in the *Babywise* book series endorses an "infant-management strategy" for moms and dads trying to "achieve excellence in parenting," stresses how important it is to train a baby, early on, to sleep alone through the night. Otherwise, Ezzo warns, sleep deprivation might "negatively impact an infant's developing central nervous system" and lead to learning disabilities. Advocates of "co-sleeping," meanwhile, warn that sleeping alone is harmful to a baby's psyche and that he should be brought into the "family bed." What about stimulation? In 1983 T. Berry Brazelton wrote that a baby arrives in the world "beautifully prepared for the role of learning about him- or herself and the world all around." Brazelton favored early, ardent stimulation—an "interactive" child. One hundred years earlier, however, L. Emmett Holt cautioned that a baby is not a "plaything." There should be "no forcing, no pressure, no undue stimulation" during the first two years of a child's life, Holt believed; the brain is growing so much during that time that overstimulation might cause "a great deal of harm." He also believed that a crying baby should never be picked up unless it is in pain. As Holt explained, a baby should be left to cry for fifteen to thirty minutes a day: "It is the baby's exercise."

The typical parenting expert, like experts in other fields, is prone to sound exceedingly sure of himself. An expert doesn't so much argue the various sides of an issue as plant his flag firmly on one side. That's because an expert whose argument reeks of restraint or nuance often doesn't get much attention. An expert must be bold if he hopes to alchemize his homespun theory into conventional wisdom. His best chance of doing so is to engage the public's emotions, for emotion is the enemy of rational argument. And as emotions go, one of them—fear—is more potent than the rest. The superpredator, Iraqi weapons of mass destruction, mad-cow disease, crib death: how can we fail to heed the expert's advice on these horrors when, like that mean uncle telling too-scary stories to too-young children, he has reduced us to quivers?

No one is more susceptible to an expert's fearmongering than a parent. Fear is in fact a major component of the act of parenting. A parent, after all, is the steward of another creature's life, a creature who in the beginning is more helpless than the newborn of nearly any other species. This leads a lot of parents to spend a lot of their parenting energy simply being scared.

The problem is that they are often scared of the wrong things. It's not their fault, really. Separating facts from rumors is always hard work, especially for a busy parent. And the white noise generated by the experts—to say nothing of the pressure exerted by fellow parents—is so overwhelming that they can barely think for themselves. The facts they do manage to glean have usually been varnished or exaggerated or otherwise taken out of context to serve an agenda that isn't their own.

Consider the parents of an eight-year-old girl named, say, Molly. Her two best friends, Amy and Imani, each live nearby. Molly's parents know that Amy's parents keep a gun in their house, so they have forbidden Molly to play there. Instead, Molly spends a lot of time at Imani's house, which has a swimming pool in the backyard. Molly's parents feel good about having made such a smart choice to protect their daughter.

But according to the data, their choice isn't smart at all. In a given year, there is one drowning of a child for every 11,000 residential pools in the United States. (In a country with 6 million pools, this means that roughly 550 children under the age of ten drown each year.) Meanwhile, there is 1 child killed by a gun for every 1 million-plus guns. (In a country with an estimated 200 million guns, this means that roughly 175 children under ten die each year from guns.) The likelihood of death by pool (1 in 11,000) versus death by gun (1 in 1 million-plus) isn't even close: Molly is far more likely to die in a swimming accident at Imani's house than in gunplay at Amy's.

But most of us are, like Molly's parents, terrible risk assessors. Peter Sandman, a self-described "risk communications consultant" in Princeton, New Jersey, made this point in early 2004 after a single case of mad-cow disease in the United States prompted an antibeef frenzy. "The basic reality," Sandman told *The New York Times*, "is that the risks that scare people and the risks that kill people are very different."

Sandman offered a comparison between mad-cow disease (a superscary but exceedingly rare threat) and the spread of food-borne pathogens in the average home kitchen (exceedingly common but somehow not very scary). "Risks that you control are much less a source of outrage than risks that are out of your control," Sandman said. "In the case of mad-cow, it feels like it's beyond my control. I can't tell if my meat has prions in it or not. I can't see it, I can't smell it. Whereas dirt in my own kitchen is very much in my own control. I can clean my sponges. I can clean the floor."

Sandman's "control" principle might also explain why most people are more scared of flying in an airplane than driving a car. Their thinking goes like this: since I control the car, I am the one keeping myself safe; since I have no control of the airplane, I am at the mercy of myriad external factors.

So which should we actually fear more, flying or driving?

It might first help to ask a more basic question: what, exactly, are we afraid of? Death, presumably. But the fear of death needs to be narrowed down. Of course we all know that we are bound to die, and we might worry about it casually. But if you are told that you have a 10 percent chance of dying within the next year, you might worry a lot more, perhaps even choosing to live your life differently. And if you are told that you have 10 percent chance of dying within the next minute, you'll probably panic. So it's the *imminent* possibility of death that drives the fear—which means that the most sensible way to calculate fear of death would be to think about it on a per-hour basis.

If you are taking a trip and have the choice of driving or flying, you might wish to consider the per-hour death rate of driving versus flying. It is true that many more people die in the United States each year in motor vehicle accidents (roughly forty thousand) than in airplane crashes (fewer than one thousand). But it's also true that most people spend a lot more time in cars than in airplanes. (More people die even in boating accidents each year than in airplane crashes; as we saw with swimming pools versus guns, water is a lot more dangerous than most people think.) The per-*hour* death rate of driving versus flying, however, is about equal. The two contraptions are equally likely (or, in truth, unlikely) to lead to death.

But fear best thrives in the present tense. That is why experts rely on it; in a world that is increasingly impatient with long-term processes, fear is a potent short-term play. Imagine that you are a government official charged with procuring the funds to fight one of two proven killers: terrorist attacks and heart disease. Which cause do you think the members of Congress will open up the coffers for? The likelihood of any given person being killed in a terrorist attack is far smaller than the likelihood that the same person will clog up his arteries with fatty food and die of heart disease. But a terrorist attack happens *now;* death by heart disease is some distant, quiet catastrophe. Terrorist acts lie beyond our control; french fries do not. Just as important as the control factor is what Peter Sandman calls the dread factor. Death by terrorist attack (or mad-cow disease) is considered wholly dreadful; death by heart disease is, for some reason, not.

Sandman is an expert who works both sides of the aisle. One day he might help a group of environmentalists expose a public health hazard. His client the next day could be a fast-food CEO trying to deal with an *E. coli* outbreak. Sandman has reduced his expertise to a tidy equation: Risk = hazard + outrage. For the CEO with the bad hamburger meat, Sandman engages in "outrage reduction"; for the environmentalists, it's "outrage increase."

Note that Sandman addresses the outrage but not the hazard itself. He concedes that outrage and hazard do not carry equal weight in his risk equation. "When hazard is high and outrage is low, people underreact," he says. "And when hazard is low and outrage is high, they overreact."

So why is a swimming pool less frightening than a gun? The thought of a child being shot through the chest with a neighbor's gun is gruesome, dramatic, horrifying—in a word, outrageous. Swimming pools do not inspire outrage. This is due in part to the familiarity factor. Just as most people spend more time in cars than in airplanes, most of us have a lot more experience swimming in pools than shooting guns. But it takes only about thirty seconds for a child to drown, and it often happens noiselessly. An infant can drown in water as shallow as a few inches. The steps to prevent drowning, meanwhile, are pretty straightforward: a watchful adult, a fence around the pool, a locked back door so a toddler doesn't slip outside unnoticed.

If every parent followed these precautions, the lives of perhaps four hundred young children could be saved each year. That would outnumber the lives saved by two of the most widely promoted inventions in recent memory: safer cribs and child car seats. The data show that car seats are, at best, nominally helpful. It is certainly safer to keep a child in the rear seat than sitting on a lap in the front seat, where in the event of an accident he essentially becomes a projectile. But the safety to be gained here is from preventing the kids from riding shotgun, not from strapping them into a $200 car seat. Nevertheless, many parents so magnify the benefit of a car seat that they trek to the local police station or firehouse to have it installed just right. Theirs is a gesture of love, surely, but also a gesture of what might be called obsessive parenting. (Obsessive parents know who they are and are generally proud of the fact; non-obsessive parents also know who the obsessives are and tend to snicker at them.)

Most innovations in the field of child safety are affiliated with— shock of shocks—a new product to be marketed. (Nearly five million car seats are sold each year.) These products are often a response to some growing scare in which, as Peter Sandman might put it, the outrage outweighs the hazard. Compare the four hundred lives that a few swimming pool precautions might save to the number of lives saved by far noisier crusades: child-resistant packaging (an estimated fifty lives a year), flame-retardant pajamas (ten lives), keeping children away from airbags in cars (fewer than five young children a year have been killed by airbags since their introduction), and safety drawstrings on children's clothing (two lives).

Hold on a minute, you say. What does it matter if parents are manipulated by experts and marketers? Shouldn't we applaud any effort, regardless of how minor or manipulative, that makes even one child safer? Don't parents already have enough to worry about? After all, parents are responsible for one of the most awesomely important feats we know: the very shaping of a child's character. Aren't they?

The most radical shift of late in the conventional wisdom on parenting has been provoked by one simple question: how much do parents really matter?

Clearly, *bad* parenting matters a great deal. As the link between abortion and crime makes clear, unwanted children—who are disproportionately subject to neglect and abuse—have worse outcomes than children who were eagerly welcomed by their parents. But how much can those eager parents actually accomplish for their children's sake?

This question represents a crescendo of decades' worth of research. A long line of studies, including research into twins who were separated at birth, had already concluded that genes alone are responsible for perhaps 50 percent of a child's personality and abilities.

So if nature accounts for half of a child's destiny, what accounts for the other half? Surely it must be the nurturing—the Baby Mozart tapes, the church sermons, the museum trips, the French lessons, the bargaining and hugging and quarreling and punishing that, in toto, constitute the act of parenting. But how then to explain another famous study, the Colorado Adoption Project, which followed the lives of 245 babies put up for adoption and found virtually *no* correlation between the child's personality traits and those of his adopted parents? Or the other studies showing that a child's character wasn't much affected whether or not he was sent to day care, whether he had one parent or two, whether his mother worked or didn't, whether he had two mommies or two daddies or one of each?

These nature-nurture discrepancies were addressed in a 1998 book by a little-known textbook author named Judith Rich Harris. *The Nurture Assumption* was in effect an attack on obsessive parenting, a book so provocative that it required two subtitles: *Why Children Turn Out the Way They Do* and *Parents Matter Less than You Think and Peers Matter More.* Harris argued, albeit gently, that parents are wrong to think they contribute so mightily to their child's personality. This belief, she wrote, was a "cultural myth." Harris argued that the top-down influence of parents is overwhelmed by the grassroots effect of peer pressure, the blunt force applied each day by friends and schoolmates.

The unlikeliness of Harris's bombshell—she was a grandmother, no less, without PhD or academic affiliation—prompted both wonder and chagrin. "The public may be forgiven for saying, 'Here we go again,' " wrote one reviewer. "One year we're told bonding is the key, the next that it's birth order. Wait, what really matters is stimulation. The first five years of life are the most important; no, the first three years; no, it's all over by the first year. Forget that: It's all genetics!"

But Harris's theory was duly endorsed by a slate of heavyweights. Among them was Steven Pinker, the cognitive psychologist and bestselling author, who in his own book *Blank Slate* called Harris's views "mind-boggling" (in a good way). "Patients in traditional forms of psychotherapy while away their fifty minutes reliving childhood conflicts and learning to blame their unhappiness on how their parents treated them," Pinker wrote. "Many biographies scavenge through the subject's childhood for the roots of the grown-up's tragedies and triumphs. 'Parenting experts' make women feel like ogres if they slip out of the house to work or skip a reading of *Goodnight Moon*. All these deeply held beliefs will have to be rethought."

Or will they? Parents *must* matter, you tell yourself. Besides, even if peers exert so much influence on a child, isn't it the parents who essentially choose a child's peers? Isn't that why parents agonize over the right neighborhood, the right school, the right circle of friends?

Still, the question of how much parents matter is a good one. It is also terribly complicated. In determining a parent's influence, which dimension of the child are we measuring: his personality? his school grades? his moral behavior? his creative abilities? his salary as an adult? And what weight should we assign each of the many inputs that affect a child's outcome: genes, family environment, socioeconomic level, schooling, discrimination, luck, illness, and so on?

For the sake of argument, let's consider the story of two boys, one white and one black.

The white boy is raised in a Chicago suburb by parents who read widely and involve themselves in school reform. His father, who has a decent manufacturing job, often takes the boy on nature hikes. His mother is a housewife who will eventually go back to college and earn a bachelor's degree in education. The boy is happy and performs very well in school. His teachers think he may be a bona fide math genius. His parents encourage him and are terribly proud when he skips a grade. He has an adoring younger brother who is also very bright. The family even holds literary salons in their home.

The black boy is born in Daytona Beach, Florida, and his mother abandons him at the age of two. His father has a good job in sales but is a heavy drinker. He often beats the little boy with the metal end of a garden hose. One night when the boy is eleven, he is decorating a tabletop Christmas tree—the first one he has ever had—when his father starts beating up a lady friend in the kitchen. He hits her so hard that some teeth fly out of her mouth and land at the base of the boy's Christmas tree, but the boy knows better than to speak up. At school he makes no effort whatsoever. Before long he is selling drugs, mugging suburbanites, carrying a gun. He makes sure to be asleep by the time his father comes home from drinking, and to be out of the house before his father awakes. The father eventually goes to jail for sexual assault. By the age of twelve, the boy is essentially fending for himself.

You don't have to believe in obsessive parenting to think that the second boy doesn't stand a chance and that the first boy has it made. What are the odds that the second boy, with the added handicap of racial discrimination, will turn out to lead a productive life? What are the odds that the first boy, so deftly primed for success, will somehow fail? And how much of his fate should each boy attribute to his parents?

One could theorize forever about what makes the perfect parent. For two reasons, the authors of this book will not do so. The first is that neither of us professes to be a parenting expert (although between us we do have six children under the age of five). The second is that we are less persuaded by parenting theory than by what the data have to say.

Certain facets of a child's outcome—personality, for instance, or creativity—are not easily measured by data. But school performance is. And since most parents would agree that education lies at the core of a child's formation, it would make sense to begin by examining a telling set of school data.

These data concern school choice, an issue that most people feel strongly about in one direction or another. True believers of school choice argue that their tax dollars buy them the right to send their children to the best school possible. Critics worry that school choice will leave behind the worst students in the worst schools. Still, just about every parent seems to believe that her child will thrive if only he can attend the *right* school, the one with an appropriate blend of academics, extracurriculars, friendliness, and safety.

School choice came early to the Chicago Public School system. That's because the CPS, like most urban school districts, had a disproportionate number of minority students. Despite the U.S. Supreme Court's 1954 ruling in *Brown v. Board of Education of Topeka*, which dictated that schools be desegregated, many black CPS students continued to attend schools that were nearly all-black. So in 1980 the U.S. Department of Justice and the Chicago Board of Education teamed up to try to better integrate the city's schools. It was decreed that incoming freshmen could apply to virtually any high school in the district.

Aside from its longevity, there are several reasons the CPS school-choice program is a good one to study. It offers a huge data set—Chicago has the third-largest school system in the country, after New York and Los Angeles—as well as an enormous amount of choice (more than sixty high schools) and flexibility. Its take-up rates are accordingly very high, with roughly half of the CPS students opting out of their neighborhood school. But the most serendipitous aspect of the CPS program—for the sake of a study, at least—is how the school-choice game was played.

As might be expected, throwing open the doors of any school to every freshman in Chicago threatened to create bedlam. The schools with good test scores and high graduation rates would be rabidly oversubscribed, making it impossible to satisfy every student's request.

In the interest of fairness, the CPS resorted to a lottery. For a researcher, this is a remarkable boon. A behavioral scientist could hardly design a better experiment in his laboratory. Just as the scientist might randomly assign one mouse to a treatment group and another to a control group, the Chicago school board effectively did the same. Imagine two students, statistically identical, each of whom wants to attend a new, better school. Thanks to how the ball bounces in the hopper, one student goes to the new school and the other stays behind. Now imagine multiplying those students by the thousands. The result is a natural experiment on a grand scale. This was hardly the goal in mind of the Chicago school officials who conceived the lottery. But when viewed in this way, the lottery offers a wonderful means of measuring just how much school choice—or, really, a better school—truly matters.

So what do the data reveal?

The answer will not be heartening to obsessive parents: in this case, school choice barely mattered at all. It is true that the Chicago students who *entered* the school-choice lottery were more likely to graduate than the students who didn't—which seems to suggest that school choice does make a difference. But that's an illusion. The proof is in this comparison: the students who won the lottery and went to a "better" school did no better than equivalent students who lost the lottery and were left behind. That is, a student who opted out of his neighborhood school was more likely to graduate whether or not he actually won the opportunity to go to a new school. What appears to be an advantage gained by going to a new school isn't connected to the new school at all. What this means is that the students—and parents—who choose to opt out tend to be smarter and more academically motivated to begin with. But statistically, they gained no academic benefit by changing schools.

And is it true that the students left behind in neighborhood schools suffered? No: they continued to test at about the same levels as before the supposed brain drain.

There was, however, one group of students in Chicago who did see a dramatic change: those who entered a technical school or career academy. These students performed substantially better than they did in their old academic settings and graduated at a much higher rate than their past performance would have predicted. So the CPS school-choice program did help prepare a small segment of otherwise struggling students for solid careers by giving them practical skills. But it doesn't appear that it made anyone much smarter.

Could it really be that school choice doesn't much matter? No self-respecting parent, obsessive or otherwise, is ready to believe that. But wait: maybe it's because the CPS study measures high-school students; maybe by then the die has already been cast. "There are too many students who arrive at high school not prepared to do high school work," Richard P. Mills, the education commissioner of New York State, noted recently, "too many students who arrive at high school reading, writing, and doing math at the elementary level. We have to correct the problem in the earlier grades."

Indeed, academic studies have substantiated Mills's anxiety. In examining the income gap between black and white adults—it is well established that blacks earn significantly less—scholars have found that the gap is virtually eradicated if the blacks' lower eighth-grade test scores are taken into account. In other words, the black-white income gap is largely a product of a black-white education gap that could have been observed many years earlier. "Reducing the black-white test score gap," wrote the authors of one study, "would do more to promote racial equality than any other strategy that commands broad political support."

So where does that black-white test gap come from? Many theories have been put forth over the years: poverty, genetic makeup, the "summer setback" phenomenon (blacks are thought to lose more ground than whites when school is out of session), racial bias in testing or in teachers' perceptions, and a black backlash against "acting white."

In a paper called "The Economics of 'Acting White,'" the young black Harvard economist Roland G. Fryer Jr. argues that some black students "have tremendous disincentives to invest in particular behaviors (i.e., education, ballet, etc.) due to the fact that they may be deemed a person who is trying to act like a white person (a.k.a. 'selling-out'). Such a label, in some neighborhoods, can carry penalties that range from being deemed a social outcast, to being beaten or killed." Fryer cites the recollections of a young Kareem Abdul-Jabbar, known then as Lew Alcindor, who had just entered the fourth grade in a new school and discovered that he was a better reader than even the seventh graders: "When the kids found this out, I became a target. . . . It was my first time away from home, my first experience in an all-black situation, and I found myself being punished for everything I'd ever been taught was right. I got all A's and was hated for it; I spoke correctly and was called a punk. I had to learn a new language simply to be able to deal with the threats. I had good manners and was a good little boy and paid for it with my hide."

Fryer is also one of the authors of "Understanding the Black-White Test Score Gap in the First Two Years of School." This paper takes advantage of a new trove of government data that helps reliably address the black-white gap. Perhaps more interestingly, the data do a nice job of answering the question that every parent—black, white, and otherwise—wants to ask: what are the factors that do and do not affect a child's performance in the early school years?

In the late 1990s, the U.S. Department of Education undertook a monumental project called the Early Childhood Longitudinal Study. The ECLS sought to measure the academic progress of more than twenty thousand children from kindergarten through the fifth grade. The subjects were chosen from across the country to represent an accurate cross section of American schoolchildren.

The ECLS measured the students' academic performance and gathered typical survey information about each child: his or her race, gender, family structure, socioeconomic status, the level of his or her parents' education, and so on. But the study went well beyond these basics. It also included interviews with the students' parents (and teachers and school administrators), posing a long list of questions more intimate than those in the typical government interview: whether the parents spanked their children, and how often; whether they took them to libraries or museums; how much television the children watched.

The result is an incredibly rich set of data—which, if the right questions are asked of it, tells some surprising stories.

How can this type of data be made to tell a reliable story? By subjecting it to the economist's favorite trick: regression analysis. No, regression analysis is not some forgotten form of psychiatric treatment. It is a powerful—if limited—tool that uses statistical techniques to identify otherwise elusive correlations.

Correlation is nothing more than a statistical term that indicates whether two variables move together. It tends to be cold outside when it snows; those two factors are positively correlated. Sunshine and rain, meanwhile, are negatively correlated. Easy enough—as long as there are only a couple of variables. But with a couple of *hundred* variables, things get harder. Regression analysis is the tool that enables an economist to sort out these huge piles of data. It does so by artificially holding constant every variable except the two he wishes to focus on, and then showing how those two co-vary.

In a perfect world, an economist could run a controlled experiment just as a physicist or a biologist does: setting up two samples, randomly manipulating one of them, and measuring the effect. But an economist rarely has the luxury of such pure experimentation. (That's why the school-choice lottery in Chicago was such a happy accident.) What an economist typically has is a data set with a great many variables, none of them randomly generated, some related and others not. From this jumble, he must determine which factors are correlated and which are not.

In the case of the ECLS data, it might help to think of regression analysis as performing the following task: converting each of those twenty thousand schoolchildren into a sort of circuit board with an identical number of switches. Each switch represents a single category of the child's data: his first-grade math score, his third-grade math score, his first-grade reading score, his third-grade reading score, his mother's education level, his father's income, the number of books in his home, the relative affluence of his neighborhood, and so on.

Now a researcher is able to tease some insights from this very complicated set of data. He can line up all the children who share many characteristics—all the circuit boards that have their switches flipped the same direction—and then pinpoint the single characteristic they *don't* share. This is how he isolates the true impact of that single switch on the sprawling circuit board. This is how the effect of that switch—and, eventually, of every switch—becomes manifest.

Let's say that we want to ask the ECLS data a fundamental question about parenting and education: does having a lot of books in your home lead your child to do well in school? Regression analysis can't quite answer that question, but it can answer a subtly different one: does a child with a lot of books in his home tend to do better than a child with no books? The difference between the first and second questions is the difference between causality (question 1) and correlation (question 2). A regression analysis can demonstrate correlation, but it doesn't prove cause. After all, there are several ways in which two variables can be correlated. X can cause Y; Y can cause X; or it may be that some other factor is causing both X and Y. A regression alone can't tell you whether it snows because it's cold, whether it's cold because it snows, or if the two just happen to go together.

The ECLS data do show, for instance, that a child with a lot of books in his home tends to test higher than a child with no books. So those factors are correlated, and that's nice to know. But higher test scores are correlated with many other factors as well. If you simply measure children with a lot of books against children with no books, the answer may not be very meaningful. Perhaps the number of books in a child's home merely indicates how much money his parents make. What we really want to do is measure two children who are alike in every way except one—in this case, the number of books in their homes—and see if that one factor makes a difference in their school performance.

It should be said that regression analysis is more art than science. (In this regard, it has a great deal in common with parenting itself.) But a skilled practitioner can use it to tell how meaningful a correlation is—and maybe even tell whether that correlation does indicate a causal relationship.

So what does an analysis of the ECLS data tell us about schoolchildren's performance? A number of things. The first one concerns the black-white test score gap.

It has long been observed that black children, even before they set foot in a classroom, underperform their white counterparts. Moreover, black children didn't measure up even when controlling for a wide array of variables. (To control for a variable is essentially to eliminate its influence, much as one golfer uses a handicap against another. In the case of an academic study such as the ECLS, a researcher might control for any number of disadvantages that one student might carry when measured against the average student.) But this new data set tells a different story. After controlling for just a few variables—including the income and education level of the child's parents and the mother's age at the birth of her first child—the gap between black and white children is virtually eliminated at the time the children enter school.

This is an encouraging finding on two fronts. It means that young black children have continued to make gains relative to their white counterparts. It also means that whatever gap remains can be linked to a handful of readily identifiable factors. The data reveal that black children who perform poorly in school do so not because they are black but because a black child is more likely to come from a low-income, low-education household. A typical black child and white child from the same socioeconomic background, however, have the same abilities in math and reading upon entering kindergarten.

Great news, right? Well, not so fast. First of all, because the average black child *is* more likely to come from a low-income, low-education household, the gap is very real: on average, black children still *are* scoring worse. Worse yet, even when the parents' income and education are controlled for, the black-white gap reappears within just two years of a child's entering school. By the end of first grade, a black child is underperforming a statistically equivalent white child. And the gap steadily grows over the second and third grades.

Why does this happen? That's a hard, complicated question. But one answer may lie in the fact that the school attended by the typical black child is not the same school attended by the typical white child, and the typical black child goes to a school that is simply . . . bad. Even fifty years after *Brown v. Board*, many

American schools are virtually segregated. The ECLS project surveyed roughly one thousand schools, taking samples of twenty children from each. In 35 percent of those schools, not a single black child was included in the sample. The typical white child in the ECLS study attends a school that is only 6 percent black; the typical black child, meanwhile, attends a school that is about 60 percent black.

Just how are the black schools bad? Not, interestingly, in the ways that schools are traditionally measured. In terms of class size, teachers' education, and computer-to-student ratio, the schools attended by blacks and whites are similar. But the typical black student's school has a far higher rate of troublesome indicators, such as gang problems, nonstudents loitering in front of the school, and lack of PTA funding. These schools offer an environment that is simply not conducive to learning.

Black students are hardly the only ones who suffer in bad schools. White children in these schools also perform poorly. In fact, there is essentially no black-white test score gap *within* a bad school in the early years once you control for students' backgrounds. But all students in a bad school, black and white, *do* lose ground to students in good schools. Perhaps educators and researchers are wrong to be so hung up on the black-white test score gap; the bad-school/good-school gap may be the more salient issue. Consider this fact: the ECLS data reveal that black students in good schools *don't* lose ground to their white counterparts, and black students in good schools outperform whites in poor schools.

So according to these data, a child's school does seem to have a clear impact on his academic progress, at least in the early years. Can the same be said for parenting? Did all those Baby Mozart tapes pay off? What about those marathon readings of *Goodnight*

Moon? Was the move to the suburbs worthwhile? Do the kids with PTA parents do better than the kids whose parents have never heard of the PTA?

The wide-ranging ECLS data offer a number of compelling correlations between a child's personal circumstances and his school performance. For instance, once all other factors are controlled for, it is clear that students from rural areas tend to do worse than average. Suburban children, meanwhile, are in the middle of the curve, while urban children tend to score higher than average. (It may be that cities attract a more educated workforce and, therefore, parents with smarter children.) On average, girls test higher than boys, and Asians test higher than whites—although blacks, as we have already established, test similarly to whites from comparable backgrounds and in comparable schools.

Knowing what you now know about regression analysis, conventional wisdom, and the art of parenting, consider the following list of sixteen factors. According to the ECLS data, eight of the factors show a strong correlation—positive or negative—with test scores. The other eight don't seem to matter. Feel free to guess which are which. Keep in mind that these results reflect only a child's early test scores, a useful but fairly narrow measurement; poor testing in early childhood isn't necessarily a great harbinger of future earnings, creativity, or happiness.

The child has highly educated parents.
The child's family is intact.
The child's parents have high socioeconomic status.
The child's parents recently moved into a better neighborhood.
The child's mother was thirty or older at the time of her first child's birth.

The child's mother didn't work between birth and kindergarten.
The child had low birthweight.
The child attended Head Start.
The child's parents speak English in the home.
The child's parents regularly take him to museums.
The child is adopted.
The child is regularly spanked.
The child's parents are involved in the PTA.
The child frequently watches television.
The child has many books in his home.
The child's parents read to him nearly every day.

Here now are the eight factors that *are* strongly correlated with test scores:

The child has highly educated parents.
The child's parents have high socioeconomic status.
The child's mother was thirty or older at the time of her first child's birth.
The child had low birthweight.
The child's parents speak English in the home.
The child is adopted.
The child's parents are involved in the PTA.
The child has many books in his home.

And the eight that aren't:

The child's family is intact.
The child's parents recently moved into a better neighborhood.
The child's mother didn't work between birth and kindergarten.

The child attended Head Start.
The child's parents regularly take him to museums.
The child is regularly spanked.
The child frequently watches television.
The child's parents read to him nearly every day.

Now, two by two:

MATTERS: *The child has highly educated parents.*

DOESN'T: *The child's family is intact.*

A child whose parents are highly educated typically does well in school; not much surprise there. A family with a lot of schooling tends to value schooling. Perhaps more important, parents with higher IQs tend to get more education, and IQ is strongly hereditary. But whether a child's family is intact doesn't seem to matter. Just as the earlier-cited studies show that family structure has little impact on a child's personality, it does not seem to affect his academic abilities either, at least in the early years. This is not to say that families ought to go around splitting up willy-nilly. It should, however, offer encouragement to the roughly twenty million American schoolchildren being raised by a single parent.

MATTERS: *The child's parents have high socioeconomic status.*

DOESN'T: *The child's parents recently moved into a better neighborhood.*

A high socioeconomic status is strongly correlated to higher test scores, which seems sensible. Socioeconomic status is a strong indicator of success in general—it suggests a higher IQ and more education—and successful parents are more likely to have successful children. But moving to a better neighborhood doesn't improve a child's chances in school. It may be that moving itself is a disruptive force; more likely, it's because a nicer house doesn't improve math or reading scores any more than nicer sneakers make you jump higher.

MATTERS: *The child's mother was thirty or older at the time of her first child's birth.*

DOESN'T: *The child's mother didn't work between birth and kindergarten.*

A woman who doesn't have her first child until she is at least thirty is likely to see that child do well in school. This mother tends to be a woman who wanted to get some advanced education or develop traction in her career. She is also likely to *want* a child more than a teenage mother wants a child. This doesn't mean that an older first-time mother is necessarily a better mother, but she has put herself—and her children—in a more advantageous position. (It is worth noting that this advantage is nonexistent for a teenage mother who waits until she is thirty to have her *second* child. The ECLS data show that her second child will perform no better than her first.) At the same time, a mother who stays home from work until her child goes to kindergarten does not seem to provide any advantage. Obsessive parents might find this lack of correlation bothersome—what was the point of all those Mommy and Me classes?—but that is what the data tell us.

MATTERS: *The child had low birthweight.*

DOESN'T: *The child attended Head Start.*

A child who had a low birthweight tends to do poorly in school. It may be that being born prematurely is simply hurtful to a child's overall well-being. It may also be that low birthweight is a strong forecaster of poor parenting, since a mother who smokes or drinks or otherwise mistreats her baby in utero isn't likely to turn things around just because the baby is born. A low-birthweight child, in turn, is more likely to be a poor child—and, therefore, more likely to attend Head Start, the federal preschool program. But according to the ECLS data, Head Start does nothing for a child's future test scores. Despite a deep reservoir of appreciation for Head Start (one of this book's authors was a charter student), we must acknowledge that it has repeatedly been proven ineffectual in the long term. Here's a likely reason: instead of spending the day with his own undereducated, overworked mother, the typical Head Start child spends the day with someone else's undereducated, overworked mother. (And a whole roomful of similarly needy children.) As it happens, fewer than 30 percent of Head Start teachers have even a bachelor's degree. And the job pays so poorly—about $21,000 for a Head Start teacher versus $40,000 for the average public-school kindergarten teacher—that it is unlikely to attract better teachers any time soon.

MATTERS: *The child's parents speak English in the home.*

DOESN'T: *The child's parents regularly take him to museums.*

A child with English-speaking parents does better in school than one whose parents don't speak English. Again, not much of a surprise. This correlation is further supported by the performance of Hispanic students in the ECLS study. As a group, Hispanic students test poorly; they are also disproportionately likely to have non-English-speaking parents. (They do, however, tend to catch up with their peers in later grades.) So how about the opposite case: what if a mother and father are not only proficient in English but spend their weekends broadening their child's cultural horizons by taking him to museums? Sorry. Culture cramming may be a foundational belief of obsessive parenting, but the ECLS data show no correlation between museum visits and test scores.

MATTERS: *The child is adopted.*

DOESN'T: *The child is regularly spanked.*

There is a strong correlation—a negative one—between adoption and school test scores. Why? Studies have shown that a child's academic abilities are far more influenced by the IQs of his biological parents than the IQs of his adoptive parents, and mothers who offer up their children for adoption tend to have significantly lower IQs than the people who are doing the adopting. There is another explanation for low-achieving adoptees which, though it may seem distasteful, jibes with the basic economic theory of self-interest: a woman who knows she will offer her baby for adoption may not take the same prenatal care as a woman who is keeping her baby. (Consider—at the risk of furthering the distasteful thinking—how you treat a car you own versus a car you are renting for the weekend.)

But if an adopted child is prone to lower test scores, a spanked child is not. This may seem surprising—not because spanking itself is necessarily detrimental but because, conventionally xpeaking, spanking is considered an unenlightened practice. We might therefore assume that parents who spank are unenlightened in other ways. Perhaps that isn't the case at all. Or perhaps there is a different spanking story to be told. Remember, the ECLS survey included direct interviews with the children's parents. So a parent would have to sit knee to knee with a government researcher and admit to spanking his child. This would suggest that a parent who does so is either unenlightened or—more interestingly—congenitally honest. It may be that honesty is more important to good parenting than spanking is to bad parenting.

MATTERS: *The child's parents are involved in the PTA.*

DOESN'T: *The child frequently watches television.*

A child whose parents are involved in the PTA tends to do well in school—which probably indicates that parents with a strong relationship to education get involved in the PTA, not that their PTA involvement somehow makes their children smarter. The ECLS data show no correlation, meanwhile, between a child's test scores and the amount of television he watches. Despite the conventional wisdom, watching television apparently does not turn a child's brain to mush. (In Finland, whose education system has been ranked the world's best, most children do not begin school until age seven but have often learned to read on their own by watching American television with Finnish subtitles.) Nor, however, does using a computer at home turn a child into Einstein: the ECLS data show no correlation between computer use and school test scores.

Now for the final pair of factors:

MATTERS: *The child has many books in his home.*

DOESN'T: *The child's parents read to him nearly every day.*

As noted earlier, a child with many books in his home has indeed been found to do well on school tests. But regularly reading to a child *doesn't* affect early childhood test scores.

This would seem to present a riddle. It bounces us back to our original question: just how much, and in what ways, do parents really matter?

Let's start with the positive correlation: books in the home equal higher test scores. Most people would look at this correlation and infer an obvious cause-and-effect relationship. To wit: a little boy named Isaiah has a lot of books at home; Isaiah does beautifully on his reading test at school; this must be because his mother or father regularly reads to him. But Isaiah's friend Emily, who also has a lot of books in her home, practically never touches them. She would rather dress up her Bratz or watch cartoons. And Emily tests just as well as Isaiah. Meanwhile, Isaiah and Emily's friend Ricky doesn't have *any* books at home. But Ricky goes to the library every day with his mother. And yet he does *worse* on his school tests than either Emily or Isaiah.

What are we to make of this? If reading books doesn't have an impact on early childhood test scores, could it be that the books' mere physical presence in the house makes the children smarter? Do books perform some kind of magical osmosis on a child's brain? If so, one might be tempted to simply deliver a truckload of books to every home that contains a preschooler.

That, in fact, is what the governor of Illinois tried to do. In early 2004, Governor Rod Blagojevich announced a plan to mail one book a month to every child in Illinois from the time they were born until they entered kindergarten. The plan would cost $26 million a year. But, Blagojevich argued, this was a vital intervention in a state where 40 percent of third graders read below their grade level. "When you own [books] and they're yours," he said, "and they just come as part of your life, all of that will contribute to a sense . . . that books should be part of your life."

So all children born in Illinois would end up with a sixty-volume library by the time they entered school. Does this mean they would all perform better on their reading tests?

Probably not. (Although we may never know for sure: in the end, the Illinois legislature rejected the book plan.) After all, the ECLS data don't say that books in the house *cause* high test scores; it says only that the two are correlated.

How should this correlation be interpreted? Here's a likely theory: most parents who buy a lot of children's books tend to be smart and well educated to begin with. (And they pass on their smarts and work ethic to their kids.) Or perhaps they care a great deal about education, and about their children in general. (Which means they create an environment that encourages and rewards learning.) Such parents may believe—as fervently as the governor of Illinois believed—that every children's book is a talisman that leads to unfettered intelligence. But they are probably wrong. A book is in fact less a cause of intelligence than an *indicator*.

So what does all this have to say about the importance of parents in general? Consider again the eight ECLS factors that are correlated with school test scores:

The child has highly educated parents.
The child's parents have high socioeconomic status.
The child's mother was thirty or older at the time of her first child's birth.
The child had low birthweight.
The child's parents speak English in the home.
The child is adopted.
The child's parents are involved in the PTA.
The child has many books in his home.

And the eight factors that are not:

The child's family is intact.
The child's parents recently moved into a better neighborhood.
The child's mother didn't work between birth and kindergarten.
The child attended Head Start.
The child's parents regularly take him to museums.
The child is regularly spanked.
The child frequently watches television.
The child's parents read to him nearly every day.

To overgeneralize a bit, the first list describes things that parents *are;* the second list describes things that parents *do.* Parents who are well educated, successful, and healthy tend to have children who test well in school; but it doesn't seem to much matter whether a child is trotted off to museums or spanked or sent to Head Start or frequently read to or plopped in front of the television.

For parents—and parenting experts—who are obsessed with

child-rearing technique, this may be sobering news. The reality is that technique looks to be highly overrated.

But this is not to say that parents don't matter. Plainly they matter a great deal. Here is the conundrum: by the time most people pick up a parenting book, it is far too late. Most of the things that matter were decided long ago—who you are, whom you married, what kind of life you lead. If you are smart, hardworking, well educated, well paid, and married to someone equally fortunate, then your children are more likely to succeed. (Nor does it hurt, in all likelihood, to be honest, thoughtful, loving, and curious about the world.) But it isn't so much a matter of what you *do* as a parent; it's who you are. In this regard, an overbearing parent is a lot like a political candidate who believes that money wins elections—whereas in truth, all the money in the world can't get a candidate elected if the voters don't like him to start with.

In a paper titled "The Nature and Nurture of Economic Outcomes," the economist Bruce Sacerdote addressed the nature-nurture debate by taking a long-term quantitative look at the effects of parenting. He used three adoption studies, two American and one British, each of them containing in-depth data about the adopted children, their adoptive parents, and their biological parents. Sacerdote found that parents who adopt children are typically smarter, better educated, and more highly paid than the baby's biological parents. But the adoptive parents' advantages had little bearing on the child's school performance. As also seen in the ECLS data, adopted children test relatively poorly in school; any influence the adoptive parents might exert is seemingly outweighed by the force of genetics. But, Sacerdote found, the parents were not powerless forever. By the time the adopted children became adults, they had veered sharply from the destiny that IQ alone might have predicted. Compared to similar children who were *not* put up for adoption, the adoptees were far more likely to attend college, to have a well-paid job, and to wait until they were out of their teens before getting married. It was the influence of the adoptive parents, Sacerdote concluded, that made the difference.

Chapter 6

**PERFECT PARENTING, PART II;
OR: WOULD A ROSHANDA BY ANY
OTHER NAME SMELL AS SWEET?**

Obsessive or not, any parent *wants* to believe that she is making a big difference in the kind of person her child turns out to be. Otherwise, why bother?

The belief in parental power is manifest in the first official act a parent commits: giving the baby a name. As any modern parent knows, the baby-naming industry is booming, as evidenced by a proliferation of books, websites, and baby-name consultants. Many parents seem to believe that a child cannot prosper unless it is hitched to the right name; names are seen to carry great aesthetic or even predictive powers.

This might explain why, in 1958, a New York City man named Robert Lane decided to call his baby son Winner. The Lanes, who lived in a housing project in Harlem, already had several children, each with a fairly typical name. But this boy—well, Robert Lane apparently had a special feeling about this one. Winner Lane: how could he fail with a name like that?

Three years later, the Lanes had another baby boy, their seventh and last child. For reasons that no one can quite pin down today, Robert decided to name this boy Loser. It doesn't appear that Robert was unhappy about the new baby; he just seemed to get a kick out of the name's bookend effect. First a Winner, now a Loser. But if Winner Lane could hardly be expected to fail, could Loser Lane possibly succeed?

Loser Lane did in fact succeed. He went to prep school on a scholarship, graduated from Lafayette College in Pennsylvania, and joined the New York Police Department (this was his mother's longtime wish), where he made detective and, eventually, sergeant. Although he never hid his name, many people were uncomfortable using it. "So I have a bunch of names," he says today, "from Jimmy to James to whatever they want to call you. Timmy. But they rarely call you Loser." Once in a while, he said, "they throw a French twist on it: 'Losier.' " To his police colleagues, he is known as Lou.

And what of his brother with the can't-miss name? The most noteworthy achievement of Winner Lane, now in his midforties, is the sheer length of his criminal record: nearly three dozen arrests for burglary, domestic violence, trespassing, resisting arrest, and other mayhem.

These days, Loser and Winner barely speak. The father who named them is no longer alive. Clearly he had the right idea—that naming is destiny—but he must have gotten the boys mixed up.

Then there is the recent case of Temptress, a fifteen-year-old girl whose misdeeds landed her in Albany County Family Court in New York. The judge, W. Dennis Duggan, had long taken note of the strange names borne by some offenders. One teenage boy, Amcher, had been named for the first thing his parents saw upon reaching the hospital: the sign for Albany Medical Center Hospital Emergency Room. But Duggan considered Temptress the most outrageous name he had come across.

"I sent her out of the courtroom so I could talk to her mother about why she named her daughter Temptress," the judge later recalled. "She said she was watching *The Cosby Show* and liked the young actress. I told her the actress's name was actually *Tempestt* Bledsoe. She said she found that out later, that they had misspelled the name. I asked her if she knew what 'temptress' meant, and she said she also found that out at some later point. Her daughter was charged with ungovernable behavior, which included bringing men into the home while the mother was at work. I asked the mother if she had ever thought the daughter was living out her name. Most all of this went completely over her head."

Was Temptress actually "living out her name," as Judge Duggan saw it? Or would she have wound up in trouble even if her mother had called her Chastity? *

It isn't much of a stretch to assume that Temptress didn't have ideal parents. Not only was her mother willing to name her Temptress in the first place, but she wasn't smart enough to know what that word even meant. Nor is it so surprising, on some level, that a boy named Amcher would end up in family court. People who can't be bothered to come up with a name for their child aren't likely to be the best parents either.

So does the name you give your child affect his life? Or is it *your* life reflected in his name? In either case, what kind of signal does a child's name send to the world—and most important, does it really matter?

* See footnote, p. 290.

• • •

As it happens, Loser and Winner, Temptress and Amcher were all black. Is this fact merely a curiosity or does it have something larger to say about names and culture?

Every generation seems to produce a few marquee academics who advance the thinking on black culture. Roland G. Fryer Jr., the young black economist who analyzed the "acting white" phenomenon and the black-white test score gap, may be among the next. His ascension has been unlikely. An indifferent high-school student from an unstable family, he went to the University of Texas at Arlington on an athletic scholarship. Two things happened to him during college: he quickly realized he would never make the NFL or the NBA; and, taking his studies seriously for the first time in his life, he found he liked them. After graduate work at Penn State and the University of Chicago, he was hired as a Harvard professor at age twenty-five. His reputation for candid thinking on race was already well established.

Fryer's mission is the study of black underachievement. "One could rattle off all the statistics about blacks not doing so well," he says. "You can look at the black-white differential in out-of-wedlock births or infant mortality or life expectancy. Blacks are the worst-performing ethnic group on SATs. Blacks earn less than whites. They are still just not doing well, period. I basically want to figure out where blacks went wrong, and I want to devote my life to this."

In addition to economic and social disparity between blacks and whites, Fryer had become intrigued by the virtual segregation of culture. Blacks and whites watch different television shows. (*Monday Night Football* is the only show that typically appears on each group's top ten list; *Seinfeld*, one of the most popular sitcoms in history, never ranked in the top fifty among blacks.) They smoke different cigarettes. (Newports enjoy a 75 percent market share among black teenagers versus 12 percent among whites; the white teenagers are mainly smoking Marlboros.) And black parents give their children names that are starkly different from white children's.

Fryer came to wonder: is distinctive black culture a *cause* of the economic disparity between blacks and whites or merely a reflection of it?

As with the ECLS study, Fryer went looking for the answer in a mountain of data: birth-certificate information for every child born in California since 1961. The data, covering more than sixteen million births, included standard items such as name, gender, race, birthweight, and the parents' marital status, as well as more telling factors about the parents: their zip code (which indicates socioeconomic status and a neighborhood's racial composition), their means of paying the hospital bill (again, an economic indicator), and their level of education.

The California data prove just how dissimilarly black and white parents name their children. White and Asian-American parents, meanwhile, give their children remarkably similar names; there is some disparity between white and Hispanic-American parents, but it is slim compared to the black-white naming gap.

The data also show the black-white gap to be a recent phenomenon. Until the early 1970s, there was a great overlap between black and white names. The typical baby girl born in a black neighborhood in 1970 was given a name that was twice as common among blacks as whites. By 1980 she received a name that was *twenty* times more common among blacks. (Boys' names moved in the same direction but less aggressively—probably because parents of all races are less adventurous with boys' names than with girls'.) Given the location and timing of this change—dense urban areas where Afro-American activism was gathering strength—the most likely cause of the explosion in distinctively black names was the Black Power movement, which sought to accentuate African culture and fight claims of black inferiority. If this naming revolution was indeed inspired by Black Power, it would be one of the movement's most enduring remnants. Afros today are rare, dashikis even rarer; Black Panther founder Bobby Seale is best known today for peddling a line of barbecue products.

A great many black names today are unique to blacks. More than 40 percent of the black girls born in California in a given year receive a name that not *one* of the roughly 100,000 baby white girls received that year. Even more remarkably, nearly 30 percent of the black girls are given a name that is unique among the names of every baby, white and black, born that year in California. (There were also 228 babies named Unique during the 1990s alone, and 1 each of Uneek, Uneque, and Uneqqee.) Even among very popular black names, there is little overlap with whites. Of the 626 baby girls named Deja in the 1990s, 591 were black. Of the 454 girls named Precious, 431 were black. Of the 318 Shanices, 310 were black.

What kind of parent is most likely to give a child such a distinctively black name? The data offer a clear answer: an unmarried, low-income, undereducated teenage mother from a black neighborhood who has a distinctively black name herself. In

Fryer's view, giving a child a superblack name is a black parent's signal of solidarity with the community. "If I start naming my kid Madison," he says, "you might think, 'Oh, you want to go live across the railroad tracks, don't you?' " If black kids who study calculus and ballet are thought to be "acting white," Fryer says, then mothers who call their babies Shanice are simply "acting black."

The California study shows that many white parents send as strong a signal in the opposite direction. More than 40 percent of the white babies are given names that are at least four times more common among whites. Consider Connor and Cody, Emily and Abigail. In one recent ten-year stretch, each of these names was given to at least two thousand babies in California—fewer than 2 percent of them black.

So what are the "whitest" names and the "blackest" names?

THE TWENTY "WHITEST" GIRL NAMES			
1. Molly	6. Madeline	11. Jenna	16. Holly
2. Amy	7. Katelyn	12. Heather	17. Allison
3. Claire	8. Emma	13. Katherine	18. Kaitlyn
4. Emily	9. Abigail	14. Caitlin	19. Hannah
5. Katie	10. Carly	15. Kaitlin	20. Kathryn

THE TWENTY "BLACKEST" GIRL NAMES

1. Imani	6. Nia	11. Jada	16. Jasmin
2. Ebony	7. Deja	12. Tierra	17. Jazmin
3. Shanice	8. Diamond	13. Tiara	18. Jasmine
4. Aaliyah	9. Asia	14. Kiara	19. Alexus
5. Precious	10. Aliyah	15. Jazmine	20. Raven

THE TWENTY "WHITEST" BOY NAMES

1. Jake	6. Dustin	11. Cole	16. Dylan
2. Connor	7. Luke	12. Lucas	17. Maxwell
3. Tanner	8. Jack	13. Bradley	18. Hunter
4. Wyatt	9. Scott	14. Jacob	19. Brett
5. Cody	10. Logan	15. Garrett	20. Colin

THE TWENTY "BLACKEST" BOY NAMES

1. DeShawn	6. Malik	11. Demetrius	16. Darius
2. DeAndre	7. Trevon	12. Reginald	17. Xavier
3. Marquis	8. Tyrone	13. Jamal	18. Terrance
4. Darnell	9. Willie	14. Maurice	19. Andre
5. Terrell	10. Dominique	15. Jalen	20. Darryl

So how does it matter if you have a very white name or a very black name? Over the years, a series of "audit studies" have tried to measure how people perceive different names. In a typical audit study, a researcher would send two identical (and fake) résumés, one with a traditionally white name and the other with an immigrant or minority-sounding name, to potential employers. The "white" résumés have always gleaned more job interviews.

According to such a study, if DeShawn Williams and Jake Williams sent identical résumés to the same employer, Jake Williams would be more likely to get a callback. The implication is that black-sounding names carry an economic penalty. Such studies are tantalizing but severely limited, for they can't explain *why* DeShawn didn't get the call. Was he rejected because the employer is a racist and is convinced that DeShawn Williams is black? Or did he reject him because "DeShawn" sounds like someone from a low-income, low-education family? A résumé is a fairly undependable set of clues—a recent study showed that more than 50 percent of them contain lies—so "DeShawn" may simply signal a disadvantaged background to an employer who believes that workers from such backgrounds are undependable.

Nor do the black-white audit studies predict what might have happened in a job interview. What if the employer *is* racist, and if he unwittingly agreed to interview a black person who happened to have a white-sounding name—would he be any more likely to hire the black applicant after meeting face-to-face? Or is the interview a painful and discouraging waste of time for the black applicant—that is, an economic penalty for having a *white*-sounding name? Along those same lines, perhaps a black person with a white name pays an economic penalty in the *black* community; and what of the potential *advantage* to be gained in the black community by having a distinctively black name? But because the audit studies can't measure the actual life outcomes of the fictitious DeShawn Williams versus Jake Williams, they can't assess the broader impact of a distinctively black name.

Maybe DeShawn should just change his name.

People do this all the time, of course. The clerks in New York City's civil court recently reported that name changes are at an all-time high. Some of the changes are purely, if bizarrely, aesthetic. A young couple named Natalie Jeremijenko and Dalton Conley recently renamed their four-year-old son Yo Xing Heyno Augustus Eisner Alexander Weiser Knuckles Jeremijenko-Conley. Some people change names for economic purposes: after a New York livery-cab driver named Michael Goldberg was shot in early 2004, it was reported that Mr. Goldberg was in fact an Indian-born Sikh who thought it advantageous to take a Jewish name upon immigrating to New York. Goldberg's decision might have puzzled some people in show business circles, where it is a time-honored tradition to change Jewish names. Thus did Issur Danielovitch become Kirk Douglas; thus did the William Morris Agency rise to prominence under its namesake, the former Zelman Moses.

The question is, would Zelman Moses have done as well had he not become William Morris? And would DeShawn Williams do any better if he called himself Jake Williams or Connor Williams? It is tempting to think so—just as it is tempting to think that a truckload of children's books will make a child smarter.

Though the audit studies can't be used to truly measure how much a name matters, the California names data can.

How? The California data included not only each baby's vital statistics but information about the mother's level of education, income, and, most significantly, her own date of birth. This last fact made it possible to identify the hundreds of thousands of California mothers who had themselves been born in California and then to link them to their *own* birth records. Now a new and extremely potent story emerged from the data: it was possible to track the life outcome of any individual woman. This is the sort of data chain that researchers dream about, making it possible to identify a set of children who were born under similar circumstances, then locate them again twenty or thirty years later to see how they turned out. Among the hundreds of thousands of such women in the California data, many bore distinctively black names and many others did not. Using regression analysis to control for other factors that might influence life trajectories, it was then possible to measure the impact of a single factor—in this case, a woman's first name—on her educational, income, and health outcomes.

So does a name matter?

The data show that, on average, a person with a distinctively black name—whether it is a woman named Imani or a man named DeShawn—*does* have a worse life outcome than a woman named Molly or a man named Jake. But it isn't the fault of their names. If two black boys, Jake Williams and DeShawn Williams, are born in the same neighborhood and into the same familial and economic circumstances, they would likely have similar life outcomes. But the kind of parents who name their son Jake *don't* tend to live in the same neighborhoods or share economic circumstances with the kind of parents who name their son DeShawn. And that's why, on average, a boy named Jake will tend to earn more money and get more education than a boy named DeShawn. A DeShawn is more likely to have been handicapped by a low-income, low-education, single-parent background. His name is an indicator—not a cause—of his outcome. Just as a child with no books in his home isn't likely to test well in school, a boy named DeShawn isn't likely to do as well in life.

And what if DeShawn *had* changed his name to Jake or Connor: would his situation improve? Here's a guess: anybody who bothers to change his name in the name of economic success is—like the high-school freshmen in Chicago who entered the school-choice lottery—at least highly motivated, and motivation is probably a stronger indicator of success than, well, a name.

Just as the ECLS data answered questions about parenting that went well beyond the black-white test gap, the California names data tell a lot of stories in addition to the one about distinctively black names. Broadly speaking, the data tell us how parents see themselves—and, more significantly, what kind of expectations they have for their children.

Here's a question to begin with: where does a name come from, anyway? Not, that is, the actual source of the name—that much is usually obvious: there's the Bible, there's the huge cluster of traditional English and Germanic and Italian and French names, there are princess names and hippie names, nostalgic names and place names. Increasingly, there are brand names (Lexus, Armani, Bacardi, Timberland) and what might be called aspirational names. The California data show eight Harvards born during the 1990s (all of them black), fifteen Yales (all white), and eighteen Princetons (all black). There were no Doctors but three Lawyers (all black), nine Judges (eight of them white), three Senators (all white), and two Presidents (both black). Then there are the in-vented names. Roland G. Fryer Jr., while discussing his names research on a radio show, took a call from a black woman who was upset with the name just given to her baby niece. It was pronounced *shuh-TEED* but was in fact spelled "Shithead." *

Shithead has yet to catch on among the masses, but other names do. How does a name migrate through the population, and why? Is it purely a matter of zeitgeist, or is there some sensible explanation? We all know that names rise and fall and rise—witness the return of Sophie and Max from near extinction—but is there a discernible pattern to these movements?

The answer lies in the California data, and the answer is yes.

Among the most interesting revelations in the data is the correlation between a baby's name and the parents' socioeconomic status. Consider the most common female names found in middle-income white households versus low-income white households. (These and other lists to follow include data from the 1990s alone, to ensure a large sample that is also current.)

MOST COMMON MIDDLE-INCOME WHITE GIRL NAMES

1. Sarah	6. Amanda	11. Nicole	16. Jennifer
2. Emily	7. Megan	12. Taylor	17. Alexandra
3. Jessica	8. Samantha	13. Elizabeth	18. Brittany
4. Lauren	9. Hannah	14. Katherine	19. Danielle
5. Ashley	10. Rachel	15. Madison	20. Rebecca

* See note, p. 289.

MOST COMMON LOW-INCOME WHITE GIRL NAMES

1. Ashley	6. Sarah	11. Emily	16. Stephanie
2. Jessica	7. Kayla	12. Nicole	17. Jennifer
3. Amanda	8. Amber	13. Elizabeth	18. Hannah
4. Samantha	9. Megan	14. Heather	19. Courtney
5. Brittany	10. Taylor	15. Alyssa	20. Rebecca

There is considerable overlap, to be sure. But keep in mind that these are the most common names of all, and consider the size of the data set. The difference between consecutive positions on these lists may represent several hundred or even several thousand children. So if Brittany is number five on the low-income list and number eighteen on the middle-income list, you can be assured that Brittany is a decidedly low-end name. Other examples are even more pronounced. Five names in each category don't appear at all in the other category's top twenty. Here are the top five names among high-end and low-end families, in order of their relative disparity with the other category:

MOST COMMON HIGH-END WHITE GIRL NAMES

1. Alexandra	4. Madison
2. Lauren	5. Rachel
3. Katherine	

MOST COMMON LOW-END WHITE GIRL NAMES

1. Amber
2. Heather
3. Kayla
4. Stephanie
5. Alyssa

And for the boys:

MOST COMMON HIGH-END WHITE BOY NAMES

1. Benjamin
2. Samuel
3. Jonathan
4. Alexander
5. Andrew

MOST COMMON LOW-END WHITE BOY NAMES

1. Cody
2. Brandon
3. Anthony
4. Justin
5. Robert

Considering the relationship between income and names, and given the fact that income and *education* are strongly correlated, it is not surprising to find a similarly strong link between the parents' level of education and the name they give their baby. Once again drawing from the pool of most common names among white children, here are the top picks of highly educated parents versus those with the least education:

MOST COMMON WHITE GIRL NAMES AMONG HIGH-EDUCATION PARENTS

1. Katherine
2. Emma
3. Alexandra
4. Julia
5. Rachel

MOST COMMON WHITE GIRL NAMES AMONG LOW-EDUCATION PARENTS

1. Kayla
2. Amber
3. Heather
4. Brittany
5. Brianna

MOST COMMON WHITE BOY NAMES AMONG HIGH-EDUCATION PARENTS

1. Benjamin
2. Samuel
3. Alexander
4. John
5. William

MOST COMMON WHITE BOY NAMES AMONG LOW-EDUCATION PARENTS

1. Cody
2. Travis
3. Brandon
4. Justin
5. Tyler

The effect is even more pronounced when the sample is widened beyond the most common names. Drawing from the entire California database, here are the names that signify the most poorly educated white parents.

**THE TWENTY WHITE GIRL NAMES
THAT BEST SIGNIFY LOW-EDUCATION PARENTS***

(AVERAGE NUMBER OF YEARS OF MOTHER'S EDUCATION IN PARENTHESES)

1.	Angel	(11.38)	11.	Jazmine	(11.94)
2.	Heaven	(11.46)	12.	Shyanne	(11.96)
3.	Misty	(11.61)	13.	Britany	(12.05)
4.	Destiny	(11.66)	14.	Mercedes	(12.06)
5.	Brenda	(11.71)	15.	Tiffanie	(12.08)
6.	Tabatha	(11.81)	16.	Ashly	(12.11)
7.	Bobbie	(11.87)	17.	Tonya	(12.13)
8.	Brandy	(11.89)	18.	Crystal	(12.15)
9.	Destinee	(11.91)	19.	Brandie	(12.16)
10.	Cindy	(11.92)	20.	Brandi	(12.17)

* WITH A MINIMUM OF 100 OCCURRENCES.

If you or someone you love is named Cindy or Brenda and is over, say, forty, and feels that those names did not formerly connote a low-education family, you are right. These names, like many others, have shifted hard and fast of late. Some of the other low-education names are obviously misspellings, whether intentional or not, of more standard names. In most cases the standard spellings of the names—Tabitha, Cheyenne, Tiffany, Brittany, and Jasmine—also signify low education. But the various spellings of even one name can reveal a strong disparity:

TEN "JASMINES" IN ASCENDING ORDER
OF MATERNAL EDUCATION

(YEARS OF MOTHER'S EDUCATION IN PARENTHESES)

1.	Jazmine (11.94)	6.	Jasmina	(12.50)
2.	Jazmyne (12.08)	7.	Jazmyn	(12.77)
3.	Jazzmin (12.14)	8.	Jasmine	(12.88)
4.	Jazzmine (12.16)	9.	Jasmin	(13.12)
5.	Jasmyne (12.18)	10.	Jasmyn	(13.23)

Here is the list of low-education white boy names. It includes the occasional misspelling (Micheal and Tylor), but more common is the nickname-as-proper-name trend.

THE TWENTY WHITE BOY NAMES
THAT BEST SIGNIFY LOW–EDUCATION PARENTS *

(YEARS OF MOTHER'S EDUCATION IN PARENTHESES)

1.	Ricky (11.55)	11.	Tommy	(11.89)
2.	Joey (11.65)	12.	Tony	(11.96)
3.	Jessie (11.66)	13.	Micheal	(11.98)
4.	Jimmy (11.66)	14.	Ronnie	(12.03)
5.	Billy (11.69)	15.	Randy	(12.07)
6.	Bobby (11.74)	16.	Jerry	(12.08)
7.	Johnny (11.75)	17.	Tylor	(12.14)
8.	Larry (11.80)	18.	Terry	(12.15)
9.	Edgar (11.81)	19.	Danny	(12.17)
10.	Steve (11.84)	20.	Harley	(12.22)

* WITH A MINIMUM OF 100 OCCURRENCES

Now for the names that signify the *highest* level of parental education. These names don't have much in common, phonetically or aesthetically, with the low-education names. The girls' names are in most regards diverse, though with a fair share of literary and otherwise artful touches. A caution to prospective parents who are shopping for a "smart" name: remember that such a name won't *make* your child smart; it will, however, give her the same name as other smart kids—at least for a while. (For a much longer and more varied list of girls' and boys' names, see pp. 290–293.)

THE TWENTY WHITE GIRL NAMES
THAT BEST SIGNIFY HIGH-EDUCATION PARENTS*

(YEARS OF MOTHER'S EDUCATION IN PARENTHESES)

1.	Lucienne	(16.60)	11.	Rotem	(16.08)
2.	Marie-Claire	(16.50)	12.	Oona	(16.00)
3.	Glynnis	(16.40)	13.	Atara	(16.00)
4.	Adair	(16.36)	14.	Linden	(15.94)
5.	Meira	(16.27)	15.	Waverly	(15.93)
6.	Beatrix	(16.26)	16.	Zofia	(15.88)
7.	Clementine	(16.23)	17.	Pascale	(15.82)
8.	Philippa	(16.21)	18.	Eleanora	(15.80)
9.	Aviva	(16.18)	19.	Elika	(15.80)
10.	Flannery	(16.10)	20.	Neeka	(15.77)

* WITH A MINIMUM OF 10 OCCURRENCES

Now for the boys' names that are turning up these days in high-education households. This list is particularly heavy on the Hebrew, with a noticeable trend toward Irish traditionalism.

THE TWENTY WHITE BOY NAMES THAT BEST SIGNIFY HIGH-EDUCATION PARENTS*

(YEARS OF MOTHER'S EDUCATION IN PARENTHESES)

1.	Dov	(16.50)	11. Finnegan	(16.13)
2.	Akiva	(16.42)	12. MacGregor	(16.10)
3.	Sander	(16.29)	13. Florian	(15.94)
4.	Yannick	(16.20)	14. Zev	(15.92)
5.	Sacha	(16.18)	15. Beckett	(15.91)
6.	Guillaume	(16.17)	16. Kia	(15.90)
7.	Elon	(16.16)	17. Ashkon	(15.84)
8.	Ansel	(16.14)	18. Harper	(15.83)
9.	Yonah	(16.14)	19. Sumner	(15.77)
10.	Tor	(16.13)	20. Calder	(15.75)

* WITH A MINIMUM OF 10 OCCURRENCES

If many names on the above lists were unfamiliar to you, don't feel bad. Even boys' names—which have always been scarcer than girls'—have been proliferating wildly. This means that even the most popular names today are less popular than they used to be. Consider the ten most popular names given to black baby boys in California in 1990 and then in 2000. The top ten in 1990 includes 3,375 babies (18.7 percent of those born that year), while the top ten in 2000 includes only 2,115 (14.6 percent of those born that year).

MOST POPULAR BLACK BOY NAMES

(NUMBER OF OCCURRENCES IN PARENTHESES)

	1990			2000	
1.	Michael	(532)	1.	Isaiah	(308)
2.	Christopher	(531)	2.	Jordan	(267)
3.	Anthony	(395)	3.	Elijah	(262)
4.	Brandon	(323)	4.	Michael	(235)
5.	James	(303)	5.	Joshua	(218)
6.	Joshua	(301)	6.	Anthony	(208)
7.	Robert	(276)	7.	Christopher	(169)
8.	David	(243)	8.	Jalen	(159)
9.	Kevin	(240)	9.	Brandon	(148)
10.	Justin	(231)	10.	Justin	(141)

In the space of ten years, even the most popular name among black baby boys (532 occurrences for Michael) became far less popular (308 occurrences for Isaiah). So parents are plainly getting more diverse with names. But there's another noteworthy shift in these lists: a very quick rate of turnover. Note that four of the 1990 names (James, Robert, David, and Kevin) fell out of the top ten by 2000. Granted, they made up the bottom half of the 1990 list. But the names that replaced them in 2000 *weren't* bottom dwellers. Three of the new names—Isaiah, Jordan, and Elijah—were in fact numbers one, two, and three in 2000. For an even more drastic example of how quickly and thoroughly a name can cycle in and out of use, consider the ten most popular names given to white girls in California in 1960 and then in 2000.

MOST POPULAR WHITE GIRL NAMES

1960		2000	
1.	Susan	1.	Emily
2.	Lisa	2.	Hannah
3.	Karen	3.	Madison
4.	Mary	4.	Sarah
5.	Cynthia	5.	Samantha
6.	Deborah	6.	Lauren
7.	Linda	7.	Ashley
8.	Patricia	8.	Emma
9.	Debra	9.	Taylor
10.	Sandra	10.	Megan

Not a single name from 1960 remains in the top ten. But, you say, it's hard to stay popular for forty years. So how about comparing today's most popular names with the top ten from only twenty years earlier?

MOST POPULAR WHITE GIRL NAMES

1980		2000	
1.	Jennifer	1.	Emily
2.	Sarah	2.	Hannah
3.	Melissa	3.	Madison
4.	Jessica	4.	Sarah
5.	Christina	5.	Samantha
6.	Amanda	6.	Lauren

7. **Nicole**	7. **Ashley**
8. **Michelle**	8. **Emma**
9. **Heather**	9. **Taylor**
10. **Amber**	10. **Megan**

A single holdover: Sarah. So where do these Emilys and Emmas and Laurens all come from? Where on earth did *Madison* come from?* It's easy enough to see that new names become very popular very fast—but why?

Let's take another look at a pair of earlier lists. Here are the most popular names given to baby girls in the 1990s among low-income families and among families of middle income or higher.

**MOST COMMON "HIGH-END"
WHITE GIRL NAMES IN THE 1990S**

1. **Alexandra**	4. **Madison**
2. **Lauren**	5. **Rachel**
3. **Katherine**	

**MOST COMMON "LOW-END"
WHITE GIRL NAMES IN THE 1990S**

1. **Amber**	4. **Stephanie**
2. **Heather**	5. **Alyssa**
3. **Kayla**	

---

* Madison almost certainly came from the 1984 movie *Splash*, starring Darryl Hannah as a mermaid who comes ashore in New York City and takes her name from the street sign for Madison Avenue. For humans, the name soon progressed from exceedingly rare to a perennial top five choice.

Notice anything? You might want to compare these names with the "Most Popular White Girl Names" list on page 202 that includes the top ten overall names from 1980 and 2000. Lauren and Madison, two of the most popular "high-end" names from the 1990s, made the 2000 top ten list. Amber and Heather, meanwhile, two of the overall most popular names from 1980, are now among the "low-end" names.

There is a clear pattern at play: once a name catches on among high-income, highly educated parents, it starts working its way down the socioeconomic ladder. Amber and Heather started out as high-end names, as did Stephanie and Brittany. For every high-end baby named Stephanie or Brittany, another five lower-income girls received those names within ten years.

So where do lower-end families go name-shopping? Many people assume that naming trends are driven by celebrities. But celebrities actually have a weak effect on baby names. As of 2000, the pop star Madonna had sold 130 million records worldwide but hadn't generated even the ten copycat namings—in California, no less—required to make the master index of four thousand names from which the sprawling list of girls' names on page 290 was drawn. Or considering all the Brittanys, Britneys, Brittanis, Brittanies, Brittneys, and Brittnis you encounter these days, you might think of Britney Spears. But she is in fact a symptom, not a cause, of the Brittany/Britney/Brittani/Brittanie/Brittney/Brittni explosion. With the most common spelling of the name, Brittany, at number eighteen among high-end families and number five among low-end families, it is surely approaching its pull date. Decades earlier, Shirley Temple was similarly a symptom of the Shirley boom, though she is often now remembered as its cause. (It should also be noted that many girls' names, including Shirley,

Carol, Leslie, Hilary, Renee, Stacy, and Tracy began life as boys' names, but girls' names almost never cross over to boys.)

So it isn't famous people who drive the name game. It is the family just a few blocks over, the one with the bigger house and newer car. The kind of families that were the first to call their daughters Amber or Heather and are now calling them Lauren or Madison. The kind of families that used to name their sons Justin or Brandon and are now calling them Alexander or Benjamin. Parents are reluctant to poach a name from someone *too* near—family members or close friends—but many parents, whether they realize it or not, like the sound of names that sound "successful."

But as a high-end name is adopted en masse, high-end parents begin to abandon it. Eventually, it is considered so common that even lower-end parents may not want it, whereby it falls out of the rotation entirely. The lower-end parents, meanwhile, go looking for the next name that the upper-end parents have broken in.

So the implication is clear: the parents of all those Alexandras, Laurens, Katherines, Madisons, and Rachels should not expect the cachet to last much longer. Those names are already on their way to overexposure. Where, then, will the new high-end names come from?

It wouldn't be surprising to find them among the "smartest" girls' and boys' names in California, listed on pages 199–200, that are still fairly obscure. Granted, some of them—Oona and Glynnis, Florian and Kia—are bound to remain obscure. The same could be surmised of most of the Hebrew names (Rotem and Zofia, Akiva and Zev), even though many of today's most mainstream names (David, Jonathan, Samuel, Benjamin, Rachel, Hannah, Sarah, Rebecca) are of course Hebrew biblical names.

Aviva may be the one modern Hebrew name that is ready to break out: it's easy to pronounce, pretty, peppy, and suitably flexible.

Drawn from a pair of "smart" databases, here is a sampling of today's high-end names. Some of them, as unlikely as it seems, are bound to become tomorrow's mainstream names. Before you scoff, ask yourself this: do any of them seem more ridiculous than "Madison" might have seemed ten years ago?

MOST POPULAR GIRLS' NAMES OF 2015?

Annika	Eleanora	Isabel	Maya
Ansley	Ella	Kate	Philippa
Ava	Emma	Lara	Phoebe
Avery	Fiona	Linden	Quinn
Aviva	Flannery	Maeve	Sophie
Clementine	Grace	Marie-Claire	Waverly

MOST POPULAR BOYS' NAMES OF 2015?

Aidan	Bennett	Johan	Reagan
Aldo	Carter	Keyon	Sander
Anderson	Cooper	Liam	Sumner
Ansel	Finnegan	Maximilian	Will
Asher	Harper	McGregor	
Beckett	Jackson	Oliver	

Obviously, a variety of motives are at work when parents consider a name for their child. They may want something traditional or something bohemian, something unique or something perfectly trendy. It would be an overstatement to suggest that all parents are looking—whether consciously or not—for a "smart" name or a "high-end" name. But they are all trying to signal *something* with a name, whether the name is Winner or Loser, Madison or Amber, Shithead or Sander, DeShawn or Jake. What the California names data suggest is that an overwhelming number of parents use a name to signal *their own expectations* of how successful their children will be. The name isn't likely to make a shard of difference. But the parents can at least feel better knowing that, from the very outset, they tried their best.

EPILOGUE: TWO PATHS TO HARVARD

And now, with all these pages behind us, an early promise has been confirmed: this book indeed has no "unifying theme."

But if there is no unifying theme to *Freakonomics*, there is at least a common thread running through the everyday application of Freakonomics. It has to do with thinking sensibly about how people behave in the real world. All it requires is a novel way of looking, of discerning, of measuring. This isn't necessarily a difficult task, nor does it require supersophisticated thinking. We have essentially tried to figure out what the typical gang member or sumo wrestler figured out on his own (although we had to do so in reverse).

Will the ability to think such thoughts improve your life materially? Probably not. Perhaps you'll put up a sturdy gate around your swimming pool or push your real-estate agent to work a little harder. But the net effect is likely to be more subtle than that.

You might become more skeptical of the conventional wisdom; you may begin looking for hints as to how things aren't quite what they seem; perhaps you will seek out some trove of data and sift through it, balancing your intelligence and your intuition to arrive at a glimmering new idea. Some of these ideas might make you uncomfortable, even unpopular. To claim that legalized abortion resulted in a massive drop in crime will inevitably lead to explosive moral reactions. But the fact of the matter is that *Freakonomics*-style thinking simply doesn't traffic in morality. As we suggested near the beginning of this book, if morality represents an ideal world, then economics represents the actual world.

The most likely result of having read this book is a simple one: you may find yourself asking a lot of questions. Many of them will lead to nothing. But some will produce answers that are interesting, even surprising. Consider the question posed at the beginning of this book's penultimate chapter: how much do parents really matter?

The data have by now made it clear that parents matter a great deal in some regards (most of which have been long determined by the time a child is born) and not at all in others (the ones we obsess about). You can't blame parents for trying to do something—anything—to help their child succeed, even if it's something as irrelevant as giving him a high-end first name.

But there is also a huge random effect that rains down on even the best parenting efforts. If you are in any way typical, you have known some intelligent and devoted parents whose child went badly off the rails. You may have also known of the opposite instance, where a child succeeds despite his parents' worst intentions and habits.

Recall for a moment the two boys, one white and one black,

who were described in chapter 5. The white boy who grew up outside Chicago had smart, solid, encouraging, loving parents who stressed education and family. The black boy from Daytona Beach was abandoned by his mother, was beaten by his father, and had become a full-fledged gangster by his teens. So what became of the two boys?

The second child, now twenty-eight years old, is Roland G. Fryer Jr., the Harvard economist studying black underachievement.

The white child also made it to Harvard. But soon after, things went badly for him. His name is Ted Kaczynski.

THE PROBABILITY THAT A REAL-ESTATE AGENT IS CHEATING YOU (AND OTHER RIDDLES OF MODERN LIFE)

Inside the curious mind of the heralded young economist Steven Levitt

BY STEPHEN J. DUBNER
THE NEW YORK TIMES MAGAZINE

The most brilliant young economist in America—the one so deemed, at least, by a jury of his elders—brakes to a stop at a traffic light on Chicago's south side. It is a sunny day in mid-June. He drives an aging green Chevy Cavalier with a dusty dashboard and a window that doesn't quite shut, producing a dull roar at highway speeds.

But the car is quiet for now, as are the noontime streets: gas stations, boundless concrete, brick buildings with plywood windows.

An elderly homeless man approaches. It says he is homeless right on his sign, which also asks for money. He wears a torn jacket, too heavy for the warm day, and a grimy red baseball cap.

The economist doesn't lock his doors or inch the car forward. Nor does he go scrounging for spare change. He just watches, as if through one-way glass. After a while, the homeless man moves along.

"He had nice headphones," says the economist, still watching in the rearview mirror. "Well, nicer than the ones I have. Otherwise, it doesn't look like he has many assets."

Steven Levitt tends to see things differently than the average person. Differently, too, than the average economist. This is either a wonderful trait or a troubling one, depending on how you feel about economists. The average economist is known to wax oracularly about any and all monetary issues. But if you were to ask Levitt his opinion of some standard economic matter, he would probably swipe the hair from his eyes and plead ignorance. "I gave up a long time ago pretending that I knew stuff I didn't know," he says. "I mean, I just—I just don't know very much about the field of economics. I'm not good at math, I don't know a lot of econometrics, and I also don't know how to do theory. If you ask me about whether the stock market's going to go up or down, if you ask me whether the economy's going to grow or shrink, if you ask me whether deflation's good or bad, if you ask me about taxes— I mean, it would be total fakery if I said I knew anything about any of those things."

In Levitt's view, economics is a science with excellent tools for gaining answers but a serious shortage of interesting questions. His particular gift is the ability to ask such questions. For instance: If drug dealers make so much money, why do they still live with their mothers? Which is more dangerous, a gun or a swimming pool? What really caused crime rates to plunge during the past decade? Do real-estate agents have their clients' best interests at heart? Why do black parents give their children names that may hurt their career prospects? Do schoolteachers cheat to meet high-stakes testing standards? Is sumo wrestling corrupt?

And how does a homeless man afford $50 headphones?

Many people—including a fair number of his peers—might not recognize Levitt's work as economics at all. But he has merely distilled the so-called dismal science down to its most primal aim: explaining how people get what they want, or need. Unlike most academics, he is unafraid of using personal observations and curiosities (though he does fear calculus). He is an intuitionist. He sifts through a pile of data to find a story that no one else had found. He devises a way to measure an effect that veteran economists had declared unmeasurable. His abiding interests—though he says he has never trafficked in them himself—are cheating, corruption and crime.

His interest in the homeless man's headphones, meanwhile, didn't last long. "Maybe," he said later, "it was just testimony to the fact I'm too disorganized to buy a set of headphones that I myself covet."

Levitt is the first to say that some of his topics border on the trivial. But he has proved to be such an ingenious researcher and clear-eyed thinker that instead of being consigned to the fringe of his field, the opposite has happened: he has shown other economists just how well their tools can make sense of the real world.

"Levitt is considered a demigod, one of the most creative people in economics and maybe in all social science," says Colin Camerer, an economist at the California Institute of Technology. "He represents something that everyone thinks they will be when they go to grad school in econ, but usually they have the creative spark bored out of them by endless math—namely, a kind of intellectual detective trying to figure stuff out."

Levitt is a populist in a field that is undergoing a bout of popularization. Undergraduates are swarming the economics departments of elite universities. Economics is seen as the ideal blend of intellectual prestige (it does offer a Nobel, after all) and practical training for a high-flying finance career (unless, like Levitt, you choose to stay in academia). At the same time, economics is ever more visible in the real world, thanks to the continuing fetishization of the stock market and the continuing fixation with Alan Greenspan.

The greatest change, however, is within the scholarly ranks. Microeconomists are gaining on the macro crowd, empiricists gaining on the theorists. Behavioral economists have called into doubt the very notion of "homo economicus," the supposedly rational decision-maker in each of us. Young economists of every stripe are more inclined to work on real-world subjects and dip into bordering disciplines—psychology, criminology, sociology, even neurology—with the intent of rescuing their science from its slavish dependence upon mathematical models.

Levitt fits everywhere and nowhere. He is a noetic butterfly that no one has pinned down—he was once offered a job on the Clinton economic team, and the Bush campaign approached him about being a crime adviser—but who is widely appreciated.

"Steve isn't really a behavioral economist, but they'd be happy to have him," says Austan Goolsbee, who teaches economics at the University of Chicago's Graduate School of Business. "He's not really an old price-theory guy, but these Chicago guys are happy to claim him. He's not really a Cambridge guy"—although Levitt went to Harvard and then M.I.T.—"but they'd love him to come back."

He has critics, to be sure. Daniel Hamermesh, a prominent labor economist at the University of Texas, has taught Levitt's paper "The Impact of Legalized Abortion on Crime" to his undergraduates. "I've gone over this paper in draft, in its printed version, at great length, and for the life of me I can't see anything wrong with it," Hamermesh says. "On the other hand, I don't believe a word of it. And his stuff on sumo wrestlers—well, this is not exactly fundamental, unless you're Japanese and weigh 500 pounds."

But at 36, Levitt is a full professor in the University of Chicago's economics department, the most legendary program in the country. (He received tenure after only two years.) He is an editor of *The Journal of Political Economy,* a leading journal in the field. And the American Economic Association recently awarded him its John Bates Clark Medal, given biennially to the country's best economist under 40.

He is a prolific and diverse writer. But his paper linking a rise in abortion to a drop in crime has made more noise than the rest combined. Levitt and his co-author, John Donohue of Stanford Law School, argued that as much as 50 percent of the huge drop in crime since the early 1990's can be traced to *Roe v. Wade.* Their thinking goes like this: the women most likely to seek an abortion—poor, single, black or teenage mothers—were the very women whose children, if born, have been shown most likely to become criminals. But since those children *weren't* born, crime began to decrease during the years they would have entered their criminal prime. In conversation, Levitt reduces the theory to a tidy syllogism: "Unwantedness leads to high crime; abortion leads to less unwantedness; abortion leads to less crime."

Levitt had already published widely about crime and punishment. One paper he wrote as a graduate student is still regularly cited. His question was disarmingly simple: Do more police translate into less crime? The answer would seem obvious—yes—but had never been proved: since the number of police officers tends to rise along with the number of crimes, the effectiveness of the police was tricky to measure.

Levitt needed a mechanism that would unlink the crime rate from police hiring. He found it within politics. He noticed that mayors and governors running for re-election often hire more police officers. By measuring *those* police increases against crime rates, he was able to determine that additional officers do indeed bring down violent crime.

That paper was later disputed—another graduate student found a serious mathematical mistake in it—but Levitt's ingenuity was obvious. He began to be acknowledged as a master of the simple, clever solution. He was the guy who, in the slapstick scene, sees all the engineers futzing with a broken machine—and then realizes that no one has thought to plug it in.

Arguing that the police help deter crime didn't make Levitt any enemies. Arguing that abortion deterred crime was another matter.

In the abortion paper, published in 2001, he and Donohue warned that their findings should not be seen "as either an endorsement of abortion or a call for intervention by the state in the fertility decisions of women." They suggested that crime might just as easily be curbed by "providing better environments for those children at greatest risk for future crime."

Still, the very topic managed to offend nearly everyone. Conservatives were enraged that abortion could be construed as a crime-fighting tool. Liberals were aghast that poor and black women were singled out. Economists grumbled that Levitt's methodology was not sound. A syllogism, after all, can be a magic trick: All cats die; Socrates died; therefore Socrates was a cat.

"I think he's enormously clever in so many areas, focusing very much on the issue of reverse causality," says Ted Joyce, an economist at Baruch College who has written a critical response to the abortion paper. "But in this case I think he ignored it, or didn't tend to it well enough."

As the news media gorged on the abortion-crime story, Levitt came under direct assault. He was called an ideologue (by conservatives and liberals alike), a eugenicist, a racist and downright evil.

In reality, he seems to be very much none of those. He has little taste for politics and less for moralizing. He is genial, low-key and unflappable, confident but not cocky. He is a respected teacher and colleague; he is a sought-after collaborator who, because of the breadth of his curiosities, often works with scholars outside his field—another rarity for an economist.

"I hesitate to use these words, but Steve is a con man, in the best sense," says Sudhir Venkatesh, a sociologist at Columbia University. "He's the Shakespearean jester. He'll make you believe his ideas were yours." Venkatesh was Levitt's co-author on "An Economic Analysis of a Drug-Selling Gang's Finances," which found that the average street dealer lives with his mother because the take-home pay is, frankly, terrible. The paper analyzed one crack gang's financial activities as if it were any corporation. (It was Venkatesh who procured the data, from a former gang member.) Such a thing had never been tried. "This lack of focus," Levitt deadpanned in one version of the paper, "is perhaps partly attributable to the fact that few economists have been involved in the study of gangs."

Levitt speaks with a boyish lisp. His appearance is High Nerd: a plaid button-down shirt, nondescript khakis and a braided belt, sensible shoes. His pocket calendar is branded with the National Bureau of Economic Research logo. "I wish he would get more than three haircuts a year," his wife, Jeannette, says, "and that he wasn't still wearing the same glasses he got 15 years ago, which weren't even in fashion then." He was a good golfer in high school but has so physically atrophied that he calls himself "the weakest human being alive" and asks Jeannette to open jars around the house.

There is nothing in his appearance or manner, in other words, that suggests a flamethrower. He will tell you that all he does is sit at his desk, day and night, wrestling with some strange mountain of data. He will tell you that he would do it free (his salary is reportedly more than $200,000), and you tend to believe him. He may be an accidental provocateur, but he is a provocateur nonetheless.

He takes particular delight in catching wrongdoers. In one paper, he devised a set of algorithms that could identify teachers in the Chicago public-school system who were cheating. "Cheating classrooms will systematically differ from other classrooms along a number of dimensions," he and his co-author, Brian Jacob of the Kennedy School of Government, wrote in "Catching Cheating Teachers." "For instance, students in cheating classrooms are likely to experience unusually large test-score gains in the year of the cheating, followed by unusually small gains or even declines in the following year when the boost attributable to cheating disappears."

Levitt used test-score data from the Chicago schools that had long been available to other researchers. There were a number of ways, he realized, that a teacher could cheat. If she were particularly brazen (and stupid), she might give students the correct answers. Or, after the test, she might actually erase students' wrong answers and fill in correct ones. A sophisticated cheater would be careful to avoid conspicuous blocks of identical answers. But Levitt was more sophisticated. "The first step in analyzing suspicious strings is to estimate the probability each child would give a particular answer on each question," he wrote. "This estimation is done using a multinomial logit framework with past test scores, demographics and socioeconomic characteristics as explanatory variables."

So by measuring any number of factors—the difficulty of a particular question, the frequency with which students got hard questions right and easy ones wrong, the degree to which certain answers were highly correlated in one classroom—Levitt identified which teachers he thought were cheating. (Perhaps just as valuable, he was also able to identify the good teachers.) The Chicago school system, rather than disputing Levitt's findings, invited him into the schools for retesting. As a result, the cheaters were fired.

Then there is his coming "Understanding Why Crime Fell in the 1990's: Four Factors That Explain the Decline and Seven That Do Not." The entire drop in crime, Levitt says, was due to more police officers, more prisoners, the waning crack epidemic and *Roe v. Wade.*

One factor that probably *didn't* make a difference, he argues, was the innovative policing strategy trumpeted in New York by Rudolph Giuliani and William Bratton.

"I think," Levitt says, "I'm pretty much alone in saying that."

He comes from a Minneapolis family of high, if unusual, achievers. His father, a medical researcher, is considered a leading authority on intestinal gas. (He bills himself as "The Man Who Gave Status to Flatus and Class to Gas.") One of Levitt's great uncles, Robert May, wrote *Rudolph the Red-Nosed Reindeer*—the book, that is; another great uncle, Johnny Marks, later wrote the song.

At Harvard, Levitt wrote his senior thesis on thoroughbred breeding and graduated summa cum laude. (He is still obsessed with horse racing. He says he believes it is corrupt and has designed a betting system—the details of which he will not share—to take advantage of the corruption.) He worked for two years as a management consultant before enrolling at M.I.T. for a doctorate in economics. The M.I.T. program was famous for its mathematical intensity. Levitt had taken exactly one math course as an undergraduate and had forgotten even that. During his first graduate class, he asked the student next to him about a formula on the board: Is there any difference between the derivative sign that's straight up-and-down and the curly one? "You are in so much trouble," he was told.

"People wrote him off," recalls Austan Goolsbee, the Chicago economist who was then a classmate. "They'd say, 'That guy has no future.'"

Levitt set his own course. Other grad students stayed up all night working on problem sets, trying to make good grades. He stayed up researching and writing. "My view was that the way you succeed in this profession is you write great papers," he says. "So I just started."

Sometimes he would begin with a question. Sometimes it was a set of data that caught his eye. He spent one entire summer typing into his computer the results of years' worth of Congressional elections. (Today, with so much information so easily available on the Internet, Levitt complains that he can't get his students to input data at all.) All he had was a vague curiosity about why incumbents were so often re-elected.

Then he happened upon a political-science book whose authors claimed that money wins elections, period. "They were trying to explain election outcomes as a function of campaign expenditures," he recalls, "completely ignoring the fact that contributors will only give money to challengers when they have a realistic chance of winning, and incumbents only spend a lot when they have a chance of losing. They convinced themselves this was the causal story even though it's so obvious in retrospect that it's a spurious effect."

Obvious, at least, to Levitt. Within five minutes, he had a vision of the paper he would write. "It came to me," he says, "in full bloom."

The problem was that his data couldn't tell him who was a good candidate and who wasn't. It was therefore impossible to tease out the effect of the money. As with the police/crime rate puzzle, he had to trick the data.

Because he himself had typed in the data, he had noticed something: often, the same two candidates faced each other multiple times. By analyzing the data from only those elections, Levitt was able to find a true result. His conclusion: campaign money has about one-tenth the impact as was commonly accepted.

An unknown graduate student, he sent his paper to *The Journal of Political Economy*—one professor told him he was crazy for even trying—where it was published. He completed his Ph.D. in three years, but because of his priorities, he says, he was "invisible" to the faculty, "a real zero." Then he stumbled upon what he now calls the turning point in his career.

He had an interview for the Society of Fellows, the venerable intellectual Harvard clubhouse that pays young scholars to do their own work, for three years, with no commitments. Levitt felt he didn't stand a chance. For starters, he didn't consider himself an intellectual. He would be interviewed over dinner by the senior fellows, a collection of world-renowned philosophers, scientists and historians. He worried he wouldn't have enough conversation for even the first course.

Instead, he was on fire. Whatever subject came up—the brain, ants, philosophy—he just happened to remember something pithy he'd read. His wit crackled as it had never crackled before. When he told them about the two summers he spent betting the horses back in Minnesota, *they ate it up!*

Finally—disquietingly—one of them said: "I'm having a hard time seeing the unifying theme of your work. Could you explain it?"

Levitt was stymied. He had no idea what his unifying theme was, or if he even had one.

Amartya Sen, the future Nobel-winning economist, jumped in and neatly summarized what he saw as Levitt's theme.

Yes, Levitt said eagerly, that's my theme.

Another fellow then offered another theme.

You're right, Levitt said, *that's* my theme.

And so it went, like dogs tugging at a bone, until the philosopher Robert Nozick interrupted. If Levitt could have been said to have an intellectual hero, it would be Nozick.

"How old are you, Steve?" he asked.

"Twenty-six."

Nozick turned to the other fellows: "He's 26 years old. Why does he need to have a unifying theme? Maybe he's going to be one of those people who's so talented he doesn't need one. He'll take a question and he'll just answer it, and it'll be fine."

The University of Chicago's economics department had a famous unifying theme—the Gospel of Free Markets, with a conservative twist—and would therefore not have seemed the most likely fit for Levitt. As he sees it, Chicago is about theory, deep thinking and big ideas, while he is about empiricism, clever thinking and "cute but ultimately insubstantial ideas."

But Chicago also had Gary Becker. To Levitt, Becker is the most influential economist of the past 50 years. Long before it was fashionable, Becker brought microeconomic theory to offbeat topics, the family and crime in particular. For years, Becker was demonized—a single phrase like "the price of children" would set off untold alarms. "I took a lot of heat over my career from people who thought my work was silly or irrelevant or not economics," Becker says. But Chicago supported him; he persevered, winning the Nobel Prize in 1992; and he became Steven Levitt's role model.

Becker told Levitt that Chicago would be a great environment for him. "Not everybody agrees with all your results," he said, "but we agree what you're doing is very interesting work, and we'll support you in that."

Levitt soon found that the support at Chicago went beyond the scholarly. The year after he was hired, his wife gave birth to their first child, Andrew. One day, just after Andrew turned a year old, he came down with a slight fever. The doctor diagnosed an ear infection. When he started vomiting the next morning, his parents took him to the hospital. A few days later he was dead of pneumococcal meningitis.

Amid the shock and grief, Levitt had an undergraduate class that needed teaching. It was Gary Becker—a Nobel laureate nearing his 70th birthday—who sat in for him. Another colleague, D. Gale Johnson, sent a condolence card that Levitt still quotes from memory.

Levitt and Johnson, an agricultural economist in his 80's, began speaking regularly. Levitt learned that Johnson's daughter was one of the first Americans to adopt a daughter from China. Soon the Levitts adopted a daughter of their own, whom they named Amanda. In addition to Amanda, they have since had a daughter, now almost 3, and a son. But Andrew's death has played on, in various ways. They have become close friends with the family of the little girl to whom they donated Andrew's liver. (They also donated his heart, but that baby died.) And not surprisingly for a scholar who pursues real-life subjects, the death also informed Levitt's work.

He and Jeannette joined a support group for grieving parents. Levitt was struck by how many children had drowned in swimming pools. They were the kinds of deaths that don't make the newspaper—unlike, for instance, a child who dies while playing with a gun.

Levitt was curious and went looking for numbers that would tell the story. He wrote up the results as an op-ed article for *The Chicago Sun-Times.* It featured the sort of plangent counterintuition for which he has become famous: "If you own a gun and have a swimming pool in the yard, the swimming pool is almost 100 times more likely to kill a child than the gun is."

Trying to get his mind off death, Levitt took up a hobby: rehabbing and selling old houses in Oak Park, where he lives. This experience has led to yet another paper, about the real-estate market. It is his most Chicago-style paper yet, a romp in price theory, a sign that the university's influence on him is perhaps as strong as his influence on it. But Levitt being Levitt, it also deals with corruption.

While negotiating to buy old houses, he found that the seller's agent often encouraged him, albeit cagily, to underbid. This seemed odd: didn't the agent represent the seller's best interest? Then he thought more about the agent's role. Like many other "experts" (auto mechanics and stockbrokers come to mind), a real-estate agent is thought to know his field far better than a lay person. A homeowner is encouraged to trust the agent's information. So if the agent brings in a low offer and says it might just be the best the homeowner can expect, the homeowner tends to believe him. But the key, Levitt determined, lay in the fact that agents "receive only a small share of the incremental profit when a house sells for a higher value." Like a stockbroker churning commissions or a bookie grabbing his vig, an agent was simply looking to make a deal, any deal. So he would push homeowners to sell too fast and too cheap.

Now if Levitt could only measure this effect. Once again, he found a clever mechanism. Using data from more than 50,000 home sales in Cook County, Ill., he compared the figures for homes *owned* by real-estate agents with those for homes for which they acted only as agents. The agents' homes stayed on the market about 10 days longer and sold for 2 percent more.

Late on a summer afternoon, Levitt is in his office, deep inside one of the university's Gothic behemoths. The ceiling is stained, the plaster around the window crumbling. He is just back from sabbatical at Stanford, and his desk is a holy mess: stacks of books and journals, a green sippy cup and a little orange squeeze hippo.

This is his afternoon to meet with students. Levitt drinks a Mountain Dew and talks softly. Some students come for research assignments, some for advice. One has just written her undergraduate thesis: "The Labor Market Consequence of Graduating College in a Bad Economy." For a thesis, Levitt tells her, it's very good. But now she wants to have it published.

"You write like a college student, and that's a problem," he says. "The thing is, you're telling a story. There's foreshadowing going on, all those tricks. You want the reader going down a particular path so when they get the results, they understand them and believe them. But you also want to be honest about your weaknesses. People are much less harsh on weaknesses that are clear than weaknesses that are hidden—as they should be."

Be honest about your weaknesses. Has there ever been a prize-winning scholar as honest about his weaknesses as Steven Levitt? He doesn't understand economics, he claims, or math. He's a little thinker in a world of big thinkers. He can't even open a jar of spaghetti sauce at home, poor guy.

Friends say that Levitt's self-deprecation is as calculated as it is genuine. Within academia, economists take pride in being the most cutthroat of a cutthroat breed. Anyone who writes papers on *Weakest Link* (contestants discriminate against Latino and elderly peers, Levitt concluded, but not blacks or women) and sumo (to best manage their tournament rankings, wrestlers often conspire to throw matches) had better not also be arrogant.

Or maybe it is not self-deprecation at all. Maybe it is self-flagellation. Maybe what Steven Levitt really wants is to graduate from his "silly" and "trivial" and "shallow" topics.

He thinks he's onto something with a new paper about black names. He wanted to know if someone with a distinctly black name suffers an economic penalty. His answer—contrary to other recent research—is no. But now he has a bigger question: Is black culture a cause of racial inequality or is it a consequence? For an economist, even for Levitt, this is new turf—"quantifying culture," he calls it. As a task, he finds it thorny, messy, perhaps impossible and deeply tantalizing.

Driving home to Oak Park that evening, his Cavalier glumly thrumming along the Eisenhower Expressway, he dutifully addresses his future. Leaving academia for a hedge fund or a government job does not interest him (though he might, on the side, start a company to catch cheating teachers). He is said to be at the top of every economics department's poaching list. But the tree he and Jeannette planted when Andrew died is getting too big to move. You get the feeling he may stay at Chicago awhile.

There are important problems, he says, that he feels ready to address.

For instance? "Tax evasion. Money-laundering. I'd like to put together a set of tools that lets us catch terrorists. I mean, that's the goal. I don't necessarily know yet how I'd go about it. But given the right data, I have little doubt that I could figure out the answer."

It might seem absurd for an economist to dream of catching terrorists. Just as it must have seemed absurd if you were a Chicago schoolteacher, called into an office and told that, ahem, the algorithms designed by that skinny man with thick glasses had determined that you are a cheater. And that you are being fired. Steven Levitt may not fully believe in himself, but he does believe in this: teachers and criminals and real-estate agents may lie, and politicians, and even C.I.A. analysts. But numbers don't.

HOODWINKED?
January 8, 2006

Our book *Freakonomics* includes a chapter titled "How Is the Ku Klux Klan Like a Group of Real-Estate Agents?" This chapter was our effort to bring to life the economic concept known as information asymmetry, a state wherein one party to a transaction has better information than another party. It is probably obvious that real-estate agents typically have better information than their clients. The Klan story was perhaps less obvious. We argued that the Klan's secrecy—its rituals, made-up language, passwords and so on—formed an information asymmetry that furthered its aim of terrorizing blacks and others.

But the Klan was not the hero of our story. The hero was a man named Stetson Kennedy, a white Floridian from an old-line family who from an early age sought to assail racial and social injustices. Out of all of his crusades—for unionism, voting rights and numberless other causes—Kennedy is best known for taking on the Klan in the 1940's. In his book *The Klan Unmasked* (originally published in 1954 as *I Rode With the Ku Klux Klan*), Kennedy describes how he adopted a false identity to infiltrate the Klan's main chapter in Atlanta, was chosen to serve as a "klavalier" (a Klan strong-arm man) and repeatedly found himself at the center of astonishing events, all the while courting great personal risk.

What did Kennedy do with all the secret Klan information he gathered? He disseminated it like mad: to state prosecutors, to human rights groups and even to broadcasters like Drew Pearson and the producers of the *Superman* radio show, who publicly aired the Klan's heretofore hidden workings. Kennedy took an information asymmetry and dumped it on its head. And in doing so, we wrote, he played a significant role in quashing the renaissance of the Klan in postwar America.

Kennedy has been duly celebrated for his activism: his friend Woody Guthrie once wrote a song about him, and a Stetson Kennedy Day was recently declared in St. John's County, Fla., where Kennedy, 89, still lives. That is where we interviewed him nearly two years ago; our account of his amazing true story was based on those interviews, *The Klan Unmasked* and a small mountain of history books and newspaper articles.

But is Kennedy's story as true as it is amazing?

That was the disturbing question that began to haunt another Florida author, Ben Green, who in 1992 began writing a book about Harry T. Moore, a black civil rights advocate who was murdered in 1951. For a time, Stetson Kennedy was a collaborator on the book. Although Green was only tangentially interested in Kennedy's Klan infiltration—it wasn't central to the Moore story—he eventually checked out Kennedy's voluminous archives, held in libraries in New York and Atlanta.

These papers charted the extraordinarily colorful life of a man who had been, among other things, a poet, a folklorist, a muckraking journalist and a union activist. But Green was dismayed to find that the story told in Kennedy's own papers seemed to be quite different from what Kennedy wrote in *The Klan Unmasked*.

In *The Klan Unmasked,* Kennedy posed as an encyclopedia salesman named John S. Perkins who, in one of his first undercover maneuvers, visits the former governor of Georgia—a reputed Klan sympathizer—and ingratiates himself by offering to distribute some hate literature. A document in Kennedy's archives, however, suggests that Kennedy had indeed met the ex-governor, but not in any undercover capacity. Rather, he had interviewed him for a book he was writing—nor did this document mention any hate literature.

A close examination of Kennedy's archives seems to reveal a recurrent theme: legitimate interviews that he conducted with Klan leaders and sympathizers would reappear in *The Klan Unmasked* in different contexts and with different facts. In a similar vein, the archives offer evidence that Kennedy covered public Klan events as a reporter but then recast them in his book as undercover exploits. Kennedy had also amassed a great deal of literature about the Klan and other hate groups that he joined, but his own archives suggest that he joined most of these groups by mail.

So did Kennedy personally infiltrate the Klan in Atlanta, as portrayed in *The Klan Unmasked*?

In his archives are a series of memos that were submitted to the Anti-Defamation League, one of several civil rights groups to which Kennedy reported. Some of the memos were written by him; others were written by a man identified as John Brown, a union worker and former Klan official who had changed his ways and offered to infiltrate the Klan. "This worker is joining the

Klan for me," Kennedy wrote in one memo in early 1946. "I am certain that he can be relied on."

In Kennedy's subsequent memos—indeed, in hundreds of pages of Kennedy's various correspondence from the era—he matter-of-factly attributed some of his most powerful Klan information to John Brown: one of the memos he declared "a report from my informant inside the Klan on the meeting of Atlanta Klan No. 1 on August 12 and Atlanta Klan No. 297 on August 15." As John Brown fed inside information to Kennedy, Kennedy would then relay it to groups like the A.D.L., as well as to prosecutors and journalists. It wasn't until he wrote *The Klan Unmasked,* several years later, that Kennedy placed himself, Zelig-like, at the center of all the action.

Ben Green, despite months spent immersed in Kennedy's archives, could not identify the man once known as John Brown. Green did manage to interview Dan Duke, a former state prosecutor who, as rendered in *The Klan Unmasked,* worked closely with Kennedy. Duke agreed that Kennedy "got inside of some [Klan] meetings" but openly disputed Kennedy's dramatized account of their relationship. "None of that happened," he told Green. In 1999, when Green finally published his Harry T. Moore book, "Before His Time," it contained a footnote labeling *The Klan Unmasked* "a novelization."

Green is not the only person to have concluded that Kennedy has bent the truth. Jim Clark, who teaches history at the University of Central Florida, says that Kennedy "built a national reputation on many things that didn't happen." Meredith Babb, director of the University Press of Florida, which has published four of Kennedy's books, now calls Kennedy "an entrepreneurial folklorist." But except for Green's footnote, they all kept quiet until the retelling of Kennedy's exploits in *Freakonomics* produced a new round of attention. Why? "It would be like killing Santa Claus," Green says. "To me, the saddest part of this story is that what he actually did wasn't enough for him, and he has felt compelled to make up, embellish or take credit for things he didn't do."

When presented with documents from his own archives and asked outright, several weeks ago over lunch near his Florida home, if *The Klan Unmasked* was "somewhat conflated or fictionalized," Kennedy said no. "There may have been a bit of dialogue that was not as I remembered it," he answered. "But beyond that, no." When pressed, Kennedy did concede that "in some cases I took the reports and actions of this other guy and incorporated them into one narrative." As it turns out, Kennedy has made such an admission at least once before. Peggy Bulger, director of the American Folklife Center in the Library of Congress, wrote a 1992 dissertation called "Stetson Kennedy: Applied Folklore and Cultural Advocacy," based in part on extensive interviews with her subject. In an endnote, Bulger writes that "Kennedy combined his personal experiences undercover with the narratives provided by John Brown in writing *I Rode With the Ku Klux Klan* in 1954."

We weren't very happy, of course, to learn that a story we included in *Freakonomics* was built on such shaky foundations— especially since the book is devoted to upending conventional wisdoms rather than reinforcing them, and concerning Stetson Kennedy, the most conventional wisdom of all is his reputation as a Klan infiltrator.

There is also the fact that in our work we make a point of depending less on anecdote in favor of data, the idea being that numbers tend to lie less baldly than people do. But the story of Stetson Kennedy was one long series of anecdotes—which, no matter how many times they were cited over the decades, were nearly all generated by the same self-interested source.

Perhaps Kennedy's long life of fighting the good fight are all that matter. Perhaps, to borrow Peggy Bulger's phraseology, a goal of "cultural advocacy" calls for the use of "applied folklore" rather than the sort of forthrightness that should be more typical of history or journalism. One thing that does remain true is that Kennedy was certainly a master of information asymmetry. Until, that is, the data caught up with him.

WHY VOTE?
November 6, 2005

Within the economics departments at certain universities, there is a famous but probably apocryphal story about two world-class economists who run into each other at the voting booth.

"What are you doing here?" one asks.

"My wife made me come," the other says.

The first economist gives a confirming nod. "The same."

After a mutually sheepish moment, one of them hatches a plan: "If you promise never to tell anyone you saw me here, I'll never tell anyone I saw you." They shake hands, finish their polling business and scurry off.

Why would an economist be embarrassed to be seen at the voting booth? Because voting exacts a cost—in time, effort, lost productivity—with no discernible payoff except perhaps some vague sense of having done your "civic duty." As the economist Patricia Funk wrote in a recent paper, "A rational individual should abstain from voting."

The odds that your vote will actually affect the outcome of a given election are very, very, very slim. This was documented by the economists Casey Mulligan and Charles Hunter, who analyzed more than 56,000 Congressional and state-legislative elections since 1898. For all the attention paid in the media to close elections, it turns out that they are exceedingly rare. The median margin of victory in the Congressional elections was 22 percent; in the state-legislature elections, it was 25 percent. Even in the closest elections, it is almost never the case that a single vote is pivotal. Of the more than 40,000 elections for state legislator that Mulligan and Hunter analyzed, comprising nearly 1 billion votes, only 7 elections were decided by a single vote, with 2 others tied. Of the more than 16,000 Congressional elections, in which many more people vote, only one election in the past 100 years—a 1910 race in Buffalo—was decided by a single vote.

But there is a more important point: the closer an election is, the more likely that its outcome will be taken out of the voters' hands—most vividly exemplified, of course, by the 2000 presidential race. It is true that the outcome of that election came down to a handful of voters; but their names were Kennedy, O'Connor, Rehnquist, Scalia and Thomas. And it was only the votes they cast while wearing their robes that mattered, not the ones they may have cast in their home precincts.

Still, people do continue to vote, in the millions. Why? Here are three possibilities:

1. Perhaps we are just not very bright and therefore wrongly believe that our votes will affect the outcome.
2. Perhaps we vote in the same spirit in which we buy lottery tickets. After all, your chances of winning a lottery and of

affecting an election are pretty similar. From a financial perspective, playing the lottery is a bad investment. But it's fun
and relatively cheap: for the price of a ticket, you buy the
right to fantasize how you'd spend the winnings—much as
you get to fantasize that your vote will have some impact on
policy.

3. Perhaps we have been socialized into the voting-as-civic-duty
idea, believing that it's a good thing for society if people vote,
even if it's not particularly good for the individual. And thus
we feel guilty for not voting.

But wait a minute, you say. If everyone thought about voting
the way economists do, we might have no elections at all. No
voter goes to the polls actually believing that her single vote will
affect the outcome, does she? And isn't it cruel to even suggest
that her vote is not worth casting?

This is indeed a slippery slope—the seemingly meaningless behavior of an individual, which, in aggregate, becomes quite meaningful. Here's a similar example in reverse. Imagine that you and
your 8-year-old daughter are taking a walk through a botanical
garden when she suddenly pulls a bright blossom off a tree.

"You shouldn't do that," you find yourself saying.

"Why not?" she asks.

"Well," you reason, "because if everyone picked one, there
wouldn't be any flowers left at all."

"Yeah, but everybody *isn't* picking them," she says with a look.
"Only me."

In the old days, there were more pragmatic incentives to vote.
Political parties regularly paid voters $5 or $10 to cast the proper
ballot; sometimes payment came in the form of a keg of whiskey,

a barrel of flour or, in the case of an 1890 New Hampshire Congressional race, a live pig.

Now as then, many people worry about low voter turnout—only slightly more than half of eligible voters participated in the last presidential election—but it might be more worthwhile to stand this problem on its head and instead ask a different question: considering that an individual's vote almost never matters, why do so many people bother to vote at all?

The answer may lie in Switzerland. That's where Patricia Funk discovered a wonderful natural experiment that allowed her to take an acute measure of voter behavior.

The Swiss love to vote—on parliamentary elections, on plebiscites, on whatever may arise. But voter participation had begun to slip over the years (maybe they stopped handing out live pigs there too), so a new option was introduced: the mail-in ballot. Whereas each voter in the U.S. must register, that isn't the case in Switzerland. Every eligible Swiss citizen began to automatically receive a ballot in the mail, which could then be completed and returned by mail.

From a social scientist's perspective, there was beauty in the setup of this postal voting scheme: because it was introduced in different cantons (the 26 statelike districts that make up Switzerland) in different years, it allowed for a sophisticated measurement of its effects over time.

Never again would any Swiss voter have to tromp to the polls during a rainstorm; the cost of casting a ballot had been lowered significantly. An economic model would therefore predict voter turnout to increase substantially. Is that what happened?

Not at all. In fact, voter turnout often *decreased*, especially in smaller cantons and in the smaller communities within cantons.

This finding may have serious implications for advocates of Internet voting—which, it has long been argued, would make voting easier and therefore increase turnout. But the Swiss model indicates that the exact opposite might hold true.

But why is this the case? Why on earth would *fewer* people vote when the cost of doing so is lowered?

It goes back to the incentives behind voting. If a given citizen doesn't stand a chance of having her vote affect the outcome, why does she bother? In Switzerland, as in the U.S., "there exists a fairly strong social norm that a good citizen should go to the polls," Funk writes. "As long as poll-voting was the only option, there was an incentive (or pressure) to go to the polls only to be *seen* handing in the vote. The motivation could be hope for social esteem, benefits from being perceived as a cooperator or just the avoidance of informal sanctions. Since in small communities, people know each other better and gossip about who fulfills civic duties and who doesn't, the benefits of norm adherence were particularly high in this type of community."

In other words, we *do* vote out of self-interest—a conclusion that will satisfy economists—but not necessarily the same self-interest as indicated by our actual ballot choice. For all the talk of how people "vote their pocketbooks," the Swiss study suggests that we may be driven to vote less by a financial incentive than a social one. It may be that the most valuable payoff of voting is simply being seen at the polling place by your friends or co-workers.

Unless, of course, you happen to be an economist.

HOW MANY LIVES DID DALE EARNHARDT SAVE?
February 19, 2006

Five years ago this weekend, Dale Earnhardt crashed into a wall during the final lap of the Daytona 500 and was instantly killed. One of the most successful, beloved and intimidating drivers in Nascar history, Earnhardt is still actively mourned. (If you watch today's Daytona 500, the first and most prominent race of the Nascar season, you will surely see his No. 3 everywhere.) Earnhardt's death was to Nascar as 9/11 was to the federal government: a wake-up call leading to a radical overhaul of safety measures. "There were three or four bad accidents in a row there over two or three years," says Matt Kenseth, an elite Nascar driver. "Nascar was always working hard on safety, but that"—Earnhardt's death—"really sped things up."

Driving a race car is an obviously hazardous pursuit. When Earnhardt died, he was the seventh driver within Nascar's three major divisions—the Craftsman Truck Series, the Busch Series and the premier circuit now known as the Nextel Cup Series—to die within a period of seven years.

And how many drivers have been killed since his death in 2001?

Zero. In more than six million miles of racing—and many, many miles in practice and qualifying laps, which are plenty dangerous—not a single driver in Nascar's three top divisions has died.

On U.S. roads, meanwhile, roughly 185,000 drivers, passengers and motorcyclists have been killed during this same time frame. Those 185,000 deaths, though, came over the course of nearly 15 trillion miles driven. This translates into one fatality for every 81 million miles driven. Although traffic accidents are the leading cause of death for Americans from ages 3 to 33, this would seem to be a pretty low death rate (especially since it includes motorcycles, which are far more dangerous than cars or trucks). How long might it take one person to drive 81 million miles? Let's say that for a solid year you did nothing but drive, 24 hours a day, at 60 miles per hour. In one year, you'd cover 525,600 miles; to reach 81 million miles, you'd have to drive around the clock for 154 years. In other words, a lot of people die on U.S. roads each year not because driving is so dangerous, but because an awful lot of people are driving an awful lot of miles.

So Nascar's record of zero deaths in five years over six million miles is perhaps not as remarkable as it first sounded. Still, driving a race car would seem to be substantially more dangerous than taking a trip to the supermarket. What has Nascar done to produce its zero-fatality record?

It's a long list. Well before Earnhardt was killed, each driver was already wearing a helmet, fireproof suit and shoes and a five-point safety harness. Months after Earnhardt's death, Nascar began requiring the use of a head-and-neck restraint that is tethered to a driver's helmet and prevents his head from flying forward or sideways in a crash. (Like many race-car drivers who are killed, Earnhardt suffered a fracture to the base of the skull.) It erected safer walls on its race tracks. And it began to zealously collect crash data. This Incident Database (which Nascar politely declined to let us examine) is gleaned from two main sources: a black box now mounted on every vehicle and the work of a new Field Investigation unit. These field investigators meticulously take key measurements on every car before every race, and then if a car is involved in a crash, they retake those measurements.

"In the past, a car would be in an accident, the driver would have no injuries and the team would load up the car and go home," says Gary Nelson, who runs Nascar's research and development center. "But now they measure every car in certain areas, and we make a log of that. Like the width of the seat—it seems simple, the width of the headrest from left to right. But in an accident, those things can bend, and the amount they bend can help us understand the energy involved. When we began, we thought our seats were adequately strong, but we found these things to be bending more than we thought. So we've come back since and rewritten the regulations."

Although it is wildly reductive to put it this way, a Nascar driver has two main goals: to win a race and to not be killed. Nascar's recent safety measures seem to have considerably reduced the likelihood of being killed. So could it be that drivers are now willing to be more reckless? When crashing is made less costly, an economist would fully expect drivers to be crashing like crazy; could it be that Nascar's safety measures have led to fewer deaths but more crashes?

A quick look at the data seems to suggest so. In last year's Nextel Cup races, there were 345 cars involved in crashes, an all-time high. But, as Matt Kenseth points out, the two cup races held during 2005 at Lowe's Motor Speedway near Charlotte, N.C., were unusually brutal—the track had a new surface that caused numerous flat tires—and may have aberrationally affected the crash count. "In Charlotte, pretty much everybody wrecked in both races," he says. "It was the fault of the track and the tires—but if you take those races out of it, crashes are probably about even." And there were actually fewer crashes in 2004 than there were in 2003. While the number of overall crashes are up a bit since Earnhardt's death (Nascar will not release annual crash counts, but one official did confirm this trend), they haven't increased nearly as much as an economist might have predicted based on how Nascar's safety measures would seem to have shifted a driver's incentives.

Maybe that's because there are other, perhaps stronger, incentives at play. The first is that Nascar has increased its penalties for reckless driving, not only fining drivers but also subtracting points in their race for the cup championship. The other lies in how the cup championship itself has been restructured. Two years ago, Nascar gave its 36-race season a playoff format. In order to qualify for the playoffs—and have a chance at winning the $6 million-plus cup championship—a driver must be among the points leaders after the first 26 races of the season. While a couple of 20th-place finishes during those first 26 races won't necessary ruin your championship hopes (each race fields a slate of 43 cars), a few bad crashes might.

So Nascar has reduced a danger incentive but imposed a financial incentive, thus maintaining the delicate and masterful balance it has cultivated: it has enough crashes to satisfy its fans but not too many to destroy the sport—or its drivers. (Nascar fans love crashes the way hockey fans love fights; when you watch the Speed Channel's edited replays of Nascar races, the plot is always the same: green flag, crash, crash, crash, crash, crash, checkered flag.)

And here lies the most startling statistic concerning Nascar and driver safety. In the past five years, more than 3,000 vehicles have crashed in Nascar's three top divisions, with zero fatalities. How does this compare with crashes on American highways? For interstate travel, there are 5.2 driver deaths per 1,000 crashes. At this rate, it would seem likely that those 3,000 Nascar crashes would have produced at least 15 deaths—and yet there have been none. To be sure, there are significant differences between Interstate driving and Nascar driving. A driver on the Interstate has to contend with poor weather, drunken drivers and cars coming at him in the opposite direction. On the other hand, a driver in the Daytona 500 is often traveling at 180 miles per hour in bumper-to-bumper traffic.

With more than 37,000 Americans dying in traffic accidents each year, it might be tempting to impose some of Nascar's safety regulations on the average driver. But considering how relatively safe it is to drive in this country, the added costs, measured in both dollars and comfort, would be steep. You might be willing to wear a five-point safety harness instead of the typical three-point lap-and-shoulder belt, and you would almost certainly be safer if you did. But are you ready to put on a helmet and fireproof suit every time you drive to the supermarket?

THE GIFT-CARD ECONOMY
January 7, 2007

What do a gym membership, a bottle of prescription pills and a holiday gift card have in common? Each of them is a thing that is bought and then often goes unused.

In their recent paper "Paying Not to Go to the Gym," the economists Stefano DellaVigna and Ulrike Malmendier showed that people who buy an annual membership to a health club overestimate by more than 70 percent how much they'll actually use it. Many people, therefore, would be better off buying monthly or daily passes.

The Cochrane Collaboration, an evidence-based health-care research group, recently issued a report about patients who fail to take their medicine. "People who are prescribed self-administered medications," it began, "typically take less than half the prescribed doses." While this may be more troubling as a medical issue than a financial one, it is nevertheless true that the medicine cabinets of America are stuffed with billions of dollars of unused prescriptions.

As for gift cards—well, let's just say there is good reason that they are known within the retail industry as a stored-value product: they store their value very well, and often permanently. The financial-services research firm TowerGroup estimates that of the $80 billion spent on gift cards in 2006, roughly $8 billion will never be redeemed—"a bigger impact on consumers," Tower notes, "than the combined total of both debit- and credit-card fraud." A survey by Marketing Workshop Inc. found that only 30 percent of recipients use a gift card within a month of receiving it, while *Consumer Reports* estimates that 19 percent of the people who received a gift card in 2005 never used it.

Considering that two-thirds of all holiday shoppers in 2006 planned to give someone else a gift card, you most likely received one yourself in recent weeks. Perhaps you are among the exceptional minority, and you have already spent it, or soon will. But the odds say that it has instead wound up in your sock drawer.

Does this mean that a gift card is a bad gift? The answer depends on whom you ask, and it also requires the asking of a separate question: What is gift-giving meant to accomplish in the first place?

An economist might describe a gift as a signaling mechanism that allows one person to tell another person that she: a) is thinking about him; b) cares about him; and c) wants to give him something that he'll value.

Of course there are many different types of recipients and relationships. It's quite easy to give gifts to people who don't have the money or the wherewithal to get things for themselves— children, for instance. Since a child can't drive himself to Toys 'R' Us and probably doesn't have much money of his own, by giving him a toy you are substantially expanding the set of things he has access to. Which makes nearly any gift meaningful.

With adults, it's a bit trickier. An adult is free to buy whatever he wants, and presumably he knows what he likes. So ideally, you'd want to give him something he might like but doesn't know about, or some kind of guilty pleasure that he wouldn't buy for himself. In either case, you are creating value for the recipient by giving him something that is actually worth more to him than the money you spent on it.

But realistically, most of our gifts fall well short of that high standard. This creates a lot of inefficiency. In 1993, the economist Joel Waldfogel addressed this subject in a paper whose continuing fame in economics circles is due in part to its wonderfully Scrooge-ish title: "The Deadweight Loss of Christmas." Since gifts "may be mismatched with the recipients' preferences," Waldfogel argued, it is likely that "the gift will leave the recipient worse off than if she had made her own consumption choice with an equal amount of cash." He concluded that "holiday gift-giving destroys between 10 percent and a third of the value of gifts."

If gift-giving destroys so much value, why not take the most efficient route and simply give cash? Obviously, some people do. In the small survey of Yale undergraduates on which Waldfogel based his paper, grandparents gave cash 42 percent of the time, and parents gave cash 10 percent of the time. But not once did a student receive cash from his or her significant other. Plainly, there are a few relationships for which a cash gift is appropriate, but in most cases, the social taboo crushes the economist's dream of such a beautifully efficient exchange.

So if cash is inappropriate, and buying gifts is inefficient, wouldn't a gift card—not quite as fungible as cash but also not nearly as coldhearted—be a perfect solution?

You could certainly make that case. And for the merchant, at least, the gift card is a godsend. Just think of it: In the weeks leading up to Christmas, millions of people visit your store or Web site and hand you billions of dollars in exchange for nothing more than a plastic I.O.U. that may never even be redeemed. Best Buy, for instance, earned $16 million last year in gift-card "breakage," which is the industry's term for card value that was bought but never redeemed. Then there's what retailers call "upspending": most customers who do use their gift cards spend some of their own money to buy merchandise that is more expensive than the value of the card.

For the giver, meanwhile, a gift card could hardly be easier. But most economists would argue that if a gift card is so transparently good for the giver, it is necessarily bad for the recipient: the fact that it can be bought so easily signals to the recipient that the giver didn't put much effort into the gift.

In the end, the value of any gift is overwhelmingly dependent on the nature of the relationship between giver and recipient. The economist Alex Tabarrok, writing recently on the Marginal Revolution blog, put an even finer point on this fact, noting that each of us has many "selves," including a "wild self," and that "we want the wild self in someone else to be wild about us." His advice? "If you want to please the economist in me, send me cash. If you want to please my wild self (you know who you are!), use your imagination."

So next year, if you need a gift for a strict rationalist, consider cash. If you want to appeal to someone's wild self, you'll have to use your imagination. And if you're hoping to send a little something extra to the shareholders of Best Buy or the Gap or Tiffany, consider a gift card.

FILLING IN THE TAX GAP
April 2, 2006

This is the time of year when American citizens inevitably think about the Internal Revenue Service and, also inevitably, about how deeply they hate it. But most people who hate the I.R.S. probably do so for the wrong reasons. They think it is a tough and cruel agency, but in fact it is not nearly as tough and cruel as it should be.

The first thing to remember is that the I.R.S. doesn't write the tax code. The agency is quick to point its finger at the true villain: "In the United States, the Congress passes tax laws and requires taxpayers to comply," its mission statement says. "The I.R.S. role is to help the large majority of compliant taxpayers with the tax law, while ensuring that the minority who are unwilling to comply pay their fair share."

So the I.R.S. is like a street cop or, more precisely, the biggest fleet of street cops in the world, who are asked to enforce laws written by a few hundred people on behalf of a few hundred million people, a great many of whom find these laws too complex, too expensive and unfair.

And yet most Americans say they are proud to pay their taxes. In an independent poll conducted last year for the I.R.S. Oversight

Board, 96 percent of the respondents agreed with the statement "It is every American's civic duty to pay their fair share of taxes," while 93 percent agreed that everyone "who cheats on their taxes should be held accountable." On the other hand, when asked what influences their decision to report and pay taxes honestly, 62 percent answered "fear of an audit," while 68 percent said it was the fact that their income was already being reported to the I.R.S. by third parties. For all the civic duty floating around, it would seem that most compliance is determined by good old-fashioned incentives.

So which of these incentives work and which do not? To find out, the I.R.S. conducted the National Research Program, a three-year study during which 46,000 randomly selected 2001 tax returns were intensively reviewed. (The I.R.S. doesn't specify what these 46,000 people were subjected to, but it may well have been the kind of inquisition that has earned the agency its horrid reputation.) Using this sample, the study found a tax gap—the difference between taxes owed and taxes actually paid—of $345 billion, or nearly one-fifth of all taxes collected by the I.R.S. This sum happens to be just a few billion dollars less than the projected federal budget deficit for 2007; it also amounts to more than $1,000 worth of cheating by every man, woman and child in the U.S.

But most people *aren't* cheating. And when you take a look at who does cheat and who doesn't, it becomes pretty clear just why people pay their taxes at all. The key statistic in the I.R.S.'s study is called the Net Misreporting Percentage. It measures the amount that was misreported on every major line item on those 46,000 returns. In the "wages, salaries, tips" category, for instance, Americans are underreporting only 1 percent of their actual income.

Meanwhile, in the "nonfarm proprietor income" category—think of self-employed workers like a restaurateur or the boss of a small construction crew—57 percent of the income goes unreported. That's $68 billion in unpaid taxes right there.

Why such a huge difference between the wage earner and a restaurateur? Simple: The only person reporting the restaurateur's income to the I.R.S. is the restaurateur himself; for the wage earner, his employer is generating a W2 to let the I.R.S. know exactly how much he has been paid. And the wage earner's taxes are automatically withheld from his every check, while the restaurateur has all year to decide if, and how much, he will pay.

Does this mean that the average self-employed worker is less honest than the average wage earner? Not necessarily. It's just that he has much more incentive to cheat. He knows that the only chance the I.R.S. has of learning his true income and expenditures is to audit him. And all he has to do is look at the I.R.S.'s infinitesimal audit rate—last year, the agency conducted face-to-face audits on just 0.19 percent of all individual taxpayers—to feel pretty confident to go ahead and cheat.

So why do people really pay their taxes: because it is the right thing to do, or because they fear getting caught if they don't? It sure seems to be the latter. A combination of good technology (employer reporting and withholding) and poor logic (most people who don't cheat radically overestimate their chances of being audited) makes the system work. And while it sounds bad to hear that Americans underpay their taxes by nearly one-fifth, the tax economist Joel Slemrod estimates that the U.S. is easily within the upper tier of worldwide compliance rates.

Still, unless you are personally cheating by one-fifth or more, you *should* be mad at the I.R.S.—not because it's too vigilant, but because it's not nearly vigilant enough. Why should you pay your fair share when the agency lets a few hundred billion dollars of other people's money go uncollected every year?

The I.R.S. itself would love to change this dynamic. In the past few years, it has increased significantly its enforcement revenue and its audit rate, despite a budget that is only fractionally larger. A main task of any I.R.S. commissioner is to beg Congress and the White House for resources. For all the obvious appeal of having the I.R.S. collect every dollar owed to the government, it is just as obviously unappealing for most politicians to advocate a more vigorous I.R.S. Michael Dukakis tried this during his 1988 presidential campaign, and—well, it didn't work.

Left to enforce a tax code no one likes upon a public that knows it can practically cheat at will, the I.R.S. does its best to fiddle around the edges. Once in a while, it hits pay dirt.

In the early 1980's, an I.R.S. research officer in Washington named John Szilagyi had seen enough random audits to know that some taxpayers were incorrectly claiming dependents for the sake of an exemption. Sometimes it was a genuine mistake (a divorced wife and husband making duplicate claims on their children), and sometimes the claims were comically fraudulent (Szilagyi recalls at least one dependent's name listed as Fluffy, who was quite obviously a pet rather than a child).

Szilagyi decided that the most efficient way to clean up this mess was to simply require taxpayers to list their children's Social Security numbers. "Initially, there was a lot of resistance to the idea," says Szilagyi, now 66 and retired to Florida. "The answer I got was that it was too much like '1984.'" The idea never made its way out of the agency.

A few years later, however, with Congress clamoring for more tax revenue, Szilagyi's idea was dug up, rushed forward and put into law for tax year 1986. When the returns started coming in the following April, Szilagyi recalls, he and his bosses were shocked: seven million dependents had suddenly vanished from the tax rolls, some incalculable combination of real pets and phantom children. Szilagyi's clever twist generated nearly $3 billion in revenues in a single year.

Szilagyi's immediate bosses felt he should get some kind of reward for his idea, but their superiors weren't convinced. So Szilagyi called his congressman, who got the reward process back on track. Finally, five years after his brainstorm became the law, Szilagyi, who earned about $80,000 annually at the time, was given a check for $25,000. By this point, his idea had generated roughly $14 billion.

Which suggests at least one legitimate reason to dislike the I.R.S.: if the agency hadn't been so stingy with Szilagyi's reward back then, it probably would have attracted a lot more of the anti-cheating wizards it really needs today.

LAID-BACK LABOR
May 6, 2007

During the late 19th century, piano manufacturing was one of New York City's largest industries. Every right-minded American family, it seemed, wanted to fill its home with music. The advent of the player piano—a music-making machine that required zero talent—drove the boom even further. By the 1920s, some 300,000 pianos were being sold in the United States each year, roughly two-thirds of them player pianos.

But a pair of newer technologies, the radio and the phonograph, soon began to drive the piano into a deep disfavor that continues to this day. Last year, Americans bought only 76,966 pianos. That's a decrease of 75 percent over a period in which the population more than doubled. As much as people may love music, most of them apparently don't feel the need to make it for themselves. According to Census Bureau statistics, only 7.3 percent of American adults have played a musical instrument in the past 12 months.

Compare this with the 17.5 percent of adults who currently engage in what the Census Bureau calls "cooking for fun." Or consider that 41 percent of households have flower gardens, 25 percent raise vegetables and 13 percent grow fruit trees—even though just 1 percent of Americans live on a farm today, down from 30 percent in 1920. On a more personal note: one of the authors of this column has a sister who runs a thriving yarn store, while the other is married to a knitting devotee who might buy $40 worth of yarn for a single scarf and then spend 10 hours knitting it. Even if her labor is valued at only $10 an hour, the scarf costs at least $140—or roughly $100 more than a similar machine-made scarf might cost.

Isn't it puzzling that so many middle-aged Americans are spending so much of their time and money performing menial labors when they don't have to? Just as the radio and phonograph proved to be powerful substitutes for the piano, the forces of technology and capitalism have greatly eased the burden of feeding and clothing ourselves. So what's with all the knitting, gardening and "cooking for fun"? Why do some forms of menial labor survive as hobbies while others have been killed off? (For instance, we can't think of a single person who, since the invention of the washing machine, practices "laundry for fun.")

Economists have been trying for decades to measure how much leisure time people have and how they spend it, but there has been precious little consensus. This is in part because it's hard to say what constitutes leisure and in part because measurements of leisure over the years have not been very consistent.

Economists typically separate our daily activities into three categories: market work (which produces income), home production (unpaid chores) and pure leisure. How, then, are we to categorize knitting, gardening and cooking? While preparing meals at home can certainly be much cheaper than dining out and therefore viewed as home production, what about the "cooking for fun" factor?

In an attempt to address such gray areas, the economists Valerie A. Ramey and Neville Francis classified certain home activities as labor and others as leisure. In their recent paper "A Century of Work and Leisure," they employed a 1985 time-use survey in which people ranked their enjoyment of various activities on a scale of 0 to 10. Knitting, gardening and cooking were in the middle of the scale, with a 7.7, 7.1 and 6.6, respectively. These ranked well behind the three favorite activities—sex, playing sports and fishing (which scored 9.3, 9.2 and 9.1)—but firmly ahead of paying bills, cleaning the house and, yes, doing the laundry (5.2, 4.9 and 4.8).

But here's where it gets tricky. Ramey and Francis decided that anything at or above a 7.3 is leisure, while anything below is home production. (Knitting, therefore, makes the grade as leisure; gardening and cooking do not.) This leads them to calculate that we spend less time doing market work today than we did in 1900 but more time in home production. Men, it seems, have contributed mightily to this upsurge: in 1920, employed men spent only two or three hours a week on home production, but they averaged 11 hours by 1965 and 16 hours by 2004.

But how many of those home-production hours are in fact leisure hours? This, it seems, is the real question here: What makes a certain activity work for one person and leisure for another?

With no disrespect toward Ramey and Francis, how about this for an alternative definition: Whether or not you're getting paid, it's work if someone else tells you to do it and leisure if you choose to do it yourself. If you are the sort of person who likes to mow his own lawn even though you can afford to pay someone to do it, consider how you'd react if your neighbor offered to pay you the going rate to mow his lawn. The odds are that you wouldn't accept his job offer.

And so a great many people who can afford not to perform menial labor choose to do so, because—well, why? An evolutionary biologist might say that embedded in our genes is a drive to feed and clothe ourselves and tame our surroundings. An economist, meanwhile, might argue that we respond to incentives that go well beyond the financial; and that, mercifully, we are left free to choose which tasks we want to do ourselves.

Granted, these choices may say a good bit about who we are and where we come from. One of us, for instance (the economist, who lives in Chicago), grew up comfortably in a Midwestern city and has fond memories of visiting his grandparents' small farm. This author recently bought an indoor hydroponic plant grower. It cost about $150 and to date has produced approximately 14 cherry tomatoes—which, once you factor in the cost of seeds, electricity and even a nominal wage for the labor, puts the average price of a single tomato at roughly $20.

The other one of us (the journalist, who lives in New York) grew up on a small farm and was regularly engaged in all sorts of sowing, mucking and reaping. He, therefore, has little vestigial desire to grow his own food—but he is happy to spend hours shopping for and preparing a special dinner for family and friends. Such dinners, even if the labor were valued at only $10 an hour, are more expensive than a commensurate takeout meal.

Maybe someday the New York guy will get to cook a meal with some of the Chicago guy's cherry tomatoes. Add in another $32 for next-day shipping, and it might become one of the most expensive meals in recent memory—and, surely, worth every penny.

A Q&A WITH THE AUTHORS

Author Q&A's have great potential but often fail because of the canned and bland questions fed to authors by their publishers — or, worse, the fawning questions invented by the authors themselves. (*Tell us, were you brilliant even as a child?*) So let's put an end to that! We asked readers of our blog, www.freakonomics.com, to ask us what they wanted to know. As you'll see, they responded with vigor.

Q: How does your collaboration work? —Ryan

A: In a word, easily. The two of us have very different skill sets. Levitt is an academic researcher and Dubner is a writer. That doesn't mean that Levitt doesn't write; he does. And Dubner does research too. But if you were to spend a day looking over our shoulders (Levitt's in Chicago and Dubner's in New York), you'd find that Levitt spends most of his day feeding numbers into a computer while Dubner spends most of his day feeding words. That said, the nature of our collaboration on a given day is dependent on the nature of the material we are working on. We e-mail back and forth voluminously; we talk on the phone so much that our wives roll their eyes. In sum, we are more like a pitcher and catcher on a baseball team than, say, a right wing and a left wing on a soccer team.

Q: Can you tell us about subjects that you researched but didn't write about, possibly because the data didn't tell you anything, it was too controversial, etc. I'd like to hear what was left behind on the editing room floor. —Mickey

A: If you think we would leave something out because it is too controversial, you obviously don't know us very well! Maybe you will be convinced after reading our second book, *SuperFreakonomics,* where we write about prostitutes, terrorists, global-warming hysterics, and profit-seeking oncologists. There are countless research projects for which we couldn't find the right data, or where the results just turned out not to be very interesting. For every 10 research ideas, only 2 will turn into academic papers and only 1 will be interesting enough for a book like this. Some readers assume that we can go out and answer any question we want, but it doesn't work that way. The downside is that all kinds of fascinating subjects have eluded our grasp (so far); the upside is that readers know the stories we *do* tell are supported by data rather than just opinion or whimsy.

Q: Am I worse off for never having read *Freakonomics?* —Terry

A: Sadly, yes. Independent testing has shown that people who read *Freakonomics* have sweeter-smelling breath, better posture, and more interesting dreams. Also, women feel no pain during childbirth; male readers find that their sperm swim faster.

Q: Are you more concerned with presenting the average citizen a new way of looking at the world or with stimulating debate among people who are familiar with economics and its methods of analysis? —Christopher Luccy

A: Well, the obvious answer would be "both." But if we had to choose one, it would surely be the former. There are a million books that explain the principles of economics, and they are widely read, usually at universities. But those books explain what economics *is;* they don't really explain how to look at the world like an economist. While this latter goal may sound like something you wouldn't wish on your worst enemy, it can in fact be made bearable—as long you cover topics that the average reader is passionate about. Sumo wrestling, for instance.

Q: How much of the book's success do you believe can be attributed to your choice of title?

A: Levitt's sister, Linda Jines, came up with the title; she is the real creative genius in the family. It's hard to know how important the title has been, but our guess is ... *very.* On the other hand, as we write in the book, the name you give your child has no discernible effect on that child's life outcome. So should we expect the same from a book title? Perhaps not; a book and a person have different qualities. Still, it's worth noting that some commercial ventures have succeeded wildly despite having names that, at first, must have seemed a detriment. Do you really think the first producers of *Oprah* had an easy time with that name? And what about ESPN?

Q: Are there any baseball stats that, when compared over a period of time or based on age, show a strong suspicion of steroid use? —Joseph Rollo

A: We've looked in the data for evidence of steroid use, as have well-known baseball statisticians like Nate Silver (who is even better-known as the proprietor of FiveThirtyEight.com). It has proven hard to find anything that looks like the smoking gun that we see on teacher cheating or sumo wrestling. At this point, what's most likely is that the effects of steroids on a baseball player's performance just aren't that stark. Sure, they get mighty beefy while taking steroids, but a lot of the power hitters were hitting home runs even when they were scrawny rookies.

Q: Tell us about the criticism you have received from traditional/academic colleagues over *Freakonomics.*—J. Plain

A: Levitt's academic colleagues tend to react in one of two ways. The majority of economists thought about it like economists: the success of *Freakonomics* probably increased the number of students wanting to take economics courses, and since the supply of economics teachers is fixed in the short run, the wages of academic economists should rise. That makes economists happy. A second group of economists decided that if Levitt could write a book that people would read, surely they could too. So there has been a flurry of "popular" books by economists—some good, some not so good. And then, inevitably, there are a handful of economists who feel that he violated the secret handshake of economics by showing the outside world that what economists do really isn't that hard or complex. They will never forgive him.

Q: What will a gallon of gas cost in 2019? What implications will this price have on our culture? —Mike Thomas

A: Economists, like everyone else, are terrible at predicting the future. But in all likelihood, a gallon of gas in 2019 will cost about the same (when adjusted for inflation) as a gallon of gas in 2009. Even if we are running out of oil (which we probably aren't), we won't be running out that soon. Perhaps the government will have the good sense to put larger taxes on gasoline, which we've advocated for a long time because of what economists call the negative externalities of driving.

Q: What do bishops and tennis professionals have in common? —Stan

A: Comfortable shoes, unusual headgear, and a lot of love.

Q: Of the examples discussed in the book, which have gained the greatest traction in the popular/political discussion? —Rick Groves

A: There has been a lot of talk about the relationship between legalized abortion and the crime rate. And some governments have cited the low wages of street-level drug dealers as an incentive to young people to go legit. But on a day-to-day level, the part of the book that's probably spurred the most *change* is our discussion of real-estate agents. The standard fixed-commission, full-service Realtor model is gradually melting away. Even the White House weighed in, with the Real Estate Settlement Procedures Act, which is meant to increase transparency between Realtors and their customers.

Q: Why do you think that the U.S. Mint is still producing pennies if the cost of physically producing a penny is much greater than the value of the resulting penny? —Dutch

A: Don't get us started! Dubner has by now become a well-known penny hawk, telling anyone who will listen—including *60 Minutes*—that the penny is a beloved artifact that should finally be put out of its misery. It represents a massive waste of time and resources. One of its strongest supporters is the zinc lobby; did you know that modern pennies happen to be made of 97.5 percent zinc? The biggest reasons to keep the penny are inertia and nostalgia, but those aren't very good reasons. Dubner counsels his children to avoid pennies at all costs, even throwing them away if necessary. For this, he has been called un-American.

Q: Why are there so few economists in politics, as it is one of the most important issues in a country? Is it that they'd rather become professors, work in the private sector, become advisers or work in the Treasury, or do they think it is too compromising? —Neil

A: You ask an intriguing and important question. Many countries around the world have elected economists as president. In the U.S., however, economists generally do not fit into the political framework well. Why? One guess is that they are trained to think rationally and tell the truth about data. As any observer of U.S. politics knows, rationality and unvarnished data are practically forbidden on the campaign trail. Politicians (and, presumably, voters) are much more interested in emotion and rhetoric. That said, some administrations (Obama's, for one) hold economists in far higher regard than others.

Q: Who would win an arm-wrestling match between Dubner and Levitt? Golf? Tennis? Chess? —Kevin

A: Dubner would definitely win arm-wrestling, Levitt would win golf. Tennis and chess would probably be hard-fought matches. Note: they are both quite good bowlers.

Q: Some people buy a book because it is interesting and well written and some people buy a book because others are reading it. To what extent do you think the success of *Freakonomics* is due to the latter rather than the former? —Euclid

A: We have wondered the same. Books being what they are— not just stories and information, but stories and information *that people like to talk about with other people*—there is obviously an extra incentive to read what everyone else is reading. Our opinion is that of all the modes of book promotion (ads, reviews, interviews, etc.), none is so powerful as good word-of-mouth.

Q: What do you guys like to read (recreationally)? —Robb

A: Levitt admits to having the reading interests of a tweener girl, the *Twilight* series and *Harry Potter* in particular. Dubner's weak spot is sports, and newspapers (the old-fashioned kind, on paper).

Q: While many of the stories and conclusions in *Freakonomics* are fascinating, there seems to be no clear methodology or set of principles that profit-maximizing executives can use in managing their business. Have you ever considered distilling the lessons (such as they are) into a handbook for the manager interested in exploiting the "hidden side" of business? —Drew

A: Drew, have you considered becoming a literary agent? (Also, we admire your ability to simultaneously flatter and condemn.) Here are the facts. For reasons that remain unclear, our publisher initially called *Freakonomics* a business book. This led to certain expectations—nearly all of which, surely, were dashed the moment any credible businessperson read the book. You are right: we do not lay out any profitable methodologies at all. That said, in recent years Levitt has done a lot of research in the business arena, which we feel may someday yield a good book that does indeed explore the "hidden side" of business.

Q: How much is all the tea in China really worth? —Dave F.

A: About $1.5 billion. But just imagine how much more valuable it would be if, like marijuana, it were illegal. (Note to selves: corner the market on Chinese tea, then bribe the government to criminalize it.)

The bulk of this book was drawn from the research of Steven D. Levitt, often done in concert with one or more collaborators. The notes below include citations for the academic papers on which the material was based; most of them are available for download at http://pricetheory.uchicago.edu/levitt/ LevittCV.html. We have also made liberal use of other scholars' research, which is cited below; we thank them not only for their work but for the subsequent conversations that allowed us to best present their ideas. Other material in this book comes from previously unpublished research or interviews by one or both of the authors. Material not listed in these notes was generally drawn from readily accessible databases, news reports, and reference works.

AN EXPLANATORY NOTE

XXI THE ITALICIZED EXCERPT originally appeared in Stephen J. Dubner, "The Probability That a Real-Estate Agent Is Cheating You (and Other Riddles of Modern Life)," *The New York Times Magazine*, August 3, 2003.

INTRODUCTION: THE HIDDEN SIDE OF EVERYTHING

1–5   THE FALL AND FALL OF CRIME: The crime-drop argument can be found in Steven D. Levitt, "Understanding Why Crime Fell in the 1990's: Four Factors That Explain the Decline and Six That Do Not," *Journal of Economic Perspectives* 18, no. 1 (2004), pp. 163–90. / **1–2 The superpredator:** See Eric Pooley, "Kids with Guns," *New York Magazine,* August 9, 1991; John J. DiIulio Jr., "The Coming of the Super-Predators," *Weekly Standard,* November 27, 1995; Tom Morganthau, "The Lull Before the Storm?" *Newsweek,* December 4, 1995; Richard Zoglin, "Now for the Bad News: A Teenage Time Bomb," *Time,* January 15, 1996; and Ted Gest, "Crime Time Bomb," *U.S. News & World Report,* March 25, 1996. / **2 James Alan Fox's dire predictions** can be found in a pair of government reports: "Trends in Juvenile Violence: A Report to the United States Attorney General on Current and Future Rates of Juvenile Offending" (Washington, D.C.: Bureau of Justice Statistics, 1996) and "Trends in Juvenile Violence: An Update" (Washington, D.C.: Bureau of Justice Statistics, 1997). / **2 President Clinton's fearful comment** came during a 1997 speech in Boston announcing new anti-crime measures; see Alison Mitchell, "Clinton Urges Campaign Against Youth Crime," *The New York Times,* February 20, 1997. / **3–4 The story of Norma McCorvey/Jane Roe:** See Douglas S. Wood, "Who Is 'Jane Roe'?: Anonymous No More, Norma McCorvey No Longer Supports Abortion Rights," CNN.com, June 18, 2003; and Norma McCorvey with Andy Meisler, *I Am Roe: My Life,* Roe v. Wade, *and Freedom of Choice* (New York: HarperCollins, 1994). / **4–5 The abortion-crime link** is laid out in John J. Donohue III and Steven D. Levitt, "The Impact of Legalized Abortion on Crime," *Quarterly Journal of Economics* 116, no. 2 (2001), pp. 379–420. Other scholars have had disagreements with portions of the theory. See Ted Joyce, "Did Legalized Abortion Lower Crime?" *Journal of Human Resources* 39, no. 1 (2004), pp. 1–28; and the Donohue-Levitt response, "Further Evidence That Legalized Abortion Lowered Crime: A Response to Joyce," *Journal of Human Resources* 39, no. 1 (2004), pp. 29–49. See also Christopher L. Foote and Christopher F. Goetz, "Testing Economic Hypotheses with State-Level Data: A Comment on Donohue and Levitt (2001)," Federal Reserve Bank of Boston working paper 05–15 (2005); and, again, the Donohue-Levitt response, "Measurement Error, Legalized Abortion, the Decline in Crime: A Response to Foote and Goetz (2005)," National Bureau of Economic Research working paper, 2006.

5–8   THE REAL REAL-ESTATE STORY: The study measuring how a real-estate agent treats the sale of her own home versus a client's home is Steven D. Levitt and Chad Syverson, "Market Distortions When Agents Are Better Informed: A Theoretical and Empirical Exploration of the Value of Information in Real Estate Transactions," National Bureau of Economic Research working paper, 2005. / **6 The lax California auto mechanics** are discussed in Thomas Hubbard, "An Empirical Examination of Moral Hazard in the Vehicle Inspection Market," *RAND Journal of Economics* 29, no. 1 (1998), pp. 406–26; and in Thomas Hubbard, "How Do Consumers Motivate Experts? Reputational Incentives in an Auto Repair Market," *Journal of Law & Economics* 45, no. 2 (2002), pp. 437–68. / **6 Doctors who perform extra C-sections** are examined in Jonathan Gruber and Maria Owings, "Physician Financial Incentives and Caesarean Section Delivery," *RAND Journal of Economics* 27, no. 1 (1996), pp. 99–123.

8–11   THE MYTH OF CAMPAIGN SPENDING is told in greater detail in a trio of papers: Steven D. Levitt, "Using Repeat Challengers to Estimate the Effect of Campaign Spending on Election Outcomes in the U.S. House," *Journal of Political Economy,* August 1994, pp. 777–98; Steven D. Levitt, "Congressional Campaign Finance Reform," *Journal of Economic Perspectives* 9 (1995), pp. 183–93; and Steven D. Levitt and James M. Snyder Jr., "The Impact of Federal Spending on House Election Outcomes," *Journal of Political Economy* 105, no. 1 (1997), pp. 30–53.

12   EIGHT GLASSES OF WATER A DAY: See Robert J. Davis, "Can Water Aid Weight Loss?" *The Wall Street Journal,* March 16, 2004, which cites an Institute of Medicine report concluding that "there is no scientific basis for the recommendation [of eight glasses of water a day] and that most people get enough water through normal consumption of foods and beverages."

13–14 ADAM SMITH is still well worth reading, of course (especially if you have infinite patience); so too is Robert Heilbroner's *The Worldly Philosophers* (New York: Simon & Schuster, 1953), which contains memorable profiles of Smith, Karl Marx, Thorstein Veblen, John Maynard Keynes, Joseph Schumpeter, and other giants of economics.

1. WHAT DO SCHOOLTEACHERS AND SUMO WRESTLERS HAVE IN COMMON?

15–16 THE ISRAELI DAY-CARE STUDY: See Uri Gneezy and Aldo Rustichini, "A Fine Is a Price," *Journal of Legal Studies* 29, no. 1 (January 2000), pp. 1–17; and Uri Gneezy, "The 'W' Effect of Incentives," University of Chicago working paper.

18–19 MURDER THROUGH THE AGES: See Manuel Eisner, "Secular Trends of Violence, Evidence, and Theoretical Interpretations," *Crime and Justice: A Review of Research* 3 (2003); also presented in Manuel Eisner, "Violence and the Rise of Modern Society," *Criminology in Cambridge*, October 2003, pp. 3–7.

20 THOMAS JEFFERSON ON CAUSE AND EFFECT: *Autobiography of Thomas Jefferson* (1829; reprint, New York: G. P. Putnam's Sons, 1914), p. 156.

20–21 BLOOD FOR MONEY: See Richard M. Titmuss, "The Gift of Blood," *Trans-action* 8 (1971); also presented in *The Philosophy of Welfare: Selected Writings by R. M. Titmuss*, ed. B. Abel-Smith and K. Titmuss (London: Allen and Unwin, 1987). See also William E. Upton, "Altruism, Attribution, and Intrinsic Motivation in the Recruitment of Blood Donors," Ph.D. diss., Cornell University, 1973.

22 WHEN SEVEN MILLION CHILDREN DISAPPEARED OVERNIGHT: See Jeffrey Liebman, "Who Are the Ineligible EITC Recipients?" *National Tax Journal* 53 (2000), pp. 1165–86. Liebman's paper was citing John Szilagyi, "Where Some of Those Dependents Went," *1990 Research Conference Report: How Do We Affect Taxpayer Behavior?* (Internal Revenue Service, March 1991), pp. 162–63.

22–35 CHEATING TEACHERS IN CHICAGO: This study, which also provides considerable background on high-stakes testing, is detailed in two papers: Brian A. Jacob and Steven D. Levitt, "Rotten Apples: An Investigation of the Prevalence and Predictors of Teacher Cheating," *Quarterly Journal of Economics* 118, no. 3 (2003), pp. 843–77; and

Brian A. Jacob and Steven D. Levitt, "Catching Cheating Teachers: The Results of an Unusual Experiment in Implementing Theory," *Brookings-Wharton Papers on Urban Affairs,* 2003, pp. 185–209. / **24 The Oakland fifth-grader with the extra-helpful teacher:** Based on an author interview with a former assistant superintendent of the Oakland Public Schools. / **32 Cheating among North Carolina teachers:** See G. H. Gay, "Standardized Tests: Irregularities in Administering of Tests Affect Test Results," *Journal of Instructional Psychology* 17, no. 2 (1990), pp. 93–103. / **33–35 The story of Arne Duncan, CEO of the Chicago schools,** was based largely on author interviews; see also Amy D'Orio, "The Outsider Comes In," *District Administration: The Magazine for K–12 Education Leaders,* August 2002; and various *Chicago Tribune* articles by Ray Quintanilla.

35–36 THE UNIVERSITY OF GEORGIA BASKETBALL TEST was made public when the university released 1,500 pages of documents in response to an investigation by the National Collegiate Athletic Association.

37 THE CHICAGO BLACK SOX: Several readers of the original version of *Freakonomics* have declared that the White Sox came to be called the Black Sox not because of the gambling scandal, but for another reason entirely. This is how the explanation plays out on the user-generated encyclopedia wikipedia.org: "The term 'Black Sox' came about earlier in [1919], when [team owner Charles] Comiskey decided to make players pay for their own laundry. The players stopped doing their laundry in protest, and as their white stockings became soiled and dark, the writers tagged them with that nickname." As endearing as this explanation may seem, Levitt and Dubner found no support for it in the historical record.

38–43 CHEATING IN SUMO: See Mark Duggan and Steven D. Levitt, "Winning Isn't Everything: Corruption in Sumo Wrestling," *American Economic Review* 92, no. 5 (December 2002), pp. 1594–1605. / **38–39 There is a lot to know about sumo,** and quite a bit can be found in these books: Mina Hall, *The Big Book of Sumo* (Berkeley, Calif.: Stonebridge Press, 1997); Keisuke Itai, *Nakabon* (Tokyo: Shogakkan Press, 2000); and Onaruto, *Yaocho* (Tokyo: Line Books, 2000). / **42–43 Two sumo whistle-blowers die mysteriously:** See Sheryl WuDunn, "Sumo Wrestlers (They're BIG) Facing a Hard Fall," *The New York Times,* June 28, 1996; and Anthony Spaeth, "Sumo Quake:

Japan's Revered Sport Is Marred by Charges of Tax Evasion, Match Fixing, Ties to Organized Crime, and Two Mysterious Deaths," reporting by Irene M. Kunii and Hiroki Tashiro, *Time* (International Edition), September 30, 1996.

44   THE BAGEL MAN: Paul Feldman was looking for a research economist to take an interest in his data, and brought himself to Steven Levitt's attention. (Several other scholars had passed.) Levitt and then Dubner subsequently visited Feldman's bagel operation near Washington, D.C. Their research led to an article that was substantially similar to the version of the story published here: Stephen J. Dubner and Steven D. Levitt, "What the Bagel Man Saw," *The New York Times Magazine,* June 6, 2004. Levitt has also written an academic paper about Feldman's bagel operation: "An Economist Sells Bagels: A Case Study in Profit Maximization," National Bureau of Economic Research working paper, 2006. / **46** *The "Beer on the Beach" study* is discussed in Richard H. Thaler, "Mental Accounting and Consumer Choice," Marketing Science 4 (Summer 1985), pp. 119–214; also worth reading is Richard H. Thaler, *The Winner's Curse: Paradoxes and Anomalies of Economic Life* (New York: Free Press, 1992).

2. HOW IS THE KU KLUX KLAN LIKE A GROUP OF REAL-ESTATE AGENTS?

51–62   SPILLING THE KLAN'S SECRETS: This section has been substantially revised since the original version of *Freakonomics* was published, owing to the authors' discovery that Stetson Kennedy—in both his memoir, *The Klan Unmasked,* and in interviews with the authors—had misrepresented his role in personally infiltrating and attacking the Klan. (See page 240 ["Hoodwinked?" *The New York Times,* January 8, 2006] for a fuller explanation of this issue.) For general Klan history, see Col. Winfield Jones, *Knights of the Ku Klux Klan* (1941); David M. Chalmers, *Hooded Americanism: The First Century of the Ku Klux Klan, 1865–1965* (Garden City, NY: Doubleday, 1965); Wyn Craig Wade, *The Fiery Cross: The Ku Klux Klan in America* (New York: Simon & Schuster, 1987); and many others. The most relevant writings of Stetson Kennedy include *Southern Exposure* (Garden City, NY: Doubleday, 1946; republished in 1991 by Florida Atlantic

University Press) and *The Klan Unmasked* (Boca Raton: Florida Atlantic University Press, 1990), which was originally published as *I Rode with the Ku Klux Klan* (London: Arco Publishers, 1954). Also helpful was Ben Green, *Before His Time: The Untold Story of Harry T. Moore, America's First Civil Rights Martyr* (New York: Simon & Schuster, 1999). Stetson Kennedy's documents relating to the Klan, as well as the reports of "John Brown" and other related material, can be found in various archives, including the Schomburg Center for Research in Black Culture, a public library in New York City; the Georgia State University Library in Atlanta; and the archives of the Anti-Defamation League in New York City. Transcripts of the Drew Pearson *Washington Merry-Go-Round* radio program can be found at http://www.aladin.wrlc.org/gsdl/collect/pearson/pearson.shtml.

62–63 **WHAT HAPPENED TO TERM-LIFE RATES?** See Jeffrey R. Brown and Austan Goolsbee, "Does the Internet Make Markets More Competitive? Evidence from the Life Insurance Industry," *Journal of Political Economy* 110, no. 3 (June 2002), pp. 481–507.

63 **SUPREME COURT JUSTICE LOUIS D. BRANDEIS** writing that "Sunlight is said to be the best of disinfectants": See Louis D. Brandeis, *Other People's Money—and How Bankers Use It* (New York: Frederick A. Stokes, 1914).

63–64 **THE BRAND-NEW USED-CAR CONUNDRUM:** This thesis, and indeed much of what we think today about "asymmetric information," stems from a paper that George A. Akerlof wrote during his first year as an assistant professor at Berkeley in 1966–67. It was rejected three times—two of the journals told Akerlof that they "did not publish papers on topics of such triviality," as he later recalled—before being published as George A. Akerlof, "The Market for 'Lemons': Quality Uncertainty and the Market Mechanism," *Quarterly Journal of Economics*, August 1970. Some thirty years later, the paper won Akerlof the Nobel Prize in Economics; he is widely considered the nicest man to have ever won the award.

66–67 **THE ENRON TAPES:** As of this writing, the tapes could be heard on http://www.cbsnews.com/stories/2004/06/01/eveningnews/main6_20626.shtml. See also Richard A. Oppel Jr., "Enron Traders on

Grandma Millie and Making Out Like Bandits," *The New York Times*, June 13, 2004.

67   ARE ANGIOPLASTIES NECESSARY? See Gina Kolata, "New Heart Studies Question the Value of Opening Arteries," *The New York Times*, March 21, 2004.

68–73   THE REAL REAL-ESTATE STORY, REVISITED: See Steven D. Levitt and Chad Syverson, "Market Distortions When Agents Are Better Informed: A Theoretical and Empirical Exploration of the Value of Information in Real-Estate Transactions," National Bureau of Economic Research working paper, 2005.

74   TRENT LOTT, NOT-SO-SECRET SEGREGATIONIST? The circumstances surrounding Lott's damaging comments are well summarized in Dan Goodgame and Karen Tumulty, "Lott: Tripped Up by History," Time.com/cnn.com, December 16, 2002.

74–77   THE WEAKEST LINK: See Steven D. Levitt, "Testing Theories of Discrimination: Evidence from *The Weakest Link*," *Journal of Law and Economics* 17 (October 2004), pp. 431–52. / **76 The theory of taste-based discrimination** originates with Gary S. Becker, *The Economics of Discrimination* (Chicago: University of Chicago Press, 1957). / **77 The theory of information-based discrimination** is derived from a number of papers, including Edmund Phelps, "A Statistical Theory of Racism and Sexism," *American Economic Review* 62, no. 4 (1972), pp. 659–61; and Kenneth Arrow, "The Theory of Discrimination," *Discrimination in Labor Markets,* ed. Orley Ashenfelter and Albert Rees (Princeton, N.J.: Princeton University Press, 1973).

77–82   THE ONLINE DATING STORY: See Günter J. Hitsch, Ali Hortaçsu, and Dan Ariely, "What Makes You Click: An Empirical Analysis of Online Dating," University of Chicago working paper, 2005.

82   VOTERS LYING ABOUT DINKINS / GIULIANI: See Timur Kuran, *Private Truths, Public Lies: The Social Consequences of Preference Falsification* (Cambridge, Mass.: Harvard University Press, 1995); also Kevin Sack, "Governor Joins Dinkins Attack Against Rival," *The New York Times,* October 27, 1989; and Sam Roberts, "Uncertainty over Polls Clouds Strategy in Mayor Race," *The New York Times,* October 31, 1989.

82–83 **VOTERS LYING ABOUT DAVID DUKE:** See Kuran, *Private Truths, Public Lies;* also Peter Applebome, "Republican Quits Louisiana Race in Effort to Defeat Ex-Klansman," *The New York Times,* October 5, 1990; and Peter Applebome, "Racial Politics in South's Contests: Hot Wind of Hate or Last Gasp?" *The New York Times,* November 5, 1990.

83 **DAVID DUKE, MASTER OF INFORMATION ABUSE:** Among the many helpful sources for this material were Karen Henderson, "David Duke's Work-Release Program," *National Public Radio,* May 14, 2004; and the exhaustive John McQuaid, "Duke's Decline," *New Orleans Times-Picayune,* April 13, 2003.

3. WHY DO DRUG DEALERS STILL LIVE WITH THEIR MOMS?

85–86 **JOHN KENNETH GALBRAITH'S "CONVENTIONAL WISDOM":** See "The Concept of the Conventional Wisdom," the second chapter of *The Affluent Society* (Boston: Houghton Mifflin, 1958).

86–87 **MITCH SNYDER AND THE HOMELESS MILLIONS:** The controversy over Snyder's activism was covered widely, particularly in Colorado newspapers, during the early 1980s and was revisited in 1990 when Snyder committed suicide. A good overview is provided in Gary S. Becker and Guity Nashat Becker, "How the Homeless 'Crisis' Was Hyped," in *The Economics of Life* (New York: McGraw-Hill, 1997), pp. 175–76; the chapter was adapted from a 1994 *Business Week* article by the same authors.

87 **THE INVENTION OF CHRONIC HALITOSIS:** The strange and compelling story of Listerine is beautifully told in James B. Twitchell, *Twenty Ads That Shook the World: The Century's Most Groundbreaking Advertising and How It Changed Us All* (New York: Crown, 2000), pp. 60–69.

87–88 **GEORGE W. BUSH AS A MAKE-BELIEVE COWBOY:** See Paul Krugman, "New Year's Resolutions," *The New York Times,* December 26, 2003.

88 **NOT AS MUCH RAPE AS IS COMMONLY THOUGHT:** The 2002 statistics from the National Crime Survey, which is designed to elicit honest responses, suggests that the lifetime risk of a woman's being the

victim of unwanted sexual activity or attempted unwanted sexual activity is about one in eight (not one in three, as is typically argued by advocates). For men, the National Crime Survey suggests a one-in-forty incidence, rather than the one-in-nine incidence cited by advocates.

88–89 NOT AS MUCH CRIME AS THERE ACTUALLY WAS: See Mark Niesse, "Report Says Atlanta Underreported Crimes to Help Land 1996 Olympics," Associated Press, February 20, 2004.

89– SUDHIR VENKATESH'S LONG, STRANGE TRIP INTO THE CRACK DEN: As
106 of this writing, Venkatesh is a professor of sociology and African American studies at Columbia University. /**89–90 The biographical material** on Venkatesh was drawn largely from author interviews; see also Jordan Marsh, "The Gang Way," *Chicago Reader,* August 8, 1997; and Robert L. Kaiser, "The Science of Fitting In," *Chicago Tribune,* December 10, 2000. / **91–95 The particulars of the crack gang** are covered in four papers by Sudhir Alladi Venkatesh and Steven D. Levitt: "The Financial Activities of an Urban Street Gang," *Quarterly Journal of Economics* 115, no. 3 (August 2000), pp. 755–89; " 'Are We a Family or a Business?' History and Disjuncture in the Urban American Street Gang," *Theory and Society* 29 (Autumn 2000), pp. 427–62; "Growing Up in the Projects: The Economic Lives of a Cohort of Men Who Came of Age in Chicago Public Housing," *American Economic Review* 91, no. 2 (2001), pp. 79–84; and "The Political Economy of an American Street Gang," American Bar Foundation working paper, 1998. See also Sudhir Alladi Venkatesh, *American Project: The Rise and Fall of a Modern Ghetto* (Cambridge, Mass.: Harvard University Press, 2000). / **101 Crack dealing as the most dangerous job in America:** According to the Bureau of Labor Statistics, the ten most dangerous legitimate occupations are timber cutters, fishers, pilots and navigators, structural metal workers, drivers/sales workers, roofers, electrical power installers, farm occupations, construction laborers, and truck drivers.

107 THE INVENTION OF NYLON STOCKINGS: It was Wallace Carothers, a young Iowa-born chemist employed by DuPont, who, after seven years of trying, found a way to blow liquid polymers through tiny nozzles to create a fiber of superstrong strands. This was nylon. Several years later, DuPont introduced nylon stockings in New York

and London. Contrary to lore, the miracle fabric's name did not derive from a combination of those two cities' names. Nor was it, as rumored, an acronym for "Now You've Lost, Old Nippon," a snub to Japan's dominant silk market. The name was actually a hepped-up rendering of "No Run," a slogan that the new stockings could not in fact uphold, but whose failure hardly diminished their success. Carothers, a longtime depressive, did not live to see his invention blossom: he killed himself in 1937 by drinking cyanide. See Matthew E. Hermes, *Enough for One Lifetime: Wallace Carothers, Inventor of Nylon* (Philadelphia: Chemical Heritage Foundation, 1996).

108   CRACK SLANG: The Greater Dallas Council on Alcohol and Drug Abuse has compiled an extraordinarily entertaining index of cocaine street names. For cocaine powder: Badrock, Bazooka, Beam, Berni, Bernice, Big C, Blast, Blizzard, Blow, Blunt, Bouncing Powder, Bump, C, Caballo, Caine, Candy, Caviar, Charlie, Chicken Scratch, Coca, Cocktail, Coconut, Coke, Cola, Damablanca, Dust, Flake, Flex, Florida Snow, Foo Foo, Freeze, G-Rock, Girl, Goofball, Happy Dust, Happy Powder, Happy Trails, Heaven, King, Lady, Lady Caine, Late Night, Line, Mama Coca, Marching Dust/Powder, Mojo, Monster, Mujer, Nieve, Nose, Nose Candy, P-Dogs, Peruvian, Powder, Press, Prime Time, Rush, Shot, Sleighride, Sniff, Snort, Snow, Snowbirds, Soda, Speedball, Sporting, Stardust, Sugar, Sweet Stuff, Toke, Trails, White Lady, White Powder, Yeyo, Zip. For smokeable cocaine: Base, Ball, Beat, Bisquits, Bones, Boost, Boulders, Brick, Bump, Cakes, Casper, Chalk, Cookies, Crumbs, Cubes, Fatbags, Freebase, Gravel, Hardball, Hell, Kibbles 'n Bits, Kryptonite, Love, Moonrocks, Nuggets, Onion, Pebbles, Piedras, Piece, Ready Rock, Roca, Rock(s), Rock Star, Scotty, Scrabble, Smoke House, Stones, Teeth, Tornado.

109   THE JOHNNY APPLESEED OF CRACK: Oscar Danilo Blandon and his purported alliance with the Central Intelligence Agency are discussed in great detail, and in a manner that stirred great controversy, in a three-part *San Jose Mercury News* series by Gary Webb, beginning on August 18, 1996. See also Tim Golden, "Though Evidence Is Thin, Tale of C.I.A. and Drugs Has a Life of Its Own," *The New York Times*, October 21, 1996; and Gary Webb, *Dark Alliance: The CIA, the Contras, and the Crack Cocaine Explosion* (New York:

Seven Stories Press, 1998). The U.S. Department of Justice later examined the matter in detail in "The C.I.A.–Contra–Crack Cocaine Controversy: A Review of the Justice Department's Investigations and Prosecutions," available as of this writing at www.usdoj.gov/oig/special/9712/ch01p1.htm.

109 GANGS IN AMERICA: See Frederick Thrasher, *The Gang* (Chicago: University of Chicago Press, 1927).

111 THE SHRINKING OF VARIOUS BLACK-WHITE GAPS, PRE-CRACK: See Rebecca Blank, "An Overview of Social and Economic Trends by Race," in *America Becoming: Racial Trends and Their Consequences,* ed. Neil J. Smelser, William Julius Wilson, and Faith Mitchell (Washington, D.C.: National Academy Press, 2001), pp. 21–40. / **111–12 Regarding black infant mortality,** see Douglas V. Almond, Kenneth Y. Chay, and Michael Greenstone, "Civil Rights, the War on Poverty, and Black-White Convergence in Infant Mortality in Mississippi," National Bureau of Economic Research working paper, 2003.

111–12 THE VARIOUS DESTRUCTIVE EFFECTS OF CRACK are discussed in Roland G. Fryer Jr., Paul Heaton, Steven D. Levitt, and Kevin Murphy, "The Impact of Crack Cocaine," University of Chicago working paper, 2005.

4. WHERE HAVE ALL THE CRIMINALS GONE?

115–17 NICOLAE CEAUŞESCU'S ABORTION BAN: Background information on Romania and the Ceauşescus was drawn from a variety of sources, including "Eastern Europe, the Third Communism," *Time,* March 18, 1966; "Ceauşescu Ruled with an Iron Grip," *The Washington Post,* December 26, 1989; Ralph Blumenthal, "The Ceauşescus: 24 Years of Fierce Repression, Isolation and Independence," *The New York Times,* December 26, 1989; Serge Schmemann, "In Cradle of Rumanian Revolt, Anger Quickly Overcame Fear," *The New York Times,* December 30, 1989; Karen Breslau, "Overplanned Parenthood: Ceauşescu's Cruel Law," *Newsweek,* January 22, 1990; and Nicolas Holman, "The Economic Legacy of Ceauşescu," *Student Economic Review,* 1994. / **116 The link between the Romanian abortion ban and life outcomes** has been explored in a pair of papers: Cristian Pop-Eleches, "The Impact of an Abortion Ban on Socio-Economic

Outcomes of Children: Evidence from Romania," Columbia University working paper, 2002; and Cristian Pop-Eleches, "The Supply of Birth Control Methods, Education and Fertility: Evidence from Romania," Columbia University working paper, 2002.

117–19 THE GREAT AMERICAN CRIME DROP: As noted earlier, this material is drawn from Steven D. Levitt, "Understanding Why Crime Fell in the 1990's: Four Factors That Explain the Decline and Six That Do Not," *Journal of Economic Perspectives* 18, no. 1 (2004), pp. 163–90. / **118 James Alan Fox's "intentional overstatement":** See Torsten Ove, "No Simple Solution for Solving Violent Crimes," *Pittsburgh Post-Gazette,* September 12, 1999.

121 POLITICIANS WERE GROWING INCREASINGLY SOFTER ON CRIME: This and a number of related issues are discussed in Gary S. Becker and Guity Nashat Becker, "Stiffer Jail Terms Will Make Gunmen More Gun-Shy," "How to Tackle Crime? Take a Tough, Head-On Stance," and "The Economic Approach to Fighting Crime," all in *The Economics of Life* (New York: McGraw-Hill, 1997), pp. 135–44; the chapters were adapted from *Business Week* articles by the same authors.

120 INCREASED RELIANCE ON PRISONS: Concerning the fifteenfold increase in drug-crime prisoners, see Ilyana Kuziemko and Steven D. Levitt, "An Empirical Analysis of Imprisoning Drug Offenders," *Journal of Public Economics* 88, nos. 9–10 (2004), pp. 2043–66. / **121–22 What if we just turn all the prisoners loose?** See William Nagel, "On Behalf of a Moratorium on Prison Construction," *Crime and Delinquency* 23 (1977), pp. 152–74. / **122 "Apparently, it takes a Ph.D. . . .":** See John J. DiIulio Jr., "Arresting Ideas: Tougher Law Enforcement Is Driving Down Urban Crime," *Policy Review,* no. 75 (Fall 1995).

122–24 CAPITAL PUNISHMENT: For a full report on New York State's failure to execute a single criminal, see "Capital Punishment in New York State: Statistics from Eight Years of Representation, 1995–2003" (New York: The Capital Defender Office, August 2003), which is available as of this writing at nycdo.org/8yr.html. More recently, New York's Court of Appeals found the death penalty itself unconstitutional, effectively halting all executions. / **123 Executing 1 criminal** translates into 7 fewer homicides: See Isaac Ehrlich, "The Deterrent Effect of Capital Punishment: A Question of Life and Death," *American Economic Review* 65 (1975), pp. 397–417; and Isaac Ehrlich, "Capital Punishment and Deterrence: Some Further Thoughts and Evidence," *Journal of Political Economy* 85 (1977), pp. 741–88. / **124 "I no longer shall tinker with the machinery of death":** From Justice Harry A. Blackmun's dissenting opinion in a 1994 Supreme Court decision denying review of a Texas death-penalty case: *Callins v. Collins,* 510 U.S. 1141 (1994); cited in *Congressional Quarterly Researcher* 5, no. 9 (March 10, 1995). It should be noted that American juries also seem to have lost their appetite for the death penalty—in part, it seems, because of the frequency with which innocent people have been executed in recent years or exonerated while on death row. During the 1990s, an average of 290 criminals were given the death sentence each year; in the first four years of the 2000s, that number had dropped to 174. See Adam Liptak, "Fewer Death Sentences Being Imposed in U.S.," *The New York Times*, September 15, 2004.

124– **DO POLICE ACTUALLY LOWER CRIME?** See Steven D. Levitt, "Using
25 Electoral Cycles in Police Hiring to Estimate the Effect of Police on Crime," *American Economic Review* 87, no. 3 (1997), pp. 270–90; Steven D. Levitt, "Why Do Increased Arrest Rates Appear to Reduce Crime: Deterrence, Incapacitation, or Measurement Error?" *Economic Inquiry* 36, no. 3 (1998), pp. 353–72; and Steven D. Levitt, "The Response of Crime Reporting Behavior to Changes in the Size of the Police Force: Implications for Studies of Police Effectiveness Using Reported Crime Data," *Journal of Quantitative Criminology* 14 (February 1998), pp. 62–81. / **125 The 1960s as a great time to be a criminal:** See Gary S. Becker and Guity Nashat Becker, *The Economics of Life* (New York: McGraw-Hill, 1997), pp. 142–43.

126– **NEW YORK CITY'S CRIME "MIRACLE":** The "Athenian period" quote
29 came from an author interview with former police captain William J. Gorta, one of CompStat's inventors. / **127 The broken window theory:** See James Q. Wilson and George L. Kelling, "Broken Windows: The Police and Neighborhood Safety," *Atlantic Monthly,* March 1982. / **129 Bratton hiring more police in Los Angeles:** See Terry McCarthy, "The Gang Buster," *Time,* January 19, 2004.

130– **GUN LAWS:** Concerning the fact that the United States has more
33 guns than it has adults, see Philip Cook and Jens Ludwig, *Guns in America: Results of a Comprehensive Survey of Gun Ownership and Use* (Washington, D.C.: Police Foundation, 1996). / **131 The gun-crime link:** See Mark Duggan, "More Guns, More Crime," *Journal of Political Economy* 109, no. 5 (2001), pp. 1086–1114. / **131 Guns in Switzerland:** See Stephen P. Halbrook, "Armed to the Teeth, and Free," *The Wall Street Journal Europe,* June 4, 1999. / **131 The impotent Brady Act:** See Jens Ludwig and Philip Cook, "Homicide and Suicide Rates Associated with Implementation of the Brady Handgun Violence Prevention Act," *Journal of the American Medical Association* 284, no. 5 (2000), pp. 585–91. / **132 Felons buying black-market guns:** See James D. Wright and Peter H. Rossi, *Armed and Considered Dangerous: A Survey of Felons and Their Firearms* (Hawthorne, N.Y.: Aldine de Gruyter, 1986). / **132 The gun-for-psychotherapy swap:** See "Wise Climb-Down, Bad Veto," *Los Angeles Times,* October 5, 1994. / **132 Why gun buybacks don't work:** See C. Callahan, F. Rivera, and T. Koepsell, "Money for Guns: Evaluation of the Seattle Gun Buy-Back Program," *Public Health Reports* 109, no. 4 (1994), pp. 472–77; David Kennedy, Anne Piehl, and Anthony Braga, "Youth Violence in Boston: Gun Markets, Serious Youth Offenders, and a Use-Reduction Strategy," *Law and Contemporary Problems* 59 (1996), pp. 147–83; and Peter Reuter and Jenny Mouzon, "Australia: A Massive Buyback of Low-Risk Guns," in *Evaluating Gun Policy: Effects on Crime and Violence,* ed. Jens Ludwig and Philip Cook (Washington, D.C.: Brookings Institution, 2003). / **133 John Lott's right-to-carry theory:** See John R. Lott Jr. and David Mustard, "Right-to-Carry Concealed Guns and the Importance of Deterrence," *Journal of Legal Studies* 26 (January 1997), pp. 1–68; and John R. Lott Jr., *More Guns, Less Crime: Understanding Crime and Gun Control Laws* (Chicago: University of Chicago Press, 1998). / **133 John Lott as Mary Rosh:** See Julian Sanchez, "The Mystery of Mary Rosh," *Reason,* May 2003; and Richard Morin, "Scholar Invents Fan to Answer His Critics," *The Washington Post,* February 1, 2003. / **133 Lott's gun theory disproved:** See Ian Ayres and John J. Donohue III, "Shooting Down the 'More Guns, Less Crime' Hypothesis," *Stanford Law Review* 55 (2003), pp. 1193–1312; and Mark

Duggan, "More Guns, More Crime," *Journal of Political Economy* 109, no. 5 (2001), pp. 1086–1114.

134–
35
THE BURSTING OF THE CRACK BUBBLE: For a discussion of crack's history and particulars, see Roland G. Fryer Jr., Paul Heaton, Steven Levitt, and Kevin Murphy, "The Impact of Crack Cocaine," University of Chicago working paper, 2005. / **134 More than 25 percent of homicides:** See Paul J. Goldstein, Henry H. Brownstein, Patrick J. Ryan, and Patricia A. Bellucci, "Crack and Homicide in New York City: A Case Study in the Epidemiology of Violence," in *Crack in America: Demon Drugs and Social Justice*, ed. Craig Reinarman and Harry G. Levine (Berkeley: University of California Press, 1997), pp. 113–30.

135–
36
THE "AGING POPULATION" THEORY: See Steven D. Levitt, "The Limited Role of Changing Age Structure in Explaining Aggregate Crime Rates," *Criminology* 37, no. 3 (1999), pp. 581–99. Although the aging theory has by now been widely discounted, learned experts continue to float it; see Matthew L. Wald, "Most Crimes of Violence and Property Hover at 30-Year Low," *The New York Times*, September 13, 2004, in which Lawrence A. Greenfield, director of the Bureau of Justice Statistics, says, "There is probably no single factor explanation for why the crime rates have been going down all these years and are now at the lowest level since we started measuring them in 1973. It probably has to do with demographics, and it probably has to do with having a lot of very high-rate offenders behind bars." / **135 "There lurks a cloud":** See James Q. Wilson, "Crime and Public Policy," in *Crime*, ed. James Q. Wilson and Joan Petersilia (San Francisco: ICS Press, 1995), p. 507.

136–
44
THE ABORTION-CRIME LINK: For an overview, see John J. Donohue III and Steven D. Levitt, "The Impact of Legalized Abortion on Crime," *Quarterly Journal of Economics* 116, no. 2 (2001), pp. 379–420; and John J. Donohue III and Steven D. Levitt, "Further Evidence That Legalized Abortion Lowered Crime: A Response to Joyce," *Journal of Human Resources* 39, no. 1 (2004), pp. 29–49. / **136 Abortion studies in Eastern Europe and Scandinavia:** See P. K. Dagg, "The Psychological Sequelae of Therapeutic Abortion—Denied and Completed," *American Journal of Psychiatry* 148, no. 5 (May 1991), pp. 578–85; and Henry David, Zdenek Dytrych, et al., *Born Unwanted: Developmental*

Effects of Denied Abortion (New York: Springer, 1988). / **137 The *Roe v.
Wade* opinion:** *Roe v. Wade*, 410 U.S. 113 (1973). / **138–39 One study
has shown that the typical child:** See Jonathan Gruber, Philip P.
Levine, and Douglas Staiger, "Abortion Legalization and Child Liv-
ing Circumstances: Who Is the 'Marginal Child'?" *Quarterly Journal
of Economics* 114 (1999), pp. 263–91. / **139 Strongest predictors of
a criminal future:** See Rolf Loeber and Magda Stouthamer-Loeber,
"Family Factors as Correlates and Predictors of Juvenile Conduct
Problems and Delinquency," *Crime and Justice*, vol. 7, ed. Michael
Tonry and Norval Morris (Chicago: University of Chicago Press,
1986); also, Robert Sampson and John Laub, *Crime in the Making:
Pathways and Turning Points Through Life* (Cambridge, Mass.: Har-
vard University Press, 1993). / **139 So does having a teenage mother:**
See William S. Comanor and Llad Phillips, "The Impact of Income
and Family Structure on Delinquency," University of California–
Santa Barbara working paper, 1999. / **139 Another study has shown
that low maternal education:** Pirkko Räsänen et al., "Maternal
Smoking During Pregnancy and Risk of Criminal Behavior Among
Adult Male Offspring in the Northern Finland 1966 Birth Cohort,"
American Journal of Psychiatry 156 (1999), pp. 857–62. / **139 Infan-
ticide fell dramatically:** See Susan Sorenson, Douglas Wiebe, and
Richard Berk, "Legalized Abortion and the Homicide of Young
Children: An Empirical Investigation," *Analyses of Social Issues and
Public Policy* 2, no. 1 (2002), pp. 239–56. / **141–42 Studies of Aus-
tralia and Canada:** See Anindya Sen, "Does Increased Abortion Lead
to Lower Crime? Evaluating the Relationship between Crime, Abor-
tion, and Fertility," unpublished manuscript; and Andrew Leigh and
Justin Wolfers, "Abortion and Crime," *AQ: Journal of Contemporary
Analysis* 72, no. 4 (2000), pp. 28–30. / **142 Many of the aborted
baby girls:** See John J. Donohue III, Jeffrey Grogger, and Steven D.
Levitt, "The Impact of Legalized Abortion on Teen Childbearing,"
University of Chicago working paper, 2002. / **142 Abortion worse
than slavery:** See Michael S. Paulsen, "Accusing Justice: Some Varia-
tions on the Themes of Robert M. Cover's *Justice Accused*," *Journal of
Law and Religion* 7, no. 33 (1989), pp. 33–97. / **143 Abortion as "the
only effective crime-prevention device":** See Anthony V. Bouza,
*The Police Mystique: An Insider's Look at Cops, Crime, and the Criminal
Justice System* (New York: Plenum, 1990). / **143 $9 million to save a**

spotted owl: See Gardner M. Brown and Jason F. Shogren, "Economics of the Endangered Species Act," *Journal of Economic Perspectives* 12, no. 3 (1998), pp. 3–20. / **143 $31 to prevent another *Exxon Valdez*–type spill:** See Glenn W. Harrison, "Assessing Damages for the Exxon Valdez Oil Spill," University of Central Florida working paper, 2004. / **144 Body-part price list:** Drawn from the state of Connecticut's Workers' Compensation Information Packet, p. 27, available as of this writing at wcc.state.ct.us/download/acrobat/info-packet.pdf.

5. WHAT MAKES A PERFECT PARENT?

147   THE EVER CHANGING WISDOM OF PARENTING EXPERTS: Ann Hulbert, *Raising America: Experts, Parents, and a Century of Advice About Children* (New York: Knopf, 2003), is an extremely helpful compendium of parenting advice. / **148 Gary Ezzo's "infant-management strategy" and sleep deprivation warning:** See Gary Ezzo and Robert Bucknam, *On Becoming Babywise* (Sisters, Ore.: Multnomah, 1995), pp. 32 and 53. / **148 T. Berry Brazelton and the "interactive" child:** T. Berry Brazelton, *Infants and Mothers: Difference in Development,* rev. ed. (New York: Delta/Seymour Lawrence, 1983), p. xxiii. / **148 L. Emmett Holt's warning against "undue stimulation":** L. Emmett Holt, *The Happy Baby* (New York: Dodd, Mead, 1924), p. 7. / **148 Crying as "the baby's exercise":** L. Emmett Holt, *The Care and Feeding of Children: A Catechism for the Use of Mothers and Children's Nurses* (New York: Appleton, 1894), p. 53.

149   A GUN OR A SWIMMING POOL? See Steven Levitt, "Pools More Dangerous than Guns," *Chicago Sun-Times*, July 28, 2001.

150–
54   PETER SANDMAN ON MAD-COW DISEASE AND OTHER RISKS: See Amanda Hesser, "Squeaky Clean? Not Even Close," *The New York Times*, January 28, 2004; and "The Peter Sandman Risk Communication Web Site," at http://www.psandman.com/index.htm.

154   HOW MUCH DO PARENTS REALLY MATTER? See Judith Rich Harris, *The Nurture Assumption: Why Children Turn Out the Way They Do* (New York: Free Press, 1998); for a Harris profile that also provides an excellent review of the nature-nurture debate, see Malcolm Gladwell, "Do Parents Matter?" *The New Yorker*, August 17, 1998;

and Carol Tavris, "Peer Pressure," *New York Times Book Review*, September 13, 1998. / **155 " 'Here we go again' ":** See Tavris, "Peer Pressure." / **155–56 Pinker called Harris's views "mind-boggling":** Steven Pinker, "Sibling Rivalry: Why the Nature/Nurture Debate Won't Go Away," *Boston Globe*, October 13, 2002, adapted from Steven Pinker, *The Blank Slate: The Modern Denial of Human Nature* (New York: Viking, 2002).

158–
61
SCHOOL CHOICE IN CHICAGO: This material is drawn from Julie Berry Cullen, Brian Jacob, and Steven D. Levitt, "The Impact of School Choice on Student Outcomes: An Analysis of the Chicago Public Schools," *Journal of Public Economics*, forthcoming; and Julie Berry Cullen, Brian Jacob, and Steven D. Levitt, "The Effect of School Choice on Student Outcomes: Evidence from Randomized Lotteries," National Bureau of Economic Research working paper, 2003.

160–
61
STUDENTS WHO ARRIVE AT HIGH SCHOOL NOT PREPARED TO DO HIGH SCHOOL WORK: See Tamar Lewin, "More Students Passing Regents, but Achievement Gap Persists," *The New York Times*, March 18, 2004.

161
THE BLACK-WHITE INCOME GAP TRACED TO EIGHTH-GRADE TEST SCORE GAP: See Derek Neal and William R. Johnson, "The Role of Pre-Market Factors in Black-White Wage Differences," *Journal of Political Economy* 104 (1996), pp. 869–95; and June O'Neill, "The Role of Human Capital in Earnings Differences Between Black and White Men," *Journal of Economic Perspectives* 4, no. 4 (1990), pp. 25–46. / **161 "Reducing the black-white test score gap":** See Christopher Jencks and Meredith Phillips, "America's Next Achievement Test: Closing the Black-White Test Score Gap," *American Prospect* 40 (September–October 1998), pp. 44–53.

161–
62
"ACTING WHITE": See David Austen-Smith and Roland G. Fryer Jr., "The Economics of 'Acting White,' " National Bureau of Economic Research working paper, 2003. / **161–62 Kareem Abdul-Jabbar:** Kareem Abdul-Jabbar and Peter Knobler, *Giant Steps* (New York: Bantam, 1983), p. 16.

162–
68
THE BLACK-WHITE TEST SCORE GAP AND THE ECLS: This material was drawn from Roland G. Fryer Jr. and Steven D. Levitt, "Understanding the Black-White Test Score Gap in the First Two Years of School,"

Review of Economics and Statistics 86, no. 2 (2004), pp. 447–64. While this paper contains little discussion of the correlation between test scores and home-based factors (television viewing, spanking, etc.), a regression of those data is included in the paper's appendix. Regarding the ECLS study itself: as of this writing, an overview of the study was posted at nces.ed.gov/ecls/.

173 ADOPTIVE PARENTS WITH HIGHER IQS THAN BIRTH MOTHER: See Bruce Sacerdote, "The Nature and Nurture of Economic Outcomes," National Bureau of Economic Research working paper, 2000.

174 FINNISH LITERACY: See Lizette Alvarez, "Educators Flocking to Finland, Land of Literate Children," *The New York Times*, April 9, 2004.

176 A BOOK FOR EVERY TOT: See John Keilman, "Governor Wants Books for Tots; Kids Would Get 60 by Age 5 in Effort to Boost Literacy," *Chicago Tribune*, January 12, 2004.

178–79 THE INFLUENCE OF ADOPTIVE PARENTS: See Sacerdote, "The Nature and Nurture of Economic Outcomes."

6. PERFECT PARENTING, PART II; OR: WOULD A ROSHANDA BY ANY OTHER NAME SMELL AS SWEET?

181–82 THE STORY OF LOSER LANE: Drawn from author interviews and from Sean Gardiner, "Winner and Loser: Names Don't Decide Destiny," *Newsday,* July 22, 2002.

182–83 THE JUDGE AND THE TEMPTRESS: Based on author interviews.

184–85 ROLAND G. FRYER AND THE STUDY OF BLACK UNDERACHIEVEMENT: Drawn from author interviews.

185 THE BLACK-WHITE CIGARETTE GAP: See Lloyd Johnston, Patrick O'Malley, Jerald Bachman, and John Schulenberg, "Cigarette Brand Preferences Among Adolescents," *Monitoring the Future Occasional Paper* 45, Institute for Social Research, University of Michigan, 1999.

185–88 BLACK NAMES (AND OTHER BLACK-WHITE CULTURE GAPS): See Roland G. Fryer Jr. and Steven D. Levitt, "The Causes and Consequences of

Distinctively Black Names," *Quarterly Journal of Economics* 119, no. 3 (August 2004), pp. 767–805.

189–90 **"WHITE" RÉSUMÉS BEATING OUT "BLACK" RÉSUMÉS:** The most recent audit study to reach such a conclusion is Marianne Bertrand and Sendhil Mullainathan, "Are Emily and Greg More Employable than Lakisha and Jamal? A Field Experiment Evidence on Labor Market Discrimination," National Bureau of Economic Research working paper, 2003.

190 **YO XING HEYNO AUGUSTUS EISNER ALEXANDER WEISER KNUCKLES JEREMIJENKO-CONLEY:** See Tara Bahrampour, "A Boy Named Yo, Etc.: Name Changes, Both Practical and Fanciful, Are on the Rise," *The New York Times,* September 25, 2003.

190 **MICHAEL GOLDBERG, INDIAN-BORN SIKH:** See Robert F. Worth, "Livery Driver Is Wounded in a Shooting," *New York Times,* February 9, 2004.

190 **WILLIAM MORRIS, NÉ ZELMAN MOSES:** Author interview with Alan Kannof, former chief operating officer of the William Morris Agency.

192 **BRAND NAMES AS FIRST NAMES:** Drawn from California birth-certificate data and also discussed in Stephanie Kang, "Naming the Baby: Parents Brand Their Tot with What's Hot," *The Wall Street Journal,* December 26, 2003.

193 **A GIRL NAMED SHITHEAD:** The woman who called the radio show to tell Roland Fryer about her niece Shithead might have been misinformed, of course, or even outright lying. Regardless, she was hardly alone in her feeling that black names sometimes go too far. Bill Cosby, during a speech in May 2004 at the NAACP's *Brown v. Board of Education* fiftieth-anniversary gala, lambasted lower-income blacks for a variety of self-destructive behaviors, including the giving of "ghetto" names. Cosby was summarily excoriated by white and black critics alike. (See Barbara Ehrenreich, "The New Cosby Kids," *The New York Times,* July 8, 2004; and Debra Dickerson, "America's Granddad Gets Ornery," *Slate,* July 13, 2004.) Soon after, the California education secretary, Richard Riordan—the wealthy, white former mayor of Los Angeles—found himself under attack for a per-

ceived racial slight. (See Tim Rutten, "Riordan Stung by 'Gotcha' News," *Los Angeles Times*, July 10, 2004.) Riordan, visiting a Santa Barbara library to promote a reading program, met a six-year-old girl named Isis. She told Riordan that her name meant "Egyptian princess"; Riordan, trying to make a joke, replied, "It means stupid, dirty girl." The resultant outrage led black activists to call for Riordan's resignation. Mervyn Dymally, a black assemblyman from Compton, explained that Isis was "a little African-American girl. Would he have done that to a white girl?" As it turned out, however, Isis *was* white. Some activists tried to keep the anti-Riordan protest alive, but Isis's mother, Trinity, encouraged everyone to relax. Her daughter, she explained, hadn't taken Riordan's joke seriously. "I got the impression," Trinity said, "that she didn't think he was very bright."

199   A MUCH LONGER LIST OF GIRLS' AND BOYS' NAMES: Here lies an arbitrary collection of names that are interesting, pretty, uncommon, very common, or somehow quintessential, along with the level of education that they signify. (Each name occurs at least ten times in the California names data.)

SOME GIRLS' NAMES
(YEARS OF MOTHER'S EDUCATION IN PARENTHESES)

Abigail (14.72), Adelaide (15.33), Alessandra (15.19), Alexandra (14.67), Alice (14.30), Alison (14.82), Allison (14.54), Amalia (15.25), Amanda (13.30), Amber (12.64), Amy (14.09), Anabelle (14.68), Anastasia (13.98), Angelina (12.74), Annabel (15.40), Anne (15.49), Anya (14.97), Ashley (12.89), Autumn (12.86), Ava (14.97), Aziza (11.52), Bailey (13.83), Beatrice (14.74), Beatriz (11.42), Belinda (12.79), Betty (11.50), Breanna (12.71), Britt (15.39), Brittany (12.87), Bronte (14.42), Brooklyn (13.50), Brooklynne (13.10), Caitlin (14.36), Caitlynn (13.03), Cammie (12.00), Campbell (15.69), Carly (14.25), Carmella (14.25), Cassandra (13.38), Cassidy (13.86), Cate (15.23), Cathleen (14.31), Cecilia (14.36), Chanel (13.00), Charisma (13.85), Charlotte (14.98), Chastity* (10.66), Cherokee (11.86), Chloe (14.52), Christina (13.59), Ciara (13.40), Cierra (12.97), Cordelia (15.19), Courtney (13.55), Crimson (11.53), Cynthia (12.79), Dahlia (14.94), Danielle

---

* Concerning the teenage girl named Temptress on p. 183: judging from Chastity's poor showing here, it is doubtful that Temptress would have gained much benefit from being called Chastity.

(13.69), Daphne (14.42), Darlene (12.22), Dawn (12.71), Deborah (13.70), December (12.00), Delilah (13.00), Denise (12.71), Deniz (15.27), Desiree (12.62), Destiny (11.65), Diamond (11.70), Diana (13.54), Diane (14.10), Dora (14.31), Eden (14.41), Eileen (14.69), Ekaterina (15.09), Elizabeth (14.25), Elizabethann (12.46), Ella (15.30), Ellen (15.17), Emerald (13.17), Emily (14.17), Emma (15.23), Faith (13.39), Florence (14.83), Francesca (14.80), Frankie (12.52), Franziska (15.18), Gabrielle (14.26), Gennifer (14.75), Georgia (14.82), Geraldine (11.83), Ginger (13.54), Grace (15.03), Gracie (13.81), Gretchen (14.91), Gwyneth (15.04), Haley (13.84), Halle (14.86), Hannah (14.44), Hilary (14.59), Hillary (13.94), Ilana (15.83), Ilene (13.59), Indigo (14.38), Isabel (15.31), Isabell (13.50), Ivy (13.43), Jacquelin (12.78), Jacqueline (14.40), Jade (13.04), Jamie (13.52), Jane (15.12), Janet (12.94), Jeanette (13.43), Jeannette (13.86), Jemma (15.04), Jennifer (13.77), Johanna (14.76), Jordan (13.85), Joyce (12.80), Juliet (14.96), Kailey (13.76), Kara (13.95), Karissa (13.05), Kate (15.23), Katelynne (12.65), Katherine (14.95), Kayla (12.96), Kelsey (14.17), Kendra (13.63), Kennedy (14.17), Kimia (15.66), Kylie (13.83), Laci (12.41), Ladonna (11.60), Lauren (14.58), Leah (14.30), Lenora (13.26), Lexington (13.44), Lexus (12.55), Liberty (13.36), Liesl (15.42), Lily (14.84), Linda (12.76), Linden (15.94), Lizabeth (13.42), Lizbeth (9.66), Lucia (13.59), Lucille (14.76), Lucy (15.01), Lydia (14.40), MacKenzie (14.44), Madeline (15.12), Madison (14.13), Mandy (13.00), Mara (15.33), Margaret (15.14), Mariah (13.00), Mary (14.20), Matisse (15.36), Maya (15.26), Meadow (12.65), Megan (13.99), Melanie (13.90), Meredith (15.57), Michaela (14.13), Micheala (12.95), Millicent (14.61), Molly (14.84), Montana (13.70), Naomi (14.05), Naseem (15.23), Natalie (14.58), Nevada (14.61), Nicole (13.77), Nora (14.88), Olive (15.64), Olivia (14.79), Paige (14.04), Paisley (13.84), Paris (13.71), Patience (11.80), Pearl (13.48), Penelope (14.53), Phoebe (15.18), Phoenix (13.28), Phyllis (11.93), Portia (15.03), Precious (11.30), Quinn (15.20), Rachel (14.51), Rachell (11.76), Rebecca (14.05), Renee (13.79), Rhiannon (13.16), Rikki (12.54), Ronnie (12.72), Rosalind (15.26), Ruby (14.26), Sabrina (13.31), Sadie (13.69), Samantha (13.37), Sarah (14.16), Sasha (14.22), Sayeh (15.25), Scarlett (13.60), Selma (12.78), September (12.80), Shannon (14.11), Shayla (12.77), Shayna (14.00), Shelby (13.42), Sherri (12.32), Shira (15.60), Shirley (12.49), Simone (14.96), Siobhan (14.88), Skylynn (12.61), Solveig (14.36), Sophie (15.45), Stacy (13.08), Stephanie (13.45), Stevie (12.67), Storm (12.31), Sunshine (12.03), Susan (13.73), Suzanne (14.37), Svetlana (11.65), Tabitha (12.49), Talia (15.27), Tallulah (14.88), Tatiana (14.42), Tatum (14.25),

Taylor (13.65), Tess (14.83), Tia (12.93), Tiffany (12.49), Tracy (13.50), Trinity (12.60), Trudy (14.88), Vanessa (12.94), Venus (12.73), Veronica (13.83), Veronique (15.80), Violet (13.72), Whitney (13.79), Willow (13.83), Yael (15.55), Yasmine (14.10), Yvonne (13.02), and Zoe (15.03).

SOME BOYS' NAMES
(YEARS OF MOTHER'S EDUCATION IN PARENTHESES)

Aaron (13.74), Abdelrahman (14.08), Ace (12.39), Adam (14.07), Aidan (15.35), Alexander (14.49), Alistair (15.34), Andrew (14.19), Aristotle (14.20), Ashley (12.95), Atticus (14.97), Baylor (14.84), Bjorn (15.12), Blane (13.55), Blue (13.85), Brian (13.92), Buck (12.81), Bud (12.21), Buddy (11.95), Caleb (13.91), Callum (15.20), Carter (14.98), Chaim (14.63), Christ (11.50), Christian (13.55), Clyde (12.94), Cooper (14.96), Dakota (12.92), Daniel (14.01), Dashiell (15.26), David (13.77), Deniz (15.65), Dylan (13.58), Eamon (15.39), Elton (12.23), Emil (14.05), Eric (14.02), Finn (15.87), Forrest (13.75), Franklin (13.55), Gabriel (14.39), Gary (12.56), Giancarlo (15.05), Giuseppe (13.24), Graydon (15.51), Gustavo (11.68), Hashem (12.76), Hugh (14.60), Hugo (13.00), Idean (14.35), Indiana (13.80), Isaiah (13.12), Jackson (15.22), Jacob (13.76), Jagger (13.27), Jamieson (15.13), Jedidiah (14.06), Jeffrey (13.88), Jeremy (13.46), Jesus (8.71), Jihad (11.60), Johan (15.11), John-Paul (14.22), Jonathan (13.86), Jordan (13.73), Jorge (10.49), Joshua (13.49), Josiah (13.98), Jules (15.48), Justice (12.45), Kai (14.85), Keanu (13.17), Keller (15.07), Kevin (14.03), Kieron (14.00), Kobe (13.12), Kramer (14.80), Kurt (14.33), Lachlan (15.60), Lars (15.09), Leo (14.76), Lev (14.35), Lincoln (14.87), Lonny (11.93), Luca (13.56), Malcolm (14.80), Marvin (11.86), Max (14.93), Maximilian (15.17), Michael (13.66), Michelangelo (15.58), Miro (15.00), Mohammad (12.45), Moises (9.69), Moses (13.11), Moshe (14.41), Muhammad (13.21), Mustafa (13.85), Nathaniel (14.13), Nicholas (14.02), Noah (14.45), Norman (12.90), Oliver (15.14), Orlando (12.72), Otto (13.73), Parker (14.69), Parsa (15.22), Patrick (14.25), Paul (14.13), Peter (15.00), Philip (14.82), Philippe (15.61), Phoenix (13.08), Presley (12.68), Quentin (13.84), Ralph (13.45), Raphael (14.63), Reagan (14.92), Rex (13.77), Rexford (14.89), Rocco (13.68), Rocky (11.47), Roland (13.95), Romain (15.69), Royce (13.73), Russell (13.68), Ryan (14.04), Sage (13.63), Saleh (10.15), Satchel (15.52), Schuyler (14.73), Sean (14.12), Sequoia (13.15), Sergei (14.28), Sergio (11.92), Shawn (12.72), Shelby (12.88), Simon (14.74), Slater (14.62), Solomon (14.20), Spencer (14.53), Stephen (14.01), Stetson (12.90), Steven (13.31), Tanner (13.82), Tariq (13.16), Tennyson (15.63), Terence

(14.36), Terry (12.16), Thaddeus (14.56), Theodore (14.61), Thomas (14.08), Timothy (13.58), Toby (13.24), Trace (14.09), Trevor (13.89), Tristan (13.95), Troy (13.52), Ulysses (14.25), Uriel (15.00), Valentino (12.25), Virgil (11.87), Vladimir (13.37), Walker (14.75), Whitney (15.58), Willem (15.38), William (14.17), Willie (12.12), Winston (15.07), Xavier (13.37), Yasser (14.25), Zachary (14.02), Zachory (11.92), Zane (13.93), and Zebulon (15.00).

202   **MOST POPULAR WHITE GIRL NAMES, 1960 AND 2000:** The California names data actually begin in 1961, but the year-to-year difference is negligible.

204   **SHIRLEY TEMPLE AS SYMPTOM, NOT CAUSE:** See Stanley Lieberson, *A Matter of Taste: How Names, Fashions, and Culture Change* (New Haven, Conn.: Yale University Press, 2000). A Harvard sociologist, Lieberson is the acknowledged master of (among other subjects) the academic study of names. For instance, *A Matter of Taste* details how, from 1960, it was American Jewish families who first popularized many girls' names (Amy, Danielle, Erica, Jennifer, Jessica, Melissa, Rachel, Rebecca, Sarah, Stacy, Stephanie, Tracy) while only a handful (Ashley, Kelly, and Kimberly) began in non-Jewish families. Another good discussion of naming habits can be found in Peggy Orenstein, "Where Have All the Lisas Gone?" *The New York Times Magazine*, July 6, 2003; if only for entertainment, see *The Sweetest Sound* (2001), Alan Berliner's documentary film about names; and for an excellent visual overview of how any given name waxes and wanes in popularity, see http://babynamewizard.com/namevoyager/lnv0105.html.

204–5   **BOYS' NAMES BECOMING GIRLS' NAMES (BUT NOT VICE VERSA):** This observation is drawn from the work of Cleveland Kent Evans, a psychologist and onomastician at Bellevue University in Bellevue, Nebraska. A sample of Evans's work is available as of this writing at academic.bellevue.edu/~CKEvans/cevans.html; see also Cleveland Kent Evans, *Unusual & Most Popular Baby Names* (Lincolnwood, Ill.: Publications International/Signet, 1994); and Cleveland Kent Evans, *The Ultimate Baby Name Book* (Lincolnwood, Ill.: Publications International/Plume, 1997).

Epilogue: Two Paths to Harvard

210–11 THE WHITE BOY WHO GREW UP OUTSIDE CHICAGO: This passage, as well as the earlier passage about the same boy on pp. 156–57, was drawn from author interviews and from Ted Kaczynski, "Truth Versus Lies," unpublished manuscript, 1998; see also Stephen J. Dubner, "I Don't Want to Live Long. I Would Rather Get the Death Penalty than Spend the Rest of My Life in Prison," *Time*, October 18, 1999.

210–11 THE BLACK BOY FROM DAYTONA BEACH: This passage, as well as the earlier passage about the same boy on p. 157, was drawn from author interviews with Roland G. Fryer Jr.

ACKNOWLEDGMENTS

Jointly, we would like to thank two people who helped nurture this book: Claire Wachtel of William Morrow and Suzanne Gluck of the William Morris Agency. This is the third book that Stephen Dubner has written under their auspices; he continues to be grateful and, on occasion, awestruck. This was the first such book for Steven Levitt; he has been duly impressed. Many thanks also to the talented and supportive colleagues in each shop: Jane Friedman, Michael Morrison, Cathy Hemming, Lisa Gallagher, Debbie Stier, Dee Dee De Bartlo, George Bick, Brian McSharry, Jennifer Pooley, Kevin Callahan, Trent Duffy, and many others at William Morrow; Tracy Fisher, Raffaella DeAngelis, Karen Gerwin, Erin Malone, Georgia Cool, Candace Finn, Andy McNicol, and many others at the William Morris Agency. We would also like to thank the various subjects of this book (especially Stetson Kennedy, Paul Feldman, Sudhir Venkatesh, Arne Duncan, and Roland Fryer) for their time and trouble. Thanks also to the friends and colleagues who helped improve the manuscript, including Melanie Thernstrom, Lisa Chase, and Colin Camerer. And to Linda Jines, who came up with the title: nicely done.

Personal Acknowledgments

I owe an enormous debt to my many co-authors and colleagues, whose great ideas fill this book, and to all the kind people who have taken the time to teach me what I know about economics and life. I am especially grateful to the University of Chicago, whose Becker Center on Chicago Price Theory provides me the ideal research home; and also to the American Bar Foundation for its collegiality and support. My wife, Jeannette, and our children, Amanda, Olivia, Nicholas, and Sophie, make every day a joy, even though we miss Andrew so much. I thank my parents, who showed me it was okay to be different. Most of all, I want to thank my good friend and co-author Stephen Dubner, who is a brilliant writer and a creative genius.

—S. D. L.

I have yet to write a book that did not germinate, or was not at least brought along, in the pages of the *The New York Times Magazine*. This one is no exception. For that I thank Hugo Lindgren, Adam Moss, and Gerry Marzorati; also, thanks to Vera Titunik and Paul Tough for inviting the Bagel Man into the *Magazine*'s pages. I am most grateful to Steven Levitt, who is so clever and wise and even kind as to make me wish—well, almost—that I had become an economist myself. Now I know why half the profession dreams of having an adjoining office to Levitt. And finally, as always, thanks and love to Ellen, Solomon, and Anya. See you at dinnertime.

—S. J. D.

of schoolteachers, 23–24, 32,
264
social, 17–18, 267
study, 23
tinkering with, 16, 20
trade-offs inherent in, 20
for voting, 238–42
infanticide, 139
information:
abuse of, 65–74, 82–83,
86–89
assumption of, 63–65
asymmetric, 63–65, 73, 234,
238
dissemination of, 63, 65, 87
expert, 65–74, 86–89
false, 66, 69, 78–79, 81–82,
86–89
media and, 87–88, 89
in personal ads, 77–82
power of, 61–63
recording of, xxv, 11, 45–48,
66–67, 94–102, 106
secret, 59–60, 63, 65–66
withholding and editing of,
73–74, 77–82
see also data
insider trading, 21, 65–66
Internal Revenue Service (IRS),
22, 251–55
Oversight Board of, 251–52
Internet, 12–13, 62–66, 73,
224–25
comparative shopping on,
62–63, 65, 73

information as currency of,
65
see also dating, online
intuition, xxv, 217
Iowa Test of Basic Skills, 23
Iraq:
U.S. invasion of, 88
weapons of mass destruction
and, 88, 149
I Rode With the Ku Klux Klan
(Kennedy), 233–34, 237

Jacob, Brian, 222
Japanese Sumo Association, 42
Jefferson, Thomas, 20
Jeremijenko, Natalie, 190
Jeremijenko-Conley, Yo
Xing Heyno Augustus
Eisner Alexander Weiser
Knuckles, 190
Jim Crow laws, 52, 112
Jines, Linda, 263
jobs, 12
interviews for, 189
loss of, 18, 120
payment for, 3
John Bates Clark Medal, xxiii,
220
Johnson, D. Gale, 228
Journal of Political Economy, 219,
225
Joyce, Ted, 221
J. T. (gang leader), 92–95,
96–106
Justice Department, U.S., 158

Lott, John R., Jr., 133
Lott, Trent, 74
Lowe's Motor Speedway, 245
lying, 66, 88, 231
lynching, 52, 56–58

McCorvey, Norma, 3–4, 12
McDonald's, 96, 100, 105, 111
macroeconomics, 218
mad-cow disease, 149, 150, 152
Madonna, 204
Mafia, 109–10
Major League baseball, 104
Malmendier, Ulrike, 247
managers, 21
Marginal Revolution blog, 250
marijuana, 268
Marketing Workshop Inc., 248
market work, 257
Marks, Johnny, 224
Massachusetts Institute of
    Technology (MIT), xxiv,
    224
mathematics, xxiv, 90, 95, 217
May, Robert, 224
measurement, xxv, 11–12, 46,
    217
  economics as science of, 11–12,
    25
  tools of, 11–12, 25
media, 104
  experts and, 87–88
  information and, 87–88, 89
Medicare, 136
Merrill Lynch, 65

microeconomics, 13, 218, 227
Mills, Richard P., 160–61
Miyake, Mitsuru, 43
Monday Night Football, 184
money:
  banking and investment of,
    12
  bribes of, 41, 42
  drug-dealing and, xxiv, 11,
    89, 96, 97–100, 101–2, 104,
    105–6, 110, 216, 221
  embezzlement of, 45
  gift cards vs., 250–51
  labor and, 257, 258–59
  laundering of, xxv
  oil and, 265
  politics and, 8–11, 12, 225
  stealing of, 45, 47
  value of, 266
Moore, Harry T., 234, 236
morality, 11, 14
  economics vs., 11, 49, 210
  incentives and, 17–18, 19–20
  self-interest and, 14
More Guns, Less Crime (J. Lott),
    133
Morris, William, 190
Moses, Zelman, 190
Mulligan, Casey, 239
murder. *See* homicide
Mussolini, Benito, 53, 60
mutual funds, 66, 67

names, 181–207, 291n–95n
  Asian-American, 185

About the Authors

Steven D. Levitt is a professor of economics at the University of Chicago and a recipient of the John Bates Clark medal, awarded to the most influential economist under the age of forty.

Stephen J. Dubner, a former writer and editor at *The New York Times Magazine,* is the author of *Turbulent Souls (Choosing My Religion), Confessions of a Hero-Worshiper,* and the children's book *The Boy with Two Belly Buttons.*